# A Triangular Conflict
## India, China and Pakistan

# A TRIANGULAR CONFLICT

## India, China and Pakistan

Col. (Retd.) S.C. Narang

PRASHANT PUBLISHING HOUSE
DELHI-110094

*Published by :*
**Prashant Publishing House**
C-34, 28 Foota Road, Gali-3,
West Karwal Nagar, Delhi-110094
Phone : 011-22963970, Mob. : 9810396373
e-mail.: prashantpublishinghouse@gmail.com

**A Triangular Conflict: India, China and Pakistan**



*First Published 2014*

**ISBN** 978-93-80565-48-4



---

**PRINTED IN INDIA**
Published by Mr. R.K. Jha M/s Prashant Publishing House and Published at H.S. Offset House Press, Delhi.

# Preface

The China-Indian War, also known as the China-Indian Border Conflict, was a war between China and India that took place in 1962. A disputed Himalayan border was the main pretext for war, but other issues played a role. There had been a series of violent border incidents after the 1959 Tibetan uprising, when India had granted asylum to the Dalai Lama. In response to Chinese incursions, India initiated a Forward Policy in which it placed outposts along the border, including several north of the McMahon Line, the eastern portion of a Line of Actual Control proclaimed by Chinese Premier Zhou Enlai in 1959.

The relation of nuclear India with nuclear China differs fundamentally from the relation with nuclear Pakistan. It is, on the one hand, less hostile and free from the kind of tension that makes a Pakistan-India confrontation an ever present possibility. In July 2009 China and India concluded their 13th round of border talks with a wide range of agreements such as the installation of a hot line between the Chinese and Indian capitals, an agreement to celebrate 60 years of diplomatic ties next year, etc. Their mutual trade, which amounted to a whopping $52 billion in 2009, is set to increase to $60 billion in 2010. In comparison, India-Pakistan trade – discounting smuggling and third party trading – amounts to less than $1 billion annually.

The Kashmir dispute dates from 1947. The partition of the Indian sub-continent along religious lines led to the formation of India and Pakistan. However, there remained the problem of over 650 states, run by princes, existing within the two newly independent countries. In theory, these princely states had the option of deciding which country to join, or of remaining independent. In practice, the restive population of each province proved decisive.

India and Pakistan have fought at least three wars over Kashmir, including the Indo-Pakistani Wars of 1947, 1965 and 1999. India and Pakistan have also been involved in several skirmishes over the Siachen Glacier. Since 1987, a disputed State election has resulted in some of the state's legislative assembly forming militant wings, creating a catalyst for insurgency. The Indian-administered Jammu and Kashmir has been the site of conflict between the Indian Armed Forces, militants, and separatists. India has furnished documentary evidence to the United Nations that these militants are supported by Pakistan, leading to a ban on some terrorist organisations, which Pakistan has yet to enforce. Former President of Pakistan and the ex-chief of Pakistan militaryPervez Musharraf, stated in an interview in London, that Pakistani government indeed helped to form underground militant groups and "turned a blind eye" towards their existence.

As the book addresses this crucial issue quite deftly, it is hoped that it would prove to be a source of great information for the reader. It an essential reading for the students taking courses on this book.

*—Editor*

# Contents

# 1

# Introduction

The recent detonation of a series of nuclear devices by India and Pakistan has increased tension in South Asia and threatens to inflame long-standing boundary disputes that India has with China and Pakistan. The disputes with China and Pakistan have already triggered several wars.

The new Hindu-nationalist government in New Delhi has reversed movement toward détente with Beijing and Islamabad. The areas in contention with China and Pakistan are among the largest land-boundary disputes in the world. The Indo-Nepali dispute over Kalapani is more recent and involves a small area.

## INDIA-CHINA (AKSAI CHIN AND ARUNACHAL PRADESH)

In the 1962 Sino-Indian War, China seized a Switzerland-sized area, Aksai Chin (Aksayqin), and overran Arunachal Pradesh (an Indian state the size of Austria). There are also other, smaller pockets of disputed area. The PRC withdrew from virtually all of Arunachal Pradesh to the Line of Actual Control (LAC), which approximates the McMahon Line that is found in a 1914 agreement initialed by British, Tibetan, and Chinese representatives. Chinese and Indian forces clashed in the Sumdorong Chu valley of Arunachal Pradesh in 1986-87. Relations began to thaw in 1988.

On 7 September 1993, China and India signed an accord to reduce tensions along their border and to respect the LAC.

During November 1996, China and India agreed to delimit the LAC and institute confidence-building measures (CBMs) along the frontier. The agreement pledged nonaggression, prior notification of large troop movements, a 10-km no-fly zone for combat aircraft, and exchange of maps to resolve disagreements about the precise location of the LAC. In August 1997 the sides ratified the CBM agreement. There seems to have been little substantive progress, except for a series of high-level visits. The most recent, on 27 April, was the first visit by a PRC Chief of Staff to India. However, two weeks before the visit the new Indian Defence Minister, George Fernandes, accused the PRC of repeated violations of Indian territory, including the construction of a helipad on "Indian" territory in the disputed zone, and of aiding Pakistan's nuclear and missile programs. On 3 May he publicly labelled China as India's number one threat and alleged that the PRC was stockpiling nuclear weapons in Tibet, expanding naval activity off the Burmese coast, and conducting surveillance against India from Burma's Coco Islands. After the visit of General Fu Quanyou and PRC protests, Fernandes said that his characterization of China as India's principal threat was a personal view, but he went on to pledge that the number of Indian troops along the frontier with China would not be reduced. Such a statement calls into question part of the agreed CBMs. (To view a map of this area click here.) China and India have yet to address their fundamental and very large land boundary disputes. Moreover, their bilateral relations are complicated by the issues of Tibet (Xizang), Sikkim, and Kashmir. India plays host to the Dalai Lama and a large number of Tibetan refugees. They present an implicit threat to Chinese control of Tibet, which it invaded in 1950. On its maps, the PRC continues to portray Sikkim, which was absorbed by India in 1974, as an independent country. In addition to the Aksai Chin, China and India dispute another section of Kashmir (the area west of Aksai Chin).

## CHINA'S BORDER SPAT WITH INDIA

The recent meeting between India's National Security Adviser MK Narayanan and China's Vice-Foreign Minister Dai

Banggio at Coonoor in Tamil Nadu was the continuation of a series of such meetings in the context of the border dispute between the two countries. While this is a good thing to go by, the main point is: what has been the actual progress in the matter? After every meeting, a standard joint communiqué is issued to the effect that the téte-a-téte was fruitful and the dialogue is being maintained in an atmosphere of friendship and mutual cooperation. Diplomatic jargon cannot be limitless; it must end somewhere.

Again, from time to time one hears of Chinese intrusion into Arunachal Pradesh, especially in the area of Sumdorong Chu Valley and the northern range of the Mishmi Hills. There is also the occasional media report that China claims this Northeastern state of ours on the grounds of a combination of history as well as geography.

India's drawback is that our foreign policy has always been linked to the vote bank. In fact it was a vote bank issue that created the border dispute with China in the first place way back in the late '50s and early '60s. The origin of this problem is worth discussing as this itself suggests the solution. Soon after China secured Tibet, Beijing sent a delegation to New Delhi under then Prime Minister Zhou en Lai with a proposal on Aksai Chin in northern Kashmir, adjacent to the Siachen Glacier. The delegation submitted to us that movement from Tibet to Sinkiang province was a huge problem because one had to traverse the inhospitable Kunlun Mountains en route. Hence it was suggested both countries could arrive at an understanding by which India could lease out Aksai Chin to China, as this would enable the latter to build an all-weather highway across this stretch of territory.

Thus movement from Tibet to Sinkiang would not then involve negotiating the Kunluns at all and India, too, could use this highway as a bonus. In any case, Aksai Chin was just an ice desert with an average height of 18,000-19,000 feet and nothing grew there, let alone having any human habitation. New Delhi reacted with its usual brash arrogance, thundering words to the effect that 'not an inch of our sacred motherland' would be given, et al. Zhou en Lai was shown the door gracelessly. The Chinese delegation went back and decided to implement a tenet in Hindi conveying the meaning that if ghee cannot be taken out by a straight finger then a crooked finger would be used! China militarily attacked India and physically captured Aksai Chin by force in late 1962 and built the desired highway through it. China is still very much in occupation of this area, cocking a snook at India now and then! On our part we bemoaned our fate, blamed Beijing for gerrymandering into our territory and generally made a political nuisance of ourselves. Nothing helped, of course.

During its attack on India, China had also deeply transgressed into what was earlier known as the North East Frontier Agency that later became Arunachal Pradesh. However, after delivering a crushing military-cum-political defeat on India, China moved back to its own side of the border in this area. This apart, China disputes an area along the Uttarkhand-Tibet border named Barahoti.

China has a strong army garrison in this area at a place called Taklakot that keeps a watching brief over Barahoti. India, therefore, has been well and truly boxed in by China, courtesy New Delhi's folly of riding the high horse with Zhou en Lai's delegation of yore. Diplomacy has never been a strong point with us and the country has suffered badly as a consequence. The science and art of statecraft continue to be subservient to the omnipotent vote bank as far as our leaders are concerned.

New Delhi, for reasons best known to itself, brought out a Lok Sabha resolution in 1994 wherein it was categorically stated that we would retake Aksai Chin by force. Obviously this resolution was nothing but a vote bank gimmick that our näive citizens — including many members of our intelligentsia — swallowed all the way. While firmly occupying Aksai Chin, China periodically needles India over Arunachal Pradesh and Barahoti. Normally, Barahoti remains dormant but Arunachal Pradesh makes news, sometimes with alarm. This has been the state of affairs since 1962. No government at New Delhi since that year has tried to accept the reality and taken any pragmatic steps to reconcile the border situation with China, notwithstanding the fact that currently our relations with China are improving virtually by the day.

The question is, what needs to be done in order to resolve the ongoing impasse? There is only one solution: India must formally accept Zhou en Lai's suggestion of yesteryear but cede Aksai Chin to China. It is doubtful whether China will accept the lease aspect now. The Chinese are a very proud race and will never climb down. In any event, China holds the aces in this matter, never mind the McMahon Line's relevancy to us.

Truth to tell, this solution was hinted by China's previous regime under President Jiang Zemin through his then Foreign Minister Tang Jiaxuan during Prime Minister AB Vajpayee's tenure. While the Sikkim issue got reconciled, Aksai Chin could not be followed through due to the change of government in India in 2004.

China is not really interested in Barahoti and Arunachal Pradesh — Beijing uses these two as pressure points on New Delhi to see reason over the border dispute, a dispute that hinges purely on Aksai Chin. The sooner we come to terms with this, the better.

## CHINA'S CLAIM TO TIBET IS FACTOR IN BORDER DISPUTE

This is perhaps the most militarized Buddhist enclave in the world. Perched above 10,000 feet in the icy reaches of the eastern Himalayas, the town of Tawang is not only home to one of Tibetan Buddhism's most sacred monasteries but also the site of a massive Indian military buildup. Convoys of army trucks haul howitzers along rutted mountain roads. Soldiers drill in muddy fields. Military bases appear every half-mile in the countryside, with watchtowers rising behind concertina wire.

A road sign on the northern edge of town helps explain the reason for all the fear and the fury: The border with China is just 23 miles away; Lhasa, the Tibetan capital, 316 miles; and Beijing 2,676 miles. "The Chinese army has a big deployment at the border, at Bumla," said Madan Singh, a junior commissioned officer who sat with a half-dozen soldiers one afternoon sipping tea beside a fog-cloaked road. "That's why we're here." Though little known to the outside world, Tawang is a flashpoint in relations between the world's two most populous nations. It is the focus of China's most delicate land-border dispute, a conflict rooted in Chinese claims of sovereignty over all of historical Tibet.

In recent months, both countries have stepped up efforts to secure their rights over this rugged patch of land. China tried to block a $2.9 billion loan to India from the Asian Development Bank on the grounds that part of the loan was slated for water projects in Arunachal Pradesh, the state that includes Tawang. It was the first time China had sought to influence the territorial dispute through a multilateral institution. Then an Indian general announced that the Indian military was deploying extra troops and fighter jets in the area. The growing belligerence has soured relations between the two Asian giants and has prompted one Indian military leader to declare that China has replaced Pakistan as India's biggest threat.

Economic progress might be expected to bring the countries closer. China and India did $52 billion of trade last year, a 34 percent increase over 2007. But businesspeople say that border tensions have infused official deliberations over business deals, dampening the willingness of Chinese and Indian companies to invest in each other's countries. "Officials start taking more time, scrutinizing things more carefully, and all that means more delays and ultimately more denials," said Ravi Bhoothalingam, a former president of the Oberoi Group, the luxury hotel chain, and a member of the Institute of Chinese Studies in New Delhi. "That's not good for business."

The roots of the conflict go back to China's territorial claims to Tibet. Not only does the Dalai Lama, the exiled spiritual leader of the Tibetans, live in the foothills of the western Himalayas with the blessing of the Indian government, but China insists that this swath of northeast India has historically been part of Tibet, and thus should be part of China. Tawang is a thickly forested area of white stupas and steep, terraced hillsides that is home to the ethnic Monpa people, who practice Tibetan Buddhism, speak a language similar to Tibetan and once paid tribute to rulers in Lhasa. The 6th Dalai Lama was born here in the 17th century.

The Chinese army occupied Tawang briefly in 1962, during a war with India fought over this and other territories along the 2,521-mile border. More than 3,100 Indian soldiers and 700 Chinese soldiers were killed and thousands wounded in the border war. War memorials highlighting China's aggressions in Tawang here are big draws for Indian tourists. "The entire border is disputed," said Ma Jiali, an India scholar at the China Institutes of Contemporary International Relations, a government-supported think tank in Beijing. "This problem hasn't been solved, and it's a huge barrier to China-India relations."

In some ways, Tawang has become a proxy battleground, too, between China and the Dalai Lama, who passed through this valley when he fled into exile in 1959. From his home in the distant hill town of Dharamsala, he wields enormous influence over Tawang. He appoints the abbot of the powerful monastery and gives financial support to institutions throughout the area. Last year, the Dalai Lama announced for the first time that Tawang is a part of India, bolstering the Indian government's territorial claims and infuriating China.

Traditional Tibetan culture runs strong in Tawang. At the Tawang monastery, an important centre of Tibetan learning, monks express apprehension about China's rule over Tibet, which the Chinese army seized in 1951. "I hate the Chinese government," said Gombu Tsering, 70, a senior monk who watches over the monastery's museum. "Tibet wasn't even a part of China. Lhasa wasn't a part of China." Few expect China to try to forcefully annex Tawang, but military skirmishes are a real danger, analysts say. The Indian military recorded 270 border violations and nearly 2,300 instances of "aggressive border patrolling" by Chinese soldiers last year, said Brahma Chellaney, a professor of strategic studies at the Centre for Policy Research, a research organization in New Delhi. Mr.

Chellaney has advised the Indian government's National Security Council.

"The India-China frontier has become more 'hot' than the India-Pakistan border," he said in an e-mail. China has grown increasingly hostile to the Dalai Lama after a severe outbreak of ethnic unrest in Tibet. This year, it turned its diplomatic guns on India. China moved in March to block a $2.9 billion loan to India from the Asian Development Bank, a multi-nation group based in Manila that has China on its board, because $60 million of the loan had been earmarked for flood-control projects in Arunachal Pradesh, the state that includes Tawang. The loan was approved in mid-June over China's heated objections.

Weeks after China first tried to block the loan, the chief of the Indian air force, now retired, told a prominent Indian newspaper that China posed a greater threat than Pakistan. Another official, J.J. Singh, the governor of Arunachal Pradesh and retired chief of the Indian army, said the next month that the Indian military was adding two divisions of troops, totalling 50,000 to 60,000 soldiers, to the border region over the next several years. Four Sukhoi fighter jets were immediately deployed to a nearby air base. Since 2005, when Chinese Prime Minister Wen Jiabao visited India, the two countries have gone through 13 rounds of bilateral negotiations over the issue. A last round was just held last month, with no results. Though China has actually resolved many of its border disputes in recent years, India remains a glaring exception.

## The Government of Tibet in Exile

From July 20 to 23, 1994, Beijing staged the Third Forum on Work in Tibet which recommended the total destruction of an entire civilization flourishing on the Tibetan Plateau for thousands of years. This cultural "empire" once encompassed far-flung areas like Buryatia, Tuva and Kalmykia in Russia; Mongolia; Laddakh, Lahaul-Spiti, Sikkim, and Arunachal Pradesh in India; Mustang, Dolpo and Solo Khumbu in Nepal; Bhutan and parts of western China.

The policy formulated in 1994 in Beijing-and these days pursued with Cultural Revolutionary zeal in Tibet-will mean the annihilation of the spiritual homeland of this shared culture. Implementation of the Third Work Forum is thus having a crippling impact on the traditional culture of millions of non-Tibetans as the well-spring of their cultural inspiration is forcibly drained and there is nothing to replenish the continuous growth and development of this distinct and highly evolved civilization.

## Losing Hearts and Minds

The decisions made at the Third Forum rest on two fundamental conclusions which Beijing drew. It realized it was losing out in two vital fields-ideology and propaganda. For a state whose existence is justified by its ideological superiority and the power of its propaganda to shape the thinking of the masses, the implications of this for the future was at best uncertain, at worst dangerous. Beijing concluded it was losing the ideological war because, despite the unrelenting assault on Tibetan Buddhism, Tibetans were as devoted to their traditional beliefs as ever. Beijing has succeeded in physically enslaving the country but it has not won over the hearts, minds and loyalty of the Tibetan populace.

Communist ideology, enforced by the military might of China, had failed to dent the heart of Buddhism. Added to this was the communist authorities' total bafflement at the non-violent policy underpinning the Middle Way Approach advocated by His Holiness the Dalai Lama to resolve the issue of Tibet's future status. For a regime which is based on Mao's dictum that political power grows out of the barrel of a gun, this supposedly eccentric philosophy which says victory lies in capturing the hearts and minds of people by the power of ideas rather than killing by the power of the gun comes as a bolt from the blue. Much of Beijing's knee-jerk reaction to, and its bafflement at, His Holiness the Dalai Lama's new policy of rapprochement lies at the heart of its new hardline policy.

Beijing considered it was losing the propaganda war because, for one reason or the other, the world's media and its pop culture considered-at least for the moment-Tibet and Tibetan

Buddhism their very own cuddly pandas. Despite its financial might China found it extremely difficult to exterminate this image of Tibet and get its voice heard on the Tibetan issue in the court of the international media. In order to address these weaknesses the Third Forum concentrated on two issues. One was to focus on Tibet's economic development in the hope that this would keep Tibetan demonstrations off the streets. This was tantamount to bribing the Tibetans with promises of riches to come if they toed the party line. The other concern was to win the coming and new generations of Tibetans over to the Chinese viewpoint.

Beijing has given up on the present generation of Tibetans as a lost cause. If the coming generations of Tibetans were also lost to the 'Dalai Clique' this, the Chinese concluded, would have dangerous consequences for Chinese rule in Tibet. The 15-year-old Gyalwa Karmapa's dramatic escape from Tibet in January 2000 was a warning to the Beijing authorities of the erosion of loyalty to China. The Karmapa's flight, and the earlier escape of Agya Rinpoche, the abbot of Kumbum Monastery, came as a huge embarrassment for China, because retaining these high lamas gave China a degree of legitimacy for its rule in Tibet. This is the reason why Beijing is enforcing with greater strictness its 1993 instruction of recalling young Tibetans studying in schools and monasteries run by Dharmasala in India. This is also the rationale for Beijing closing down schools in Tibet which are privately run by Tibetans.

For these reasons Tibet today is in the throes of a second Cultural Revolution as the Chinese authorities step up their long-term strategy to exterminate Tibet's distinct cultural and ethnic identity. The authorities are pursuing a four-pronged strategy to achieve their final objective. They have stepped up repression while employing their huge propaganda machine to paint a rosy picture of Tibet. They have quickened the pace of economic development to dampen Tibetan nationalism and are simultaneously moving more Chinese settlers onto the Tibetan Plateau to change Tibet's demographic composition and to ease social unrest because of mounting unemployment back in China.

The Third Work Forum on Tibet was convened by the top Chinese leadership and was presided over by President Jiang Zemin. The authorities have now enshrined this Work Forum as the most "important strategic policy to rejuvenate Tibet" and have hailed its directives as the new manifesto for party work on the plateau. The significance of the Third Work Forum lies in the fact that it overturned the more liberal policies laid out for Tibet's "development" by the First and Second Work Forums held in 1980 and 1984.

The first two work forums were initiated by the late Hu Yaobang, then Secretary General of the Chinese Communist Party. This liberal and somewhat maverick leader is credited with masterminding a series of measures to improve the social, economic and political conditions in Tibet. The brief spell of liberalization markedly improved the living conditions of the majority of Tibetans and contributed to a more relaxed intellectual and social climate.

The Third Work Forum reversed these policies and reinstated hardline measures under which Tibet is still reeling today. The Tibetans in Tibet perceive the current repressive policies as a second Cultural Revolution. The question is why did China choose to jettison its earlier more liberal policies and adopt a manifesto which is leading to the systematic destruction of Tibet's distinct culture. The answer lies in domestic and international events which forced China to formulate a series of hardline policies on Tibet which eventually crystallized into the Third Work Forum for Tibet. The world which confronted China in the late 1980s and early 1990s was a frightening one.

Starting from 1987, Tibet was rocked by a string of protest demonstrations, which called for Tibetan independence. One of the largest demonstrations which erupted on March 5, 1989 in Lhasa, forced the authorities to impose martial law on the city. These demonstrations are now seen to have been an inspiration behind the outburst of Chinese students' pro-democracy uprisings. The authorities saw the series of Tiananmen Square demonstrations as a sign of their Central Government losing control, and in an attempt to regain supremacy, the authorities slaughtered-perhaps hundreds if not thousands of students on

June 4, 1989. These demonstrations were a chilling replay to the authorities of the May 4, 1919 student demonstrations in Beijing which signalled a political and cultural awakening across the erstwhile Middle Kingdom.

Bejing's fears of losing control were exacerbated by external events which saw the unraveling of the communist world. The Solidarity Movement in Poland, the fall of the Berlin Wall, and the implosion of the Soviet Union fed Beijing's paranoia over threats to the Chinese Communist Party hold on power. Official China's fears were further inflamed by the rapidly changing attitude of the broad masses as they turned back from communism to traditional beliefs like Confucionism, Buddhism, Islam, Christianity and indigenous folk cults. In the eyes of ordinary citizens communism was becoming totally discredited and this, more than anything else, was the biggest nightmare for China's leadership. The leadership's justification for staying in power was being disavowed by the masses. For a one-party dictatorship this historically indicates the first step along the slippery road to dissolution and removal of power.

For these reasons the Chinese leadership then reverted to its earlier view that traditional beliefs were its real enemy. In competing with Buddhism, Confucionism, Islam, Christianity and other isms, communism was losing out in terms of its ability to retain the loyalty and allegiance of the masses. The leadership revived the old aphorisms once served up to the Tibetan people to justify their policies to destroy Tibetan Buddhism during the Cultural Revolution. Bewildered Tibetans were then told that just as there cannot be two suns in the sky, so there cannot be both Buddhism and socialism in Tibet. Inevitably Buddhism then had to give way to socialism. And again, today, religion is being blatantly sublimated to Chinese state power.

These were the fears of the Chinese leaders when they met in Beijing in 1994 to hammer out their new Tibet initiatives. For the Chinese authorities Tibet is an especially sensitive issue because of their conviction that hostile Western forces are using the issue of Tibet to "westernize" China and to lead to its territorial fragmentation. The third generation Chinese leaders came to the conclusion that stability in Tibet was vital to the stability of China as a whole. Earlier, Tibet was merely of peripheral concern to the vital interests of China's sprawling communist empire. Now, with the Third Work Forum, the authorities were saying, "We must clearly understand that we must do our work in Tibet not only for the sake our of own region's stability and development, not only for the interests of our people, but also for the sake of the whole nation's stability and development."

In Tibet, China faced peculiar problems because of the inherent strength of Tibetan Buddhism and the depth of devotion of the populace to His Holiness the Dalai Lama. The sustained burst of religious revival that followed in the wake of the brief spell of liberalization in Tibet confirmed the leadership's worst fears that decades of concerted assault on Tibetan culture and religion had not extinguished the people's traditional beliefs and values. From merely nuisance value, the Chinese leadership now viewed Tibetan Buddhism as a very real and imminent threat to the stability of Chinese rule in Tibet.

At the same time the Chinese leadership's attitude towards His Holiness the Dalai Lama changed. From being an uncertain ally in the peace process in Tibet, the current Chinese leadership now saw him as a full-blown "enemy". A top-level conclave held in Beijing on March 10, 1993 concluded that, "There are different factions within the Dalai Clique; they are, however, unanimous in their political nature and position. They differ from each other in ideological viewpoints and ways of expressing them. Different strategies must be adopted to use their differences, to deal with them differently in order to divide and destroy them."

Repeated statements by high-level officials describe the struggle against "splittism", the official term for Tibetan independence, as a "life-and-death struggle". At the 1994 annual meeting of the "TAR" Communist Party Committee to brief members on the policy thrust of the Third Work Forum on Tibet, Raidi, deputy Secretary of the Committee said, "Up to now, his (the Dalai Lama's) standpoint on Tibet's independence has never changed, and we must reveal his double-faced true colour. The focal point in our region in the struggle against splittism is to oppose the Dalai Clique. As the saying goes, to kill a serpent, one must first cut off its head."

In short, the Third Work Forum decided that Beijing was in a position to solve the Tibet issue without the Dalai Lama's involvement. It abandoned the earlier liberal policy of including His Holiness the Dalai Lama in any future settlement of Tibet's status. His Holiness the Dalai Lama was clearly singled out as the cause of China's "Tibet problem".

The Third Work Forum also abandoned the policy of granting concessions to Tibet because of the plateau's "special characteristics". This policy had been the cornerstone of recommendations made by the First and Second Tibet Work Forums.

To carry out its new hardline policies in Tibet, Beijing appointed Chen Kuiyuan as the "TAR" Party Secretary in 1992. Chen Kuiyuan's appointment is significant because he had a track record for being a tough and ruthless administrator. He had already served as the First Secretary of the Chinese Communist Party in Inner Mongolia and is credited with repressing the rebellious Mongols, many of whom refer to him as "the butcher". Chen Kuiyuan was especially recommended to the post by Hu Jintao, the current Vice-President of China, who was then the First Secretary of the Chinese Communist Party in Tibet.

## Tackling Tibetan Nationalism

The Third Work Forum policies chalked out for Tibet contained four key elements. China stepped up the scale of repression in Tibet. External propaganda work was escalated. The pace of economic development in Tibet-and its corollary of encouraging more Chinese settlers and businessmen to take advantage of the economic boom on the "roof of the world"-was also increased. In short, Beijing had decided to tackle Tibetan nationalism head-on and observers are still assessing the consequences on both Chinese rule in Tibet and on the populace.

Beijing remains convinced that these key components of its current policy will stabilize Chinese rule over Tibet and solve once and for all, the vexed problem of its negative image over the way Tibet has been handled. One main target of the current policy of repression is Tibetan Buddhism. Chinese leaders are increasingly alarmed by the proliferation of monasteries and temples which the period of liberalization spawned throughout Tibet: they are seen as the bastions of Tibetan nationalism. The authorities have set up "Democratic Management Committees" to control monasteries and nunneries and created "Work Inspection Teams" to supervise the "education" of monks and nuns.

A major thrust is underway to break the bond of loyalty between the clergy in Tibet and His Holiness the Dalai Lama in India. Campaigns like "Strike Hard" and "Patriotic Re-education", unleashed in 1996, are aimed at crippling the rise of Tibetan Buddhism which the authorities suspect is weaning the loyalty of the Tibetan people away from the communist party and towards His Holiness the Dalai Lama. One salient feature of the "Strike Hard" campaign is how differently it is interpreted in China and Tibet. China's "Strike Hard" campaign was started to weed out corruption. Tibet's version is used as a political tool to eliminate those whom the authorities label "splittists". In Tibet, rather than striking at corruption, the authorities turn a blind eye to this social disease in the hope that it will erode the traditional morality of Tibetans and undermine Tibetan Buddhism.

In fact, at a secret meeting held in December 1999 in Chengdu, capital of Sichuan province, Chen Kuiyuan, the hardline Party Secretary of "TAR" recommended to the Central Chinese Government that an all-out effort must be made to eradicate Tibetan Buddhism and culture from the face of the earth so that no memory of them will be left in the minds of coming generations of Tibetans-except as museum pieces.

Chen Kuiyuan stated that the main cause of instability is the existence of the Dalai Lama and his Government-in-Exile in Dharamsala and these must be "uprooted". He recommended that Tibet, Tibetan people and Tibetan Buddhism-in other words the very name of Tibet-must be destroyed and the "Tibet Autonomous Region" be merged with provinces like Sichuan.

While treating Tibetans to boot-heel subjugation at home, internationally China was on an overdrive propaganda blitz. At a brainstorming conclave held on March 10, 1993, Zeng Jian-hui, Vice-Minister of the Propaganda Ministry, told participants, "The propaganda work on the question of Tibet is one of the focal points of the entire external propaganda work...With regard to attacks by the West and the Dalai Clique and their frequent activities, our external propaganda should launch offensive. We should expand our spheres of influence; in particular, we should infiltrate our propaganda into the mainstream life of the West.

"Firstly we should continue to send Tibetan scholars and Tibetan singing and dancing troupes abroad to lecture and perform. Secondly, relevant embassies and consulates should aim at the public opinion and the activities of the Dalai Clique in the countries where they are stationed and utilize speeches, picture exhibitions, special articles and other forms to carry out propaganda work, so as to win over officials and people of those countries... We should reinforce the work of utilizing the power of foreign propaganda. A few years ago, in the light of the situation of that time, we made arrangements for foreign journalists to visit Tibet."

The September 3, 2000 edition of *People's Daily* carried a story headlined "Tibet Welcomes Foreign Journalists for Objective Reporting". It stated that "A senior Tibetan official said Sunday that Tibet welcomes foreign journalists to come for objective and just reporting, but not those who take distorted views. Raidi, Deputy Secretary of the Tibet Autonomous Regional Committee of the Communist Party of China and Chairman of the Standing Committee of the Tibetan Autonomous Regional People's Congress, made the remarks at a meeting here with a press delegation of Thailand." In this context, it is interesting to note that N. Ram, the editor of India's *Frontline* magazine, devoted 36 pages of the September 15, 2000 issue to promote the Chinese line and recommended that the Indian Government expel the Central Tibetan Administration from Indian soil for being the main stumbling block to normal relations between India and China. It is difficult to assess to what extent the views contained in his stupendous reporting marathon are his own.

These editorial outbursts are in line with policy decisions outlined in the early nineties. During a two-day secret conclave in March 1993 in Chengdu, Vice-Minister Zeng Jian-hui, told participants, "All foreigners that we entertain and send to Tibet must have a relatively objective opinion of Tibet. We should use people from abroad to carry out the propaganda on Tibet for us, which is more powerful than if we do it."

Along with its external public relations strategy, China is presently carrying out a potentially much more dangerous policy of speeding up the pace of Tibet's economic development and its related drive to bring more Chinese settlers onto the Tibetan Plateau. Beijing's Western China Development Programme, which incorporates Tibet in its ambit, is devised to shift the focus of China's economic activities from Coastal China to the interior-both to narrow the imbalance in the level of economic development between the two regions and to ease population pressure on the coastal areas which attract millions of migrant workers. The focus of Beijing's Western China Economic Development Programme in Tibet is to exploit the plateau's still untapped minerals and other natural resources and to upgrade Tibet's infrastructure-like roads and telecommunications-to facilitate transportation of these resources to China. The other purpose of the heightened level of economic activity is to divert the Tibetans' attention from their political fate to focus on their livelihood-thus undermining Tibetan nationalism. The Chinese authorities aim to manipulate the situation in Tibet still further by bringing in more Chinese settlers who would then demographically cement Chinese rule once and for all. These current hardline policies and their implementation in Tibet are impacting the stalled Sino-Tibetan Dialogue and will vitally affect the ability of Tibetans to survive as a distinct people and culture.

## Beijing's Flawed Perceptions

The basic flaws in China's new policy in its search to resolve the problem of Tibet is thinking the solution can exclude the involvement of His Holiness the Dalai Lama. The other is in attempting to solve the problem over the heads of Tibet's citizens.

These two fundamental mistakes will exacerbate China's Tibet problem, not solve it. The reason lies in the history of Tibet and in the sentiments of the people. The institution of the Dalai Lamas of Tibet is more than 600 years old, if we start from the birth of the first Dalai Lama in 1391. In the course of its growth and development, the very institution itself came to symbolize fundamental beliefs and the political destiny of the nation. The bond between the Dalai Lamas and the Tibetan people is fundamental and unbreakable; any attempt, however sustained, will never succeed in driving a wedge between the two.

Consequently, China's current policy of forcing Tibetans-especially monks and nuns-to denounce His Holiness the Dalai Lama and pledge loyalty to the Chinese Communist Party will prove counterproductive. In view of this the Third Work Forum's basic assumption that in the case of Tibet time is on the side of China, and that Beijing can stall the problem of Tibet till the demise of the present Dalai Lama whereupon the issue of Tibet will solve itself, is fatally flawed-based as it is on a mistaken perception of the role played by the institution of the Dalai Lamas in the development of Tibetan history.

This assumption, if not reviewed, revised and abandoned, will prove catastrophic for the Chinese leadership and for those who chose to turn their whimsical personal analysis into state policy. The reason is simple. The Chinese Communist Party was founded in the 1920s and came to power in 1949. Within this short span of time the masses have lost faith in communist ideology, and members of the party these days pay mere lip service to the ideological justifications of the party. Conversely, the institution of the Dalai Lamas as a political force is more than 300 years old. These days the Dalai Lama is recognized by Tibetans throughout the world as the heart of Tibetan nationalism. How can a party which has lost its soul outlast an institution which symbolizes the very soul of a people? For these reasons it is imperative for China to review and re-assess its current hardline stance towards Tibet. China must re-start its stalled peace process over Tibet and consider His Holiness the Dalai Lama as a vital and active partner in the procedures. If China does this it will have won a powerful ally and companion along the road to peace, stability and continued prosperity.

## GLOBAL VARIABLES LEADING TO CONFLICT: CHINA FACTOR

The systemic level variables motivating China towards conflict, like in India, revolved around Chinese national interests, the system's influence on Chinese behaviour through structural constraints, and the role of anarchy in the system. Because of the anarchic structure of the international system, China is no different than India and state security must be its prime end. China's membership in the communist bloc does not grant it any guarantee of protection, and therefore its national interests are calculated in ways of maximizing national security. As such we shall discuss the three main interests affected by the border dispute with India.

As in India's case, the delineation of official borders for the PRC was a prime interest in order to gain legitimacy in the international system. This legitimacy is rooted within the conventions of the Westphalian system, where borders are paramount as they define the extent of sovereignty and political self-determination. The PRC's inheritance of territory which was divided by Western imperialists had a strong legal and pragmatic interest in negotiating legitimate borders with its neighbours. The basis of Chinese territorial definition was on the extent of historical holdings, but the PRC had determined in 1950 to negotiate borders based off the alignments they had inherited. This meant that China would not bog itself down in unreasonable claims in Indochina or other areas of traditional imperial suzerainty. This mentality guided border settlement by peaceful means with Burma, Nepal, Pakistan, Afghanistan, Mongolia, Cambodia, and Laos. Peaceful settlement of the Sino-Indian border however, was not possible due to Indian unwillingness to negotiate based on the perceived legitimacy of the McMahon Line.

A second national interest challenged by the border dispute with India was the Chinese right to non-intervention of foreigners in their domestic affairs. This principle of domestic sanctity from outside interference is also one of the rights of states in the Westphalian system. Chinese security was undermined by India's role in manipulating domestic events in both Tibet and in Ladakh. The Indian military's establishment of forward posts and patrols of the Ladakh region, beginning in 1960, was direct interference in Chinese domestic areas. While it was true China did not have legal sovereignty over the Ladakh area due to its position south of the McMahon Line, that argument remains moot as international boundaries must be agreed upon at least bilaterally, and the PRC gave it no such recognition. Furthermore, Ladakh, and more importantly the Aksai-Chin plain was a strategically important tract of land connecting Xinjiang and Tibet.

Indian interference in Tibet after the 1959 uprising was also taken as a direct violation of domestic sanctity, and a challenge to Chinese security and interests. The PRC became aware of Indian efforts to covertly aid the Dalai Lama and Tibetan separatists shortly after the PLA moved in to suppress the uprising. In fact, India had gone so far as to allow the CIA bases of operation along the border for a covert campaign in Tibet from 1957 to 1961. Furthermore, a series of four Indian military bases were constructed and manned in Tibet north of the McMahon Line. These actions illustrated India's desire to keep Tibet as a buffer state, and recognize Chinese suzerainty instead of sovereignty in the region, thus directly challenging China's security.

The Chinese interest of maintaining a secure border with India was also threatened by the border dispute. Reinforcement of Tibet after 1959, the Aksai-Chin road way, and Chinese military patrols of the border were an attempt to maintain their territorial integrity. This added military presence created a security dilemma for India, and they began building up and strengthening their own military capacity near contested areas. The adoption of a forward Indian military policy in 1960, coupled with Indian scouting patrols across the border and the construction of military posts around Ladakh and Tibet severely undermined Chinese border security. This led to the PLA "digging in" around contested border areas and effectively militarizing the border.

China's response to the Indian military buildup as well as their covert programs in contested border areas was constrained by the structure of the international environment. A major constraining force on Chinese action was the geostrategic situation in Asia during the late 1950's. Beginning in 1950 with the Korean War, the major battles of the Cold War were fought in Asia in the West's effort to contain the communist bloc. The PRC had to contend with anti-Chinese forces in South Korea, a U.S. backed ROC in Taiwan, a U.S.-fortified Japan, and increasing U.S. involvement in Indochina by 1960. These numerous threats on China's Western front were significant, and severely limited their maneuverability in other areas of concern. Unbeknownst to the West, the PRC was increasingly unable to depend on the support of the communist bloc due to increasing belligerence from the U.S.S.R. on various diplomatic and territorial issues. The Soviets pressured the PRC to acknowledge Indian border claims, and Sino-Soviet relations strained under their own border issues.

Acknowledging the limiting effects of these security threats on Chinese military power, the PRC advocated a policy of peaceful border settlement. China used this policy to its advantage and scored a critical victory in neutralizing a potential Pakistani threat to their security interests by a warming of relations. The geostrategic environment in which the PRC found itself was one of being surrounded by a ring of hostile states. Indian diplomatic intransigence on border issues and known subversion in Tibet added another threat in that ring. Thus, the structure of the international environment drove the PRC to rely on diplomacy to achieve its interests against minor powers in order to preserve its military power for guarding its borders against larger threats. This situation explains a seemingly coincidental rapprochement in relations with Pakistan, India's arch-rival, while Sino-Indian relations simultaneously deteriorated in 1959.

This hostile geostrategic environment ruled out the option of using military force to settle the border dispute with India because of the potential pitfall of starting a two front war. Thus PRC actions along the Indian border were limited by the international structure to defensive posturing, deterrence, and entrenchment. This is illustrated by the numerous Chinese overtures to Indian representatives to keep patrols 20km behind each border. Rapprochement with Pakistan was pragmatic in the freedom of action the PRC gained by not needing to guard the Sino-Pakistani border heavily. Therefore, Chinese policy was constrained by the system to not initiate force against India in order to settle the border dispute, but instead to bolster its defenses. However, the PRC declared that "force would be met with force" on the border issue, and this is evidenced by the PLA counter offensives launched on October 20 and November 16, 1962.

Finally, the anarchy present in the international system played a significant role in the actions of the PRC on the border issue. Unlike their Indian counterparts, China properly assessed the international situation and never lost sight of the fact that only China could assure Chinese security. The emerging Sino-Soviet split was a key element in the PRC's unwillingness to rely on outside support for their interests. Not only did the Soviets urge China to a settlement counter to their interests, but they openly aided India in both the construction of a domestic MIG program and a pledge to help them develop nuclear energy. Simultaneously, Soviet aid to China was severely cut including assistance in developing a nuclear program. Clearly a common Soviet-Sino communist ideology was unimportant to their "allies," as they even ventured to grant India great power status through nuclear development.

In addition to the Soviet military aid was U.S. support of India in the form of agricultural assistance and millions in financial aid packages. Although India pledged neutrality, the PRC clearly believed that they were in the West's bloc. Indian based CIA operations into Tibet and India's role in the Korean War helped bolster this perception. Unable to rely on either superpower for protection or intervention on their behalf, the PRC assessed that any military movements in securing the border would have to be proportional, decisive, and most importantly retaliatory. This assessment was gained from a rational calculation of the potential geostrategic and political consequences of a PLA initiation of force. While neither the PRC nor India possessed nuclear weapons, they feared a PLA offensive into India would be interpreted by the West as communist advance and therefore provoke a nuclear response. In the wake of the Taiwan Straits Crisis, and keeping in mind Sino-Soviet agitation, China was unwilling to risk a potential nuclear strike from the West, especially without full Soviet support. This being the case, China resolved that its armed response to Indian aggression would be purely political. The PRC would paint itself as the victim of aggression, but would then unleash a massive but calculated counterattack to force diplomatic concessions by India on the border issue, thereby resolving the issue once and for all. While the systems level of analysis plainly explains both the motives and limitations of India and China leading to the Sino-Indian War, it is contended that the model overlooks key motivations of either state leading to conflict.

## GLOBAL VARIABLES LEADING TO CONFLICT: INDIA FACTOR

The three main variables motivating Indian behaviour towards conflict with China on the systemic level are: Indian national interests, the system's influence on Indian behaviour through structural constraints, and the relationship between Indian perception of the international structure and reality. To begin a systemic explanation of India's actions we must first identify its national interests, as it is what drives Indian action throughout the international structure. According to neorealist thought the primary end of all states is security. This being the case, not only is security the primary Indian national interest, but any issue relating to national security becomes a primary interest.

Official borders, and their enforcement is a primary interest of each state for obvious reasons. However, in the Indian case this issue takes on greater importance than it otherwise would for other nations. This can be attributed to two factors. The most prevalent factor was that India bordered a nation which not only questioned the legitimacy of the established border, but also violated it. The second factor is the modern international system is formed by the interaction of nation-states, which as defined by the Westphalian system are the only entities capable of legitimately exercising sovereignty.

A key component of nation-state status under the Westphalian system is the existence of demarcated and respected borders. These borders represent the extent of national sovereignty and define where each nation's authority begins and ends. The questioning of India's established border by China undermines both Indian sovereignty and security. Security is undermined first by the direct military and administrative challenge to Indian territory, and second by delegitimizing India's position as a nation-state. If India can neither defend nor define borders respected by other nations, other states may begin to question their position as a nation-state in the system and then their sovereignty. This was a chief concern for India as they regarded the Chinese threat to their border as one compromising their "independence, self-determination, and position as a great power in Asia".

Another issue of national security relating to Indian interests was defense of the McMahon Line. Two key issues aided the creation of security dilemma situation along the McMahon Line. The first was the discovery of the Chinese road connecting Xinjiang and Tibet through the Aksai-Chin area in 1957. The second was the imposition of martial law on Tibet in 1959 by the PLA. China argued that completion of the road southeast of the McMahon Line in Aksai-Chin was simply the reestablishment of a historical commerce route from Xinjiang to Tibet. This road not only represented a blatant Chinese violation of India's McMahon Line border, but it also caused armed tension in the region. Shortly after the roads discovery, PLA frontier guards began patrolling the Aksai-Chin region, but never more than 20km away from the road's location. The issue of the road in Aksai-Chin and the PLA's role in Tibet in 1959 became linked since the majority of Chinese troops entered Tibet via the road from Xinjiang. The surge of PLA soldiers into Tibet aroused suspicions of a forcible border assertion by the PRC. These tensions were heightened by the flight of the Dalai Lama from Lhasa, and the closure of Tibet to commercial and cultural access by India, guaranteed in the 1951 treaty. Defensive maneuvers or not, these activities created a security dilemma along the border as India felt that Tibet was "essential for mastery over South Asia, and the most economical method for guaranteeing India's security". Forced to account for increasing Chinese military power near or past the McMahon Line, India responded by deploying their military in forward positions along the border with China as early as 1960. Accounting for India's national interest with force posturing, they attempted to both affirm the legitimacy of the McMahon Line as a border and to account for the security dilemma created by the hardening of PLA positions in Tibet and Aksai-Chin.

The second way a systemic level analysis accounts for the 1962 war is the manner in which India's policy was defined by the structure of the international system. In looking at the geostrategic positioning of India within the system, it is immediately apparent that they attempted to remain neutral or unaligned in the bipolar structure. India remained a powerful enough state to deter the third world adventurism of either bloc within its territory, but weak enough to be challenged by hostile neighbours. An excellent example of this was the persistent threat of Pakistan on their Northwestern border. The poor relationship of Pakistan and India is rooted in domestic level variables, but a systemic level cause was a disputed claim over the sovereignty of Kashmir. Both sides claim the right to sovereignty over Kashmir, and this has resulted in a heavily armed border. Additionally, appearances of a Sino-Pakistani agreement to hem in India developed with Chinese diplomatic overtures to Pakistan for peaceful border settlement beginning in 1961. This forced India to take a hard-line stance in their border dispute with China out of fear that concessions would show weakness, and endanger their control of Kashmir in a Domino-Theory type logic train.

Another structural element of the international system was the existence of nuclear weapons. Nuclear weapons invalidated traditional calculations of deterrence, and thus the great powers were those whom possessed them. In India's regional calculations neither themselves, nor did any other surrounding nations possess nuclear weapons keeping intact the use of deterrence as a method of securing or defending interests. This being the case, the option of engaging in armed conflict with surrounding nations remained possible as long as in India's force calculations they were superior to their target. A prime example of India's employment of force to further interests was their invasion of Portuguese controlled Goa on December 17, 1961. This use of force to assert sovereignty over perceived territory is an excellent precedent for the October 9, 1962 offensive against the PLA in Ladakh. Force against PLA incursions remained off the table as long as the Indian military believed their strategic position and capabilities to be inferior to the Chinese. Returning from a 1960 diplomatic tour of the U.S., Nehru expressed the idea that due to Soviet and Western military aid, "the military balance had changed in favour of India". Thus in the absence of nuclear weapons, India disregarded the Chinese effort at deterrence and employed the use of force to settle their territorial claims.

Finally, it is necessary to point out how India's perception of the international system, which differed from reality, influenced their decision to employ force against the PRC. India perceived the international system as open to change from a bipolar to a multi-polar structure. This was based in their success of remaining unaligned to either bloc, while still receiving significant military and economic aid from both camps. Given India's strategic geographic position in the system, both superpowers sought to gain the allegiance of India to their side through the use of aid. Understanding this, India played both sides against each other, and assumed that either superpower would be willing to intervene on their behalf in the event of Sino-Indian hostilities for pragmatic and alliance building reasons. Thus, India viewed its use of force as a no lose situation. Either the force would succeed in attaining their national interests, or if Indian power proved to be inadequate, "the superpowers would intervene to prevent any large-scale war between India and China;" therefore, bailing out India from a potential catastrophe. This perception of Indian value to either superpower and the general misperception of the international system would cost them.

Ultimately the Indians failed to acknowledge that while the interests of the superpowers may partially depend on India's well being, the system is ultimately in anarchy and each nation is responsible for assuring their own security. Additionally, India had miscalculated both the willingness and ability of the superpowers to intervene on their behalf. In reality the Soviet Union could not exercise restraint on Chinese actions or compel them to drop the border issue. The Sino-Soviet split had not yet occurred, but its origin is in the late 1950's, and the attempt to restrain PRC actions towards India was a contributing factor in the decline of Soviet influence. Indian belief in U.S. intervention was based on a miscalculation of U.S. interests in Asia, as well as willingness to repel PRC advance based on the Domino Theory. While the U.S. intervened in Korea, Taiwan, and Indochina, India overlooked the essential element common to each. This element was the inability of each nation to resist communist advance on its own. In this case, the projected image of Indian power was a liability. The realities of the international system and its anarchic nature would ensure that their decision to use force would not be consequence free. Now the Chinese causes for war will be evaluated at the systemic level.

## ALTERNATIVE EXPLANATIONS OF CONFLICT: DOMESTIC LEVEL ANALYSIS

A valid criticism of a systemic level approach to explaining conflict is that it overlooks key variables and differences between states in the assumption that all states are equal due to constraints that the structure of the international system places upon them. Singer argues that at this level of analysis "actors are characterized and their behaviour predicted in relatively gross and general terms". To account for the generalization of state behaviour inherent in a systemic level analysis a brief domestic level analysis explaining the Sino-Indian war will be attempted. Based on Vertberger's literature review on the subject, my domestic level analysis will be limited to the most influential domestic variable driving China and India to war; ideological and political considerations.

Indian ideological and political causes for war centered on the belief in non-alignment as a viable alternative to the bipolar system. The source of Indian non-aligned thought was that the Cold War was a conflict between the imperialist Western nations, and therefore newly independent former colonies had no reason or interest in siding with their former masters. The Indians by remaining non-aligned, hoped to establish a third pole of power in the international system organized by the nations of the Third World. This third bloc of nations would fight for issues that really mattered to them such as ending colonialism, racial discrimination, and raising living standards in the developing world. Nehru envisioned that this Third World bloc would act as an arbiter in the West's conflict, thereby gaining both moral authority and legitimacy.

In concert with the Bandung Conference in 1955 and the Sino-Indian Panchsheel Agreement, Nehru hoped to expand his concept of non-alignment into a full-blown pan-Asianism movement. This pan-Asianism was based in the common historical experience of colonialism that these nations shared, but Nehru failed to account for historical differences and regional rivalries. Nehru asserted that, "the basic challenge in Southeast Asia is between India and China," but he forgot this reality in supporting an Asian solidarity bloc. Nehru, and India's conception of a non-aligned third world was based on not only its viability, but that India would be both the natural and unchallenged leader of such a group. Traditional Sino-Indian rivalry for influence in Asia challenged Indian thinking as China asserted its right to be the leader of such a group. The need to exert its regional great power status over China led to diplomatic intransigence on the issue of border negotiations. Thus, India saw Chinese dispute of border areas to be a political challenge to their right to lead Asia, and in turn pushed backed in order to show strength.

Chinese ideological and political causes for war centered on the belief that its Maoist interpretation of communist revolution was not only correct, but purer than the Soviet model. This dispute on the merits of Maoism over Leninism was focused squarely on the Soviet Union's insistence on backing the Indian position in the border dispute through political and military aid. The PRC challenged Soviet actions on three points; that their diplomatic position showed a lack of solidarity with a fellow communist nation, that Soviet support of a bourgeoisie regime in India would not forward the goal of communist revolution, and that India wasn't truly non-aligned but in fact in league with the imperialists. Soviet military aid inflamed the PRC, especially in light of Soviet cuts to Chinese aid, because it appeared as if the Soviets were turning their backs on a Marxist brother. Furthermore, the PRC believed that only through struggle and challenge, not foreign aid, could they achieve the end of global Marxist revolution. Finally, Indian overtures to the West for aid, and their assistance to the West in fomenting problems on China's border led the PRC on a quest to convince the Soviets that they were being used. The PRC concluded that superior PLA military forces and position in the region would force the Indians to rely on Western intervention to bail them out in the event of hostilities. This would both expose the Indians as true imperialists, and score an ideological victory against the Soviet Union in the enlarging diplomatic split.

The domestic level analysis contends that it is domestic differences between states that drive them towards conflict. Examining the most influential domestic factors (according to scholars on the subject) on Chinese and Indian decision making leading to the 1962 war, it seems as if ideology had differing levels of importance for each nation. Indian ideology and their belief in leading a pan-Asian bloc nationalized tensions with China, creating a zero-sum game. If the Indian's backed down they would seem weak, and to avoid this they took a non-compromising stand on border issues. In China, Maoist ideology was more so an issue with hierarchy within the Soviet bloc than with Indian recalcitrance on border issues. The PRC actively believed the Indians not to be non-aligned, but this was not important as ideologically they did not pose a threat to the Chinese communist system. As such, Chinese ideology was not as important in crafting policy, and Zhou Enlai was able to take a pragmatic stand. As Singer points out the overgeneralization of a systemic analysis, he also points out that a domestic analysis suffers from the same weakness but instead an undue focus on state differences. The domestic analysis helps us better understand the importance of the border issue in each nation's context, but in this case it does not adequately explain the actions undertaken by either regime. Furthermore, only with a systemic level analysis can we explore the limitation on action caused by the international structure on each state. Ultimately, Chinese ideology does not explain why they did not take the offensive to oust India as imperialists, or why India decided to change its military policy towards an aggressive forward base strategy. Therefore, a systemic level analysis is more suited to explaining the actions leading to the Sino-Indian War.

While valid alternative theoretical models explaining the causes for war exist, a neorealist systems-level analysis best explains the factors leading India and China to war in 1962. Keeping in mind the historical context of generally cordial Sino-Indian relations prior to 1959 it seems unlikely that solely ideological differences drove the two nations to war. If ideology was such an important motivator behind the militarization of the Sino-Indian border dispute, then it is unlikely conflict would have waited to develop until 1962. Additionally, if Sino-Indian rivalry for dominance in Asia was so virulent why did India recognize PRC sovereignty in Tibet in 1951, and later agree to a mutual treaty of peaceful coexistence in 1954? A domestic level analysis cannot account for these otherwise amicable diplomatic relations.

What a systemic level analysis reveals is certain changes in national interests, geostrategic positions, and the anarchy of the international system brought both nations closer to the precipice of conflict. Various actions and reactions by both nations along the border created a security dilemma for each, and this brought the border dispute to the forefront of Sino-Indian relations. Furthermore, India believed they had the power to reshape the international system from a bipolar to multi-polar world. Their lack of either nuclear capability or significant conventional power exposed their status as simply a minor power of strategic importance in the international system. Thus either superpower was only motivated to preserve their security so long as it was in their interests to do so, and not as an ultimate necessity contrary to Indian belief. The ultimate cause for war in 1962 was India's assertion that it was a major power in world affairs. China's incentive in limiting their defeat of the Indian military was motivated by their interest in de-legitimizing the McMahon Line and consolidating their sovereignty in Tibet. The systems level analysis reveals not only what urged each nation to war, but also explains how the anarchy of the system limited the extent of the fighting.

## INDIA-PAKISTAN-CHINA (KASHMIR)

When India and Pakistan became independent of Great Britain in 1947, the various princely states, including that of Jammu and Kashmir, could accede to either country. An armed revolt of Muslim peasantry against the Maharaja of Jammu and Kashmir prompted the Maharaja to accede to India in order to gain military aid. Pakistan objected and the countries went to war. The matter was taken up by the UN Security Council in 1948, which adopted a resolution calling for the restoration of order, the withdrawal of Pakistani forces and reduction of Indian forces, and a UN plebiscite. India and Pakistan objected to various of these provisions. They went to war over Kashmir again in 1965. In 1971 India intervened in Pakistan's civil war that led to the independence of Bangladesh. India and Pakistan came close to war over Kashmir in 1990. (To view a map of this area click here.)

UN observers monitor part of the Indo-Pakistani cease-fire line. The current line was established by the 1972 Simla accord and approximately follows the 1949 Cease-fire Line. The coordinates of the Simla line have not been published, and the line was never delimited in the forbidding Siachin Glacier, near the Chinese frontier, where India and Pakistan frequently trade artillery rounds. Firing incidents and allegations of infiltration are chronic along the entire cease-fire line.

The Indian-controlled part of Jammu and Kashmir became a state in 1974. The parts of Kashmir controlled by Pakistan, Azad Kashmir and the Northern Areas, have anomalous status as administered territories. In 1963 China and Pakistan delimited a boundary that India claims illegally gave part of Kashmir to China. In 1987 a Sino-Pakistani protocol formalized demarcation of their boundary. The termination of this boundary at the Karakoram Pass on the Chinese line of control suggests that Pakistan recognizes Chinese sovereignty over Aksai Chin, which is part of the former Princely State of Kashmir.

India and Pakistan have held sporadic talks. In June 1997, they agreed to eight issues for discussion, including the issue of Kashmir and their maritime boundary. Pakistan wants to set-up a separate task force on Kashmir; India has resisted the idea. Talks have made little progress due to changes in the respective governments. The recent efforts by US Ambassador Richardson to resolve the dispute seem to have been blown out of the water by Indian and Pakistani nuclear tests.

## RESOLVING THE BOUNDARY DISPUTE: CHINA'S REASONS AND INDIA'S CHOICES

The final settlement of the Sino-Indian territorial and

boundary dispute is not a question of 'if' but 'when'. Four pertinent reasons suggest that China can be ultimately trusted to settle the dispute. On its part, India can take certain steps to ensure that China's reasons do not alter and that 'compromise' is seen as mutually beneficial.

One, China has steadily resolved its territorial disputes with almost all of its 15 land neighbours. Negotiations with the Soviet Union and Vietnam began in 1964 and 1977 respectively. However, it was not until much later that the negotiation processes fructified; it was only in October 2004 that the eastern sector of the Sino-Russian border was finally resolved with the signing of the Supplementary Agreement. With Vietnam, China signed a land boundary agreement in 1999, although they continue to meet regularly at the governmental level to thrash out details pertaining to the Beibu Gulf and the placement of border markers. Therefore, boundary negotiations between China and its other neighbours have been long and arduous affairs. The slowness of the boundary negotiations between India and China needs to be seen in this context.

Two, China has settled 17 of its 23 territorial disputes since 1949, according to M. Taylor Fravel, Assistant Professor of Political Science at MIT. Fravel suggests that regime insecurity and legitimacy crises in peripheral border regions best explain why China not only made concessions but also favoured the peaceful resolution of its territorial disputes. Despite a significant rise in China's economic and military strength vis-a-vis weaker neighbours, China received less than 50 per cent of the contested land. China's 'peaceful development' and 'new security concept' are directly responsible for the gradual stabilization of its borders-both concepts demand peaceful and stable borders for sustained economic growth.

Three, the absence of territorial disputes on China's western flank is a consequence of its 'western development' strategy. Starting with Myanmar and Nepal in the 1960s, a flurry of diplomatic activity saw the resolution of China's borders with Tajikistan and Kazakhstan (in 2002), Kyrgyzstan (in September 2004), Russia (in October 2004), and Mongolia (in November

2005). The pacification of China's western border is driven by the need to build cross-border linkages for economic development as well as the suppression of the three evils-separatism, extremism and terrorism. China's two westernmost provinces that border India, Xinjiang and Tibet, are important to China not least due to the fear that an economic imbalance can potentially fuel secessionist sentiments amongst the Uighurs and Tibetans.

Four, China is likely to reserve the use of force to settle heartland disputes. The hard component of China's comprehensive national strength will continue to dictate an inflexible stance on Taiwan's reunification as well as territorial conflicts of strategic value. Therefore, China is unlikely to make concessions on approximately 30,000 square kilometres of Aksai Chin, not least due to the fact that the Karakoram highway that traverses it provides a strategic link between Pakistan, and China and a shorter route between Tibet and Xinjiang. However, even in the case of disputes over territory of great economic value, such as the South China Sea, China has emphasized the joint development and exploitation of resources, albeit without making any concessions.

As emerging powers, India and China will continue to be pitted against each other. The sheer size and altitude of the disputed area is likely to make demarcation a difficult and lengthy process. However, India can take certain steps to ensure it remains in China's interest to settle the dispute. India must do its utmost to convince China that it is not the target of the newly sealed Indo-US strategic relationship. India must clarify that the support for Tibetans in India is humanitarian and cultural and not a challenge to China's sovereign territoriality. China's friendship with Pakistan cannot be wished away; however, India can make itself important to China by promising trade and joint border development projects that make good business sense. India's inclusion into the Shanghai Cooperation Organisation as an observer in July 2005 was an important recognition of India's commitment to curbing cross-border terrorism.

Even though there are reasons to believe that China is not a revisionist state determined to use force to uphold its territorial claims, proactive steps to create lobbies with vested interests in resolving the dispute must be taken. The seventh round of Sino-Indian border talks in March 2006 helped provide a 'constructive and friendly' atmosphere. It is time for India and China to carry that forward and focus on opening Nathu La for trade, reviving the Stilwell Road for trade across India's northeast, building border free trade zones similar to the Sino-Kazakh one and establishing independent inter-linkages between border regions through transport linkages akin to the Kashgar (Xinjiang, China)-Gilgit (Northern Areas, Pakistan) bus service. Discussion on the Sino-Indian boundary talks must therefore go beyond the rhetoric on China's 'concirclement' of India; it must emphasize the domestic constraints and foreign policy concerns of the Chinese government and the resolution of territorial disputes that such a study reveals.

## BEIJING'S RESPONSE TO INDIA-PAKISTAN TENSIONS AFTER 9/11

Since the late 1990s, China had become increasingly concerned over the gradual shift in the regional balance of power in South Asia, driven by the steady rise of India coupled with the growing US-India entente and the talk of "India as a counterweight to China" in Washington's policy circles, and by Pakistan's gradual descent into the ranks of failed states. Since the end of the Cold War, a politically dysfunctional and economically bankrupt Pakistan's flirtation with Islamic extremism and terrorism, coupled with its nuclear and missile programs, had alienated Washington.

However, the 11 September 2001 attacks changed all that. Pakistan saw an opportunity to revive its past close relations with the United States, shed its near pariah status, and enhance its economic and strategic position vis-à-vis India by instantaneously becoming a "frontline state" in the international coalition fighting global terrorism. In return, Washington lifted sanctions and agreed to provide Pakistan with billions of dollars in aid and debt rescheduling. From Washington's perspective, courting Musharraf made geopolitical sense because the Pakistani military not only knew a great deal about the Taliban, Osama bin Laden, and al Qaeda, but also because any US military operation against Afghanistan could not be successful without the bases, logistics, personnel, and airspace in neighbouring Pakistan. In Beijing, as a result, there were great expectations of a sharp downturn in US-India relations, because in many ways what happens on the Indian subcontinent is unavoidably a zero-sum game and Pakistan's new relationship with the United States did affect India negatively.

However, tensions between South Asia's nuclear-armed rivals rose sharply after the terrorist attacks at the Kashmir Assembly in October 2001 and the Indian Parliament on 13 December 2001. The attack on the Indian Parliament triggered a major deployment of Indian troops along the border with Pakistan, with Islamabad responding in kind. New Delhi warned of retaliatory, punitive military strikes against terrorist camps inside Pakistani-controlled Kashmir. Although the Chinese Foreign Ministry spokesperson condemned these attacks, Chinese leaders and South Asia watchers were much more circumspect and ambivalent while lauding Pakistan's contribution to the war against terrorism. A South Asia specialist from China's National Defence University, Wang Baofu, noted with satisfaction that under the new circumstances, "The United States, considering its own security interests, readjusted its policies toward South Asian countries and started paying more attention to the important role of Pakistan in the anti-terrorism war, therefore arousing the vigilance and jealousy of India." Wang criticized India for "defin[ing] resistance activities in Kashmir as terrorism by taking advantage of the US anti-terrorism war in Afghanistan, thus putting more pressure on Pakistan through the United States," and praised General Musharraf for his "clear-cut attitude toward fighting against international terrorism)." Such a stance was not unexpected. For almost a decade, China had rejected India's proposal to issue a joint declaration against terrorism lest it be interpreted as a condemnation of Pakistan. Pakistan President General

Musharraf made three trips to Beijing in less than a year (in December 2001, January 2002, and August 2002) for urgent security consultations with President Jiang Zemin and Premier Zhu Rongji and reportedly obtained "firm assurances of support in the event of a war" with India. At the time of heightened tensions in mid-January 2002, General Zhang Wannian, Vice-Chairman of China's Central Military Commission, met with General Muhammad Aziz Khan, Chairman of Pakistan's Joint Chiefs of the Staff Committee, and was quoted as telling Khan: "For many years the militaries of our two nations have maintained exchanges and cooperation at the highest and all levels and in every field. This fully embodies the all-weather friendship our nations maintain." Zhang's reference to "cooperation... inevery field" (meaning the nuclear and missile fields) was a thinly veiled warning to India to back off. Later, Beijing matched words with deeds by rushing two dozen F-7 jet fighters, nuclear and missile components, and other weapon systems to shore up Pakistani defenses in the tense border face-off.Asecret "futuristic arms development cooperation" agreement was signed during General Musharraf's five-day visit to China in December 2001 to construct, among other weapons, an all-solid-fuel Shaheen III missile with a range of 3,500-4,000 kilometers to target all major Indian cities. The People's Liberation Army (PLA) troops from the Military Regions of Chengdu and Lanzhou and their respective subdivisions, the Xizang (Tibet) and Wulumuqi (Urumqi), along China's southern borders, were also put on alert in January to test their war preparedness should the conflict in the Indian subcontinent spill over onto Chinese soil.

The Chinese leaders had reportedly conveyed the following message to Musharraf: "China hopes Pakistan will not initiate any assault. Pakistan should not get involved in wars and instead focus on economic construction. However, if a war does break out between India and Pakistan, Beijing will firmly stand on the side of Islamabad." Soon thereafter, President Musharraf in a televised speech on 12 January 2002 announced a crackdown on extremist organizations waging jihad from Pakistani territory, and as a result, Indo-Pakistani tensions somewhat subsided. The Chinese media claimed some credit for "mediating" between the two sub-continental rivals despite the Indian government's aversion to the dreaded "m" word: "Mediated by the United States, China, Britain, and Russia, leaders of India and Pakistan recently expressed their desire to try to control the tense situation." 12 Interestingly, this stance contradicted then Indian Foreign Minister Jaswant Singh's statement during Premier Zhu's visit to New Delhi in January 2002 that "China has neither any intention, nor shall it play any mediatory role between India and Pakistan." Not only that, the Chinese Foreign Minister also succeeded in persuading his Russian counterpart to issue a "Joint Declaration on the India-Pakistan Situation," signaling to New Delhi that, for the first time, Beijing and Moscow had a unified stand on the dispute. In concrete policy terms, it meant that New Delhi could no longer count on the Russian veto in the UN Security Council in the event of a war.

Then came the 14 May 2002 terrorist attack on a military base in Jammu that killed 34 people, mostly women and children, once again escalating tensions along the border where more than one million troops backed by heavy armor, warplanes, and missiles were deployed. There was renewed tough talk of war, including nuclear war, on both sides of the border. Beijing called for restraint from both India and Pakistan and emphasized the need for peaceful dialogue to settle outstanding disputes. Chinese Defence Minister Chi Haotian also urged both countries to desist from a military conflict and not to threaten each other with nuclear weapons. Describing the US diplomatic moves (i.e., the dispatch of Deputy Secretary of State Richard Armitage and Defence Secretary Donald Rumsfeld in early June 2002) to defuse the India-Pakistan military stand-off as "too little too late," the state-run media accused Washington of showing "no genuine desire to resolve the Kashmir issue." It noted that Washington had clearly not taken the tensions very seriously when it went on with a ten-day joint military maneuver with India on 16-26 May 2002, thereby implying that the Indo-US joint military exercise had emboldened India to up the ante against Pakistan. On 15 May, a Chinese official accompanying

Foreign Minister Tang Jiaxuan during his visit to Islamabad told Pakistani journalists that China would back Pakistan in any conflict with India. Concerned over the "one-sided nature of public appeals" from Washington, Moscow, London, Paris, and Tokyo to General Musharraf to halt "cross-border terrorism" into Indian Kashmir, Chinese Foreign Minister Tang Jiaxuan told US Secretary of State Colin Powell on 27 May 2002 that "the international community should encourage direct dialogue between India and Pakistan in a more balanced and fair manner, which is the most effective way to lead South Asia towards peace and stability." Apparently, the growing threat of nuclear war and the prospect of Pakistani nuclear weapons falling into the hands of Islamic terrorists have made Washington lean heavily on Islamabad. In contrast, Beijing repeatedly asked New Delhi to do more to end the military stand-off while publicly calling for restraint by both sides and claiming to be even-handed. China continued to covertly side with its long-term ally, however, and is providing military wherewithal to Pakistan.

Meanwhile, in yet another television address on 27 May, Musharraf pledged that all militant infiltration across the Line of Control (LoC) would end, and he announced the banning of Lashkar-e-Toiba, the Jaish-e-Mohammad, and the Harkat-ul-Mujahideen—the three "*jihadi*" outfits at the forefront of terrorist activity in Indian Kashmir. From New Delhi's perspective, India's military deployment had succeeded in bringing the international focus on Pakistan as the home of pan-Islamic *jihadis* after the war in Afghanistan.

At the Conference on Interaction and Confidence Building Measures in Asia held in Kazakhstan in early June 2002, Chinese President Jiang Zemin pressed Indian Prime Minister Vajpayee to enter into direct talks with Pakistani President Musharraf to prevent the Kashmir conflict from exploding into a full-scale war. But the Indian government was so irked over Musharraf's playing of "the China card" that Vajpayee refused to budge. Later, in an interview with *The Washington Post*, the Indian Prime Minister complained that he saw "no basic change in China's policy. China continues to help Pakistan acquire weapons and equipment." In an article titled "Beijing as Guarantor of Pakistan's Security," a Russian weekly, *Nezavisimoye Voyennoye Obozreniye* (Independent Military Review), had reported that new security commitments have indeed been made to Pakistan by China since 9/11.[18] New Delhi expressed its displeasure with Beijing by postponing scheduled visits by Indian Army Chief Padmanabhan and Prime Minister Vajpayee to China in October and November 2002.

## The Nuclear Connection

There were other grounds for the cooling of relations between Beijing and New Delhi. In his testimony before the US Senate governmental affairs subcommittee in early June 2002, the Assistant Secretary of State for Nonproliferation, John S. Wolf, revealed that "China recently provided Islamabad with missile-related technologies, which include dual-use missile-related items, raw materials, and other accessories essential for missile manufacturing." In a sense, China's nuclear and missile assistance to a volatile Pakistan over the last two decades has now created the risk of a conventional conflict swiftly escalating into nuclear war. Beijing has not only provided Islamabad with nuclear bombs, uranium, and plants (all three Pakistani nuclear plants—Kahuta, Khushab, and Chasma— have been built with Chinese assistance) but also their delivery systems: readyto-launch M-9 (Ghaznavi/Hatf), M-11 (Shaheen), and a number of Dong Feng 21 (Ghauri) ballistic missiles. This cooperation has continued despite Beijing's growing concerns over the "Talibanization" of the Pakistani state and society. When Islamabad carried out a series of missile tests amidst heightened tensions apparently to warn New Delhi to back off, the Indian government drew the international community's attention to the Pakistani missiles' China connection. "We are not impressed by these missile antics, particularly when all that is demonstrated is borrowed or imported ability.... The technology used in the missiles is not their own but clandestinely acquired from other countries," said a spokesperson of the Indian External Affairs Ministry.

Pakistan's test of its nuclear-capable, medium-range, Shaheen ballistic missile in early October 2002, just days before the parliamentary elections, once again provoked India to level accusations of missile technology proliferation by China. India's outspoken Defence Minister, George Fernandes, long a critic of China, said that Pakistan's military had always depended on support from China ever since it was carved out as a homeland for South Asia's Muslims in 1947 following decolonization of British India. "Everyone knows what Pakistan will be without China. Its ego is boosted purely by the support it gets from China," Fernandes said at a party convention in Mumbai. Earlier, when India weaponized its nuclear capability through a series of tests in May 1998, Fernandes had described "China [as] the mother of Pakistan's nuclear bomb" and claimed that India's aim was to counter China's capability rather than Pakistan's, drawing protests from Beijing. When Pakistan came in the firing line following revelations in the US media about the missiles-for-nukes barter deal with North Korea, New Delhi argued that blame should also be put on China for making Pakistan a nuclear weapons state.

For New Delhi, Beijing's military alliance with Islamabad remains a sore point because the Sino-Pakistani nuclear nexus has introduced a new element of uncertainty and complexity in sub-continental strategic equations. While the attention of world leaders and the media has been focused on the nightmarish scenario of a nuclear Armageddon in South Asia and large-scale mutual assured destruction leading to the deaths of 12 to 30 million people, strategic circles in Islamabad and New Delhi have been discussing the pros and cons of a short, limited nuclear war in Kashmir. Media reports based on intelligence leaks have revealed the forward deployment by the Pakistani military of low-yield (five kilotons or less) tactical nuclear weapons (TNWs). Such small battlefield nuclear weapons have a one-mile destruction radius and could be used effectively against large troop concentrations and advancing tank formations along the LoC in Kashmir.

The Pakistanis seem to have taken a page out of China's book on tactical nuclear warfighting capability. Just as persistent

Sino-Soviet disputes and the Soviet Union's conventional military superiority during the 1970s and 1980s gave China strong incentives to develop and deploy TNWs, the decade-long India-Pakistan border tensions and India's conventional superiority may have added momentum to Islamabad's efforts to deploy TNWs. Most of Pakistan's missiles acquired from China, such as the M-9, are short-range, solid-fueled, mobile, nuclear-capable missiles and can be used in a tactical mode. Asked to comment on reports that Pakistan has acquired TNWs, the Deputy Chief of the Indian Army, Lieutenant General Raj Kadyan, was quoted as saying that the "Indian Army has trained itself to cope with a tactical nuclear strike in the battlefield." Tactical nukes can be launched over an unpopulated area from field artillery guns or aircraft to halt an enemy advance or in an effort to intimidate a numerically stronger enemy. Since the damage is localized or confined to a certain area, the danger of affecting the civilian population is greatly reduced as compared to a strategic nuclear weapon of the Hiroshima kind and therefore need not evoke massive retaliation by enemy forces. The mountainous terrain in Kashmir provides the perfect setting for their use.

In addition to the United States and Russia, only China is believed to have a large stockpile of about 120 TNWs or "baby nukes." Some of these were apparently delivered to Pakistan following the visit of PLA Deputy Chief and military intelligence boss General Xiong Guangkai (arguably China's most important military figure and the man who calls Pakistan "China's Israel") to Islamabad in early March 2002.27 If the reports of China's transfer of TNWs to Pakistan are indeed true, the question then is: Would India, which does not possess TNWs but has strategic nuclear weapons in abundance, keep a nuclear conflict limited or escalate it to the strategic level and respond with massive retaliation? Though New Delhi has long maintained that even a tactical nuclear strike on its forces would be treated as a nuclear first strike, and would invite massive retaliation, some Pakistani generals believe that a tactical strike would circumvent retaliation from India, since such an attack on an advancing tank regiment or infantry battalion (in contrast to a strategic strike killing millions of civilians), would not be provocation enough for all-out retaliation. They contend that the many layers of bureaucracy surrounding India's nuclear capability, the strength of world public opinion, and the fact that strategic command remains in civilian hands places severe doubts on India's willingness and ability to retaliate with a massive nuclear strike against an opponent, particularly in the face of only a limited tactical strike from Pakistan.

Some analysts attribute the recent lessening of tensions to the belated recognition in India's strategic circles that New Delhi cannot afford to dismiss Pakistan's repeated threats of using nuclear weapons as "mere posturing" or "bluffing" on Islamabad's part. They point to the Pakistani military's strong aversion to fighting a 1965-or 1971-type conventional war with India and offer this as the rationale behind Islamabad's decision to pull back from the brink on several occasions in recent history (in 1987, 1990, 1999, and 2002). Others believe that the tendency of Indian strategic planners to discount the threat of nuclear escalation may well be based on some fundamentally erroneous assumptions:

- That the United States cannot allow Pakistan to be the first Islamic country to use nuclear weapons to settle a territorial dispute, as it would mean the end of the global nonproliferation regime and encourage other countries to go nuclear to settle their territorial disputes as well.
- That the presence of US forces in Pakistan will be a constraining factor.
- That the international community (the United States, United Kingdom, China, or the United Nations) will intervene in time to prevent such a catastrophe.
- And that India can count on American and Israeli military support to seize or take out Pakistan's nuclear and missile infrastructure. These assumptions do not seem to be based on cold, clear-headed calculations of the strategic interests and influence of major powers (especially the United States and China) and may well

be a sign of wishful thinking on India's part. It is worth noting that new strategic and geopolitical realities emerging in Asia since 9/11 have put a question mark over Beijing's older certainties, assumptions, and beliefs.

## China's Concerns

Much to Jiang and his Politburo's chagrin, the US-led war on terrorism has developed in ways that could not have been foreseen, with potentially disastrous consequences for China's core strategic interests. A major unintended (and unsettling, from Beijing's standpoint) consequence has been not only to checkmate and roll back China's recent strategic expansion moves in Central, South, and Southeast Asia, thereby severely constricting the strategic latitude that China has enjoyed since the Cold War, but also to tilt the regional balance of power decisively in Washington's favour within a short period. The supposedly brief Unipolar moment in history seems to have turned into a long-lasting Imperial moment—a Pax Americana *par excellence*. More important, recent developments show how tenuous Chinese power remains when compared to that of the United States.

The fast-changing strategic scene not only undercuts Chinese ambitions to expand Beijing's power and influence in Asia, but also hems in the one country in the world with the most demonstrable capacity to act independently of the United States. Not surprisingly, the beginning of 2002 saw Chinese leaders and generals shedding their earlier inhibitions about publicly expressing concern over the growing "southern discomfort"—that is, ever-expanding US military power and presence in southern Asia after 9/11. China's Chief of the General Staff Fu Quanyou warned the United States against using the war on terrorism to dominate global affairs by saying "counter-terrorism should not be used to practice hegemony." On an official visit in April 2002 in Iran, Jiang Zemin openly repudiated the US stance against the Iranian and Iraqi regimes, saying, "Our opinion [on terrorism] is not the same as the United States." In Germany, he told the *Welt am Sonntag*: "We all want to fight terrorism. But the states involved in the fight against terror each have their own specific viewpoint." China's initial optimism that new Sino-US-Pakistan triangular cooperation in the aftermath of 11 September 2001 would wean Washington away from New Delhi turned out to be wishful thinking as Bush Administration officials went out of their way to assure India that America's intensifying alliance with Pakistan would not come at India's expense. If anything, the current crisis has strengthened the American commitment to building stronger relations, including defence ties, with South Asia's preeminent power. However, China does not want to see India increasing its power, stature, and profile regionally or internationally. Beijing shares Islamabad's deep mistrust of India's strategic ambitions and seeks to prevent India's emergence as a peer competitor and a major strategic rival in Asia. That is why Chinese strategists have long argued that China's pursuit of great power status is a historical right and perfectly legitimate but India's pursuit of great power status is illegitimate, wrong, dangerous, and a sign of hegemonic, imperial behaviour. For its part, New Delhi has long accused Beijing of doing everything it can to undermine India's interests and using its ties with other states to contain India. Beijing is also alarmed over the growing talk in some con-servative policy circles in Washington and New Delhi of India emerging as a counterweight to China on the one hand and the fragile, radical Islamic states of West Asia on the other.

Earlier, when President Bush unveiled his missile defence plan, New Delhi responded far more positively than did most US allies. Some Indian strategic thinkers even see in the emerging US-India quasi-alliance an opportunity for "payback" to China. As G. Parthasarthy, former Indian Ambassador to Pakistan and Burma, put it: "Whether it was the Bangladesh conflict of 1971, or in the Clinton-Jiang Declaration in the aftermath of our nuclear tests, China has never hesitated to use its leverage with the Americans to undermine our security." Growing Chinese strategic pressure on the Malacca Straits has already led to maritime collaboration between India and the United States, with their navies jointly patrolling the straits. More significantly, US-India strategic engagement has scaled new heights with the announcement of a series of measures usually reserved for close US allies and friends: joint military exercises in Alaska that would boost India's high-altitude warfare capabilities in the Himalayan glaciers of northern Kashmir where it faces Pakistan and China; sale of military hardware including radars, aircraft engines, and surveillance equipment to India; joint naval exercises and the training of India's special forces; and intelligence sharing as well as the joint naval patrols in the Straits of Malacca. Washington also reportedly gave the green light for Israel to proceed with selling the Phalcon airborne early warning and control system (AWACS) to India—something that was earlier denied to China for fear of enhancing Beijing's air surveillance and early warning capabilities in the Taiwan Strait.

All of these measures send an implicit signal to China of India's growing military prowess. In a cover story in the authoritative *Beijing Review*, one of China's noted South Asia specialists expressed concern over the US sale of arms to India which "enables it to become the first country to have close military relations with the world's two big powers—the United States and Russia." To make matters worse, in early May 2002 Prime Minister Koizumi of Japan, Beijing's other Asian rival, which sees China representing a clear and future threat to its security, called for a broadening of Japan's security cooperation with India.

Many Chinese strategists believe India is using the war on terrorism as a pretext to militarily subdue Pakistan or to destabilize and dismember the country. Pakistan is the only country that stands up to India and thereby prevents Indian hegemony over the region, thus fulfilling a key objective of China's South Asia policy. 39 As South Asia watcher Ehsan Ahrari points out: "India may end up intensifying its own rivalry with China by remaining steadfast in its insistence that Musharraf kowtow to its demands, especially if China calculates that US-India ties are harming its own regional interests. China, though still concerned about the continued activism of Islamist groups in Pakistan and contiguous areas, is not at all willing to see the regional balance of power significantly tilt in favour of India." Though Beijing welcomes the new US commitment to prop up Beijing's "all-weather friend" after a decade of abandonment and estrangement, most Chinese strategists worry about the destabilizing consequences of a prolonged US military presence in Pakistan and increased influence on the future of Sino-Pakistan ties as well as on Pakistan's domestic stability. The Chinese are also believed to be "highly uncomfortable" with the four US military bases in Pakistan. Of special concern to Beijing is the US presence at Pasni in the Baluchistan region of Pakistan, where China is constructing a deep-water naval port at Gwadar, the inland Makran coastal highway linking it with Karachi, and several oil and gas pipeline projects.

Beijing has long been eyeing its construction of the naval base at Gwadar, at the mouth of the Strait of Hormuz in the Persian Gulf, as a bulwark against the US presence and India's growing naval power. Furthermore, the US military presence in Pakistan could sharpen the divide within the Pakistani military into pro-West and pro-Beijing factions, with China supporting the latter to regain ground lost since 9/11.44 The pro-Beijing lobby within the Pakistani military is reportedly getting restive and waiting to strike if and when General Musharraf falters. The pro-China faction within the Pakistani military could also join hands with the pro-Islamic fundamentalist faction opposing the US military presence on Pakistan's soil. Alternatively, it could throw its support behind those nationalist elements that find Pakistan's loss of its "strategic depth" in Afghanistan for elusive diplomatic gains very hard to digest. The US arms sales to India and joint US-Indian military exercises may further sour China's and Pakistan's willingness to assist Washington in its war on terrorism.

## War Scenarios

It is said that each conflict simply prepares the ground for the next one or every war contains the seeds of another. The AfghanWar of the 1980s against the Soviet occupation culminated in the war on terrorism in 2001. Whether the war on terrorism will lead to another war or a clash of civilizations or a nuclear jihad in South Asia, only time will tell. Pakistan is, in the words of former Italian Foreign Minister Gianni De Michelis, "the fuse of the world." The provinces close to the Afghan border and home to the US military bases are now controlled by Islamic parties that created the Taliban and are openly sympathetic to the aims and ideals of al Qaeda. The rising anti-American sentiment in Pakistan as demonstrated in the recent elections has made the country increasingly unstable. Violence levels in Indian Kashmir also continue to rise. Many observers believe that Washington may have to rethink its strategy vis-à-vis Islamabad if the war on terrorism is to be won decisively. The complete dismantling of the al Qaeda terrorist infrastructure in Pakistan seems unlikely because of the apprehension within the Pakistani military that doing so would devalue Pakistan's importance in the US security strategy and once again make the United States turn its back on the country and make the country vulnerable to Western pressure and sanctions. It would also deprive Pakistan of invaluable Western aid and leverage vis-à-vis Washington and New Delhi.

One Chinese national security analyst argues that "what worries China more is the possibility that it could be drawn into a conflict, not between Pakistan and India per se, but between Pakistan and the United States, with the latter using India as a surrogate." With the top al Qaeda and Taliban leadership fleeing into Pakistan's Wild West and Pakistani-held Kashmir, Beijing knows full well that Pakistan is no longer the "frontline state" in the war on terrorism that it once was; it is, in fact, the battlefield in the war on terror. Should the India-Pakistani conflict escalate into a nuclear one, neither the geopolitical nor the radioactive fallout will remain limited to South Asia. Indeed, the most worrisome scenario would be one where Pakistan is losing a conventional conflict and uses tactical nuclear weapons in a desperate effort to win or to salvage a face-saving defeat that would allow the regime to survive. (The risk-taking nature of the Pakistani military leadership suggests that such a scenario cannot be completely ruled out.) Should India respond by launching strategic nuclear strikes resulting in the complete destruction of the Pakistani state, China would find it difficult to sit idly by. The next India-Pakistan war also could bring the United States and Pakistan on a collision course, with or without India acting as a US partner. Such a development would obviously present China with difficult choices. Open support for its closest ally would jeopardize China's relations with the United States and India. But nonintervention on Pakistan's behalf could encourage India to solve "the Pakistan problem" once and for all, with or without a nuclear exchange, and thereby tilt the regional balance of power decisively in its favour. As Zhang Xiaodong put it: "There is the real possibility that a new Indian-Pakistani war will take place in the future. This war would be disastrous, as it would change the whole political balance in Central and South Asia," which is currently tilted in China's favour. Unrestrained Indian power could eventually threaten China's security along its soft underbelly—Tibet and Xinjiang.

Should post-Musharraf Pakistan disintegrate or be taken over by Islamic extremists, a new level of instability would rock the region and increase tensions among Pakistan, India, and China. Another dreadful scenario is one in which Chinese-made Pakistani nuclear weapons fall into the hands of the United States, Israel, or even India in the event of a civil war should al Qaeda or the Taliban declare jihad against Pakistan—the weakest ally in the US-led anti-terrorism coalition. 51 India would be tempted to militarily intervene in Pakistan if Islamists gain control over the nuclear weapons of its neighbour, either through a coup or civil war. Such a scenario could reveal information regarding China's own nuclear program and the extent of help provided by Beijing to Islamabad. The scenario of Pakistan in splinters, with one piece becoming a radical Muslim state in possession of nuclear weapons, can no longer be simply rejected as an alarmist fantasy.

## Difficult Choices

These scenarios put Beijing on the horns of a dilemma. Some Chinese strategists see in the current South Asian crisis an opportunity to recover lost ground and thwart India's ambitions to challenge China's future economic and military primacy in Asia. Should another war between India and Pakistan break out, New Delhi's high hopes of an India-US alliance to counter China may never materialize, a welcome development from China's perspective. Some hawks in the PLAsee China even benefiting from an India-Pakistani nuclear war. Hideaki Kase, a former special advisor to Japanese Premiers Takeo Fukuda and Yasuhiro Nakasone, believes that "China wants an Indo-Pakistan war, possibly a nuclear conflict, to weaken India." At the time of the 1999 Kargil War, one Chinese military official had reportedly told a Western diplomat that "should India and Pakistan destroy themselves in a nuclear war, there would be peace along China's southwestern frontiers for at least three decades, and Beijing needs 20 to 30 years to consolidate its hold over restive Tibet and Xinjiang provinces." However, this remains a minority viewpoint, as a nuclear war would have worldwide repercussions in terms of global economic depression, humanitarian crises, WMD proliferation, and China's developmental priorities.

Most Chinese analysts and policymakers believe that Beijing should have absolutely minimum involvement in a situation where there can be no clear winners. Some argue that Beijing should seize the opportunity to coordinate its South Asia policy with Washington as it is in the interests of both countries to avert the world's first nuclear exchange and to use India-Pakistan tensions to strengthen Sino-US ties.

While the Pakistanis are confident that if war comes with India, China will throw its weight behind Pakistan, diplomatically as well as militarily, the Indians remain adamant that the Chinese would not do so for fear of India playing "the Taiwan and Tibet cards." Interestingly, on 31 May 2002, the day Pakistan's new UN Ambassador, Munir Akram, issued an explicit nuclear warning to India, a Chinese Foreign Ministry spokesman denied a *Times of India* report that Chinese President Jiang Zemin had assured a US congressional delegation that China would not favour Pakistan in the existing tensions, and claimed that the report was "not based on facts."

A Chinese South Asia analyst at Fudan University in Shanghai, Shen Dingli, told *The Wall Street Journal*: "China needs to send a message: For my own security I will intervene." Though Beijing may not overtly intervene in a limited war, China's geopolitical imperative requires it to come to Pakistan's defence if the latter's existence as a nation-state is threatened by India. Clearly, there is a great deal more to the Chinese role in South Asia than meets the eye. In the final analysis, Beijing's response to the next India-Pakistan war will be shaped by its desire to protect Chinese national interests, no matter what the cost.

Geostrategic concerns require China to covertly side with Pakistan, while publicly calling for restraint by both sides and appearing to be even-handed. In the triangular power balance game, the South Asian military balance of power is neither pro-India nor pro-Pakistan, it has always been pro-China. And Beijing will take all means possible, including war, to ensure that the regional power balance does not tilt in India's favour. Even in the absence of a war, Pakistan hopes to continue to reap significant military and economic payoffs not only from the intensifying Sino-Indian geopolitical rivalry in southern Asia but also from what many believe is the coming showdown between China and the United States, which will further increase the significance of China's strategic ties with Pakistan. In the meantime, a major consolation for Beijing is that a stronger Pakistan aided by the United States, Western Europe, Japan, and international financial institutions would be better able to balance and contain rival India.

# 2

# Globalization Impact on Threat Perceptions in India, Pakistan and China

For the purpose of this book, South Asia has been taken to cover India, Afghanistan, Pakistan, Bangladesh, Sri Lanka, Nepal, Bhutan and the Maldives. Even though China is not considered a part of South Asia, it has common borders with some of the countries of the region and their threat perceptions are influenced by the China factor.

There cannot, therefore, be any meaningful discussion on this subject without a reference to this factor. South Asia, as defined above, covers only about 10 per cent of the total land area of the Asian continent, but about 40 per cent of Asia's total population and between 45 and 50 per cent of Asia's Muslim population live in this area.

Many analysts in India, including this writer, make a distinction between the Indian sub-continent and South Asia. When they talk of the Indian sub-continent, they have in mind India, Pakistan, Bangladesh, Nepal and Bhutan. Of these, India, Pakistan and Bangladesh constituted one political entity before the British left the sub-continent in 1947. Pakistan was born in 1947 through the partition of the British India and Bangladesh was born in 1971 through the partition of Pakistan after a war of liberation waged by the Bengalis of the then East Pakistan, with Indian assistance.

Indian analysts, who talk of the Indian sub-continent, wish to keep in mind, in their analyses, the common historical, political, religious and cultural heritage of these three countries. The term sub-continent is used less and less in Pakistan and Bangladesh. The political leadership and the policy-makers in these two countries do not wish to be reminded of this common heritage. Any highlighting of this common heritage by Indian analysts is viewed by them with suspicion—— as indicating a hidden desire to reverse history and undo the 1947 partition. They, therefore, talk only of South Asia and have, for all practical purposes, banished any reference to the sub-continent from their strategic discourse. This has to be kept in mind since complexes arising from sub-continental memories tend to influence their mind-set and threat perceptions and have stood in the way of the progress of globalization in this area. They view any Indian enthusiasm for globalization as a concealed attempt towards political and economic re-subcontinentalisation.

## THE INDIA FACTOR

The India factor has had an impact on the threat perceptions of all the countries of this region except Afghanistan and the Maldives. This arises due to the following reasons:

- Asymmetry in size, human and material resources and economic and military potential.
- Perceived Indian willingness/tendency to assert its national interests even if they be detrimental to those of the neighbours. Examples: India's role in the creation of Bangladesh, alleged Indian support to the Tamils of Sri Lanka.
- Perceived Indian encouragement of its political favourites in the countries of the region. Examples: India's alleged soft corner for the opposition Awami League in Bangladesh and for the democratic forces in Nepal.
- Continuing differences relating to territory (Kashmir with Pakistan) and utilization of water resources (Pakistan and Bangladesh).

The other countries, except Afghanistan and the Maldives, tend to guard themselves against these factors by avoiding too close economic linkages with India, which comes in the way of the region as a whole benefiting from the fruits of globalization, by developing economic and military linkages with China and by supporting Chinese aspirations for a role in regional organizations such as the SAARC as an observer.

Pakistan and Bangladesh embarked on a policy of liberalization of their economies before India. Despite this, their economic development has not been as satisfactory as they would have like it to be. Amongst the reasons, one could cite the bad internal security situation, which keeps foreign investors away despite a favourable policy framework; political instability due to periodic interventions by the Army in politics; inadequate investment in a modern education system due to the diversion of the limited resources to meet military and strategic needs; and failure to diversify the economy. Pakistan's economy continues to be largely a three-commodity (cotton and cotton textiles, leather goods and sports articles) and one-port (Karachi) economy. Bangladesh's economy continues to be largely textiles, jute and raw materials dependent.

Though India embarked on the liberalization of its economy only from 1991 onwards, its economy has made impressive progress freeing it from its past dependence on traditional goods such as textiles, tea etc. India's rapid diversification and development of its economy have been facilitated by the facts that democracy has taken firm roots in the country; that its internal security problems, though serious, are confined to areas in which the foreign investors are presently not interested; and that its founding fathers had shown foresight in investing heavily on a modern education system, including institutes of excellence in technology, which have significantly contributed to its emergence as a leading Information Technology (IT) power.

Complexes and concerns arising from the India factor continue to come in the way of the normalization of trade relations between Pakistan and India, the improvement in the trade relations between India and Bangladesh and progress towards the integration of the economies of the region through appropriate institutional and policy frameworks. Political factors continue to receive priority over economic and prejudices and fears continue to rule out pragmatism.

However, economic realities ultimately have a way of asserting themselves. One could already see a beginning of it in Pakistan. Its rulers and policy-makers have realized that a favourable policy frame-work and wide-ranging reforms alone will not attract foreign investors. They also need a market and consumers large enough to make their investments adequately profitable. Pakistan does not provide such a market and such a reservoir of consumers. Unless the foreign investors perceive the sub-continent as a whole as a single economic entity and market and are able to sell their products anywhere within this entity, they are reluctant to invest in Pakistan or Bangladesh alone, without guarantees of access to the Indian market.

The realization of this ground reality has already brought about a significant change in Pakistan's policy since Gen. Pervez Musharraf came to power in October, 1999. While continuing to oppose the normalization of economic relations with India till the differences over Jammu & Kashmir (J&K) are settled, he has made an exception in respect of energy supplies. He is prepared now to allow the foreign investors investing heavily in the construction of oil and gas pipelines to Pakistan from Iran or Turkmenistan to cater to the requirements of the Indian market too in order to make their investments adequately profitable. Significantly, even the religious fundamentalist parties, who continue to insist on a policy of "Kashmir first and the rest later", have not objected to what Gen. Musharraf describes as the stand-alone exception. If this exception materializes and if the benefits of it are felt by the Pakistani people, this will become more and more a rule than a mere exception.

Such a realization is yet to come about in Bangladesh. The trade relations between India and Bangladesh are not as restricted as those between India and Pakistan. There is a much, much freer flow of trade between the two countries. While encouraging a greater flow of trade with China,

Bangladesh continues to prevent pragmatism, profitability and mutual benefits from having a free play to contribute to a rapid expansion of the bilateral economic relations with India.

Four examples could be cited as illustrations of the Bangladesh attitude:

- It refuses to sell its surplus gas to India on the ostensible ground that it wants to conserve it for its future use. At the same time, it has reportedly entered into negotiations with China for selling it through a pipeline to China via Myanmar.
- It refuses to grant transit rights to India to facilitate the movement of Indian goods to India's northeast.
- It has been reluctant to permit a pipeline to bring gas from the Arakan area of Myanmar to India pass through Bangladesh territory.
- During the period from July to December, 2005, the value of Chinese exports to Bangladesh amounted to US $ 1.03 billion and Chinese imports from Bangladesh only US $ 27.9 million. During the same period, the value of Indian exports to Bangladesh amounted to US $ 820 million and imports from Bangladesh to US $ 105 million. India's imports from Bangladesh are still small, but they are four times the value of Chinese imports from Bangladesh. Chinese exports to Bangladesh are nearly 25 per cent more than those of India. And yet, while Bangladesh nurses a grudge against India on the ground that it has allegedly been dumping its goods in Bangladesh and has not been buying enough from there, it does not voice a similar grievance against China.

Feelings of insecurity, an aggressive inferiority complex, and a Me-too syndrome continue to influence policy-making in Pakistan. What India does, it must do too. What India gets, it must get too. One saw an example of this syndrome in action during the recent visit of President George Bush to India and Pakistan, when, during Mr. Bush's talks in Islamabad, Gen. Musharraf reportedly pleaded with him to reach with Pakistan an agreement on co-operation in the development of civilian nuclear energy similar to the agreement offered to India. Mr. Bush had to point out to him that the needs and circumstances of the two countries are different.

These factors——feelings of insecurity, the inferiority complex and the Me-too syndrome—will continue to influence the Pakistani mind-set and policy-making in the short and medium terms. Though there has been progress in the identification and implementation of confidence-building measures and in the promotion of people-to-people contacts, the relationship between the two countries will continue to be fragile and the exploitation of the opportunities for beneficial co-operation provided by globalization will be slow.

While Pakistan's longing for the acquisition of J&K and its painful memories of 1971 could explain its attitude to India, no convincing explanation is possible for the behaviour of Bangladesh. While there are differences between India and Bangladesh over the utilization of river waters, there are no major differences over territory compared to the Kashmir issue with Pakistan and Bangladesh has no negative memories of India's military might in action against it. The anti-Indian reflexes in Bangladesh are largely confined to the present ruling formation headed by Begum Khalida Zia and are not shared by the opposition headed by the Awami League, which was in the forefront of its independence struggle.

India-Bangladesh relations will continue to zigzag—— improving when the Awami League is in power and stagnating, if not declining, when the Bangladesh National Party comes to power. Globalization has not made any significant difference to this zigzag and is unlikely to do so in the short and medium terms.

## THE PAKISTAN FACTOR

A reference has already been made to the Pakistan factor while discussing India-Pakistan relations. Two other aspects, which have not been touched upon earlier, need to be highlighted. The first relates to Pakistan's use of terrorism as a covert weapon to achieve its strategic objective of forcing a change in the status quo in Jammu and Kashmir. The second relates to its long-nourished objective of acquiring a strategic depth vis-a-vis India by bringing Afghanistan under its control and by establishing military and strategic linkages with Iran.

It was these objectives, which led Pakistan to set up a clandestine infrastructure not only in its territory, but also in Afghan territory for training and arming terrorists for use against India. It was from this infrastructure that Al Qaeda, the Taliban and the various terrorist organizations, which are members of the International Islamic Front (IIF) of bin Laden came. This infrastructure continues to function undisturbed creating national security problems not only for India and Afghanistan, but also for other countries.

Pakistan's strategic relationship with Iran, the foundations for which were laid by the late Zulfiquar Ali Bhutto and the Shah of Iran, led to the flow of funds from Iran for Pakistan's military nuclear programme to produce what was described as the world's first Islamic atomic bomb. The recent enquiries by the International Atomic Energy Agency (IAEA) of Vienna into Iran's clandestine nuclear programme have brought out the covert role of Dr. A. Q. Khan, the so-called father of Pakistan's Islamic bomb, in assisting Irán to become the world's second Islamic military nuclear power.

Will the so-called Islamic bomb developed by Pakistan with funds not only from Iran, but also from Saudi Arabia and Libya and any similar bomb developed by Iran with Pakistani complicity fall into the hands of Al Qaeda, the IIF and organizations such as the Lashkar-e-Toiba (LET) and become the world's first jihadi atomic bomb? It is fears caused by the spectre of a jihadi bomb in the hands of the terrorists that should explain India's vote in the IAEA in favour of a continued role by the Agency to pre-empt this danger. Afghanistan, a pre-2001 failed State, is yet to start benefiting from the fruits of globalization. India's efforts to develop trade links with Afghanistan and bring it into the global economic mainstream continue to be thwarted by Pakistan's refusal to grant Indian businessmen transit rights to Afghanistan through Pakistani territory.

## The Non-state Actors

The US-orchestrated covert war against the Soviet troops in Afghanistan in the 1980s turned the region into a play ground for non-State actors of various hues, persuasions and motives——— jihadi and sectarian terrorists, trans-national crime mafia groups, narcotics producers and smugglers and money-laundering gangs. These non-State actors turned Afghanistan into a failed State and almost caused the collapse of the Pakistani economy before 2001.

The anti-communist jihadi terrorism of the 1980s gave place to the anti-modernisation terrorism of the 1990s personified by the Taliban, which, in turn, has given way to the revanchist terrorism of the present decade personified by Al Qaeda and the International Islamic Front (IIF). The recently in a keynote addresss to an international conference on terrorism organized the Intelligence Summit of Washington DC from February 18 to 20, 2006, Al Qaeda and the IIF are revanchist in character, medieval in their objectives and frighteningly modern in their methods of operation.

Even more than four years after the so-called war on international terrorism was launched on October 7, 2001, the international community is not yet able to get the better of a determined, well-motivated and elusive enemy. Two of the four epicenters of international jihadi terrorism are located in this area. The first is in the Waziristan area of Pakistan, from where Al Qaeda, the Taliban, the Islamic Movement of Uzbekistan (IMU), the Jundullah (Army of Allah) and the other components of the IIF are making a determined bid to stage a come-back in Afghanistan and Osama bin Laden is planning another 9/11 in US territory. This is also the epicenter from which the continuing use of terrorism against India is fuelled. The second epicenter is located in Bangladesh, which has become an alternate command and control for jihadi terrorists from the Harkat-ul-Jihad-al-Islami (HUJI) and the LET operating in Indian territory. The epicenter in Bangladesh has also serious implications for the future security and stability of Myanmar and Southern Thailand.

Narcotics production in Afghanistan has again increased significantly and the resulting cash flow has nullified any benefits to the war on terrorism from the campaign against terrorism funding mounted after 9/11 under the UN Security Council Resolution No.1373. There is no trust deficit coming in the way of networking and co-operation among the non-State actors. As a result, the non-State actors have benefited more than the State actors of the region from the fruits of networking, freer flow of human beings, the communications revolution and the innovations in science and technology. Al Qaeda and the IIF are making better use of the Internet than the State actors.

Globalization has given rise to two parallel trends towards a radicalization of sections of the youth of South Asia. The first trend is a radicalization of sections of the youth of all communities due to continuing economic and social disparities despite the growing economic prosperity. Uneven distribution of the newly-created wealth and opportunities is a major cause of this trend. There are more haves than in the past, but the number of have-nots is still very high and is more than the total population of many countries of the world. For example, in India, about 260 million people are still below the poverty line.

There has been an aggravation of the divide between the privileged and the under-privileged and of the feelings of relative deprivation among different layers of the society. The result: Ideology, which, according to conventional wisdom, should have become increasingly irrelevant in pragmatism-driven economies, has assumed a new relevance. One sees this in the resurgence and aggravation of ideological terrorism. Example—the Maoists of India and Nepal. The second trend is the growing radicalization of sections of the Muslim youth, more due to religious than economic reasons. Anger against the non-Muslims, who are projected as the enemies of Islam for allegedly committing various wrongs against the Muslims, has given rise to a new kind of terrorism personified by Al Qaeda and the International Islamic Front (IIF). Innovations in science and technology, knowledge of Information Technology and modern means of communication are sought to be used by the revanchist terrorist elements not as forces of creation, but of destruction, not to integrate, but to disintegrate.

The tensions caused by the old divide between the developed and the developing or the under-developed have been reduced, but the attempts by these elements to create a new divide between Islam and the rest have brought in new threats to peace, security and prosperity. As a result of these trends, dealing with threats to internal security has become an overriding preoccupation of the states of the region, consuming a considerable proportion of their resources, time and attention. Linkages between sources of internal and external threats to security are stronger in the South Asian region than in any other region of Asia. Exploitation of internal tensions by external actors—State as well as non-State—for strategic reasons has come in the way of the region reaping the full benefits of the process of integration and globalization.

The result: Greater progress towards integration with the societies and economies of countries outside the region than of countries in the region. Example: the countries of the region moving closer to those of Southeast Asia, bilaterally as well as multilaterally, than to each other. There has been a positive change in the relations of the countries of the region with countries outside the region such as the US, China, Japan etc., but there has been little change in their relations with each other. Countries outside the region such as the USA, China and Japan are viewed with decreasing suspicion and increasing comfort. There is consequently a greater comfort level in the relations of the countries of this region with such powers outside the region.

However, there are incipient positive trends, which are having an impact on inter as well as intra-regional relationships, despite continuing inter-regional sources of discord. Example: Energy requirements driving India and Pakistan on the one side and India and China on the other towards solutions based on co-operation rather than competition in their energy quest. The likelihood of threats to regional and global trade has been driving the countries of Asia towards a search for co-operative counter-terrorism and maritime security initiatives and mechanisms. However, the persistence of traditional distrustful mindsets in the South Asian region makes the search for such co-operative security mechanisms fractional rather than well-integrated. Example: Pakistan's attempts to keep India out of the co-operative mechanisms in the Gulf area despite India's support for the association of Pakistan with the ASEAN Regional Forum. The trust deficit, which is a defining characteristic of the threat perceptions in the South Asian region, will continue to make the progress towards inter-regional integration slow and halting in the short and medium terms, but it is bound to acquire the needed momentum as the compulsions of economics acquire predominance over traditional sources of mistrust and discord.

## THE CHINA FACTOR

China is not a South Asian power, but it has acquired a significant South Asian presence, by skilfully exploiting the complexes and reflexes of the countries of the region vis-a-vis India. Amongst the steps it has taken to make its presence felt in this region are:

- The clandestine supply of nuclear and missile technologies to Pakistan, which might one day fall into the hands of Al Qaeda and other jihadi terrorist organizations should the jihadis capture power in Pakistan.
- Strengthening Pakistan's military capability in the Army, the Air Force and the Navy in order to reduce its feeling of insecurity vis-a-vis India.
- Strengthening Pakistan's strategic infrastructure through projects such as the construction of the Gwadar port on the Baloch coast and the Mekran Highway connecting Gwadar with Karachi.
- Strengthening Pakistan's IT capability.
- Strengthening Bangladesh's military capability.
- Helping Bangladesh in the development of its energy resources.

- The reported offer of assistance to Bangladesh for setting up facilities for research into the peaceful uses of nuclear energy.
- Reported military supplies to the royal regime in Nepal at a time when India has cut down its military supplies in view of the suppression of democracy by the King.
- Reported assistance to Sri Lanka for the development of the Hambantota port.

These developments are viewed by many analysts, including this writer, as an attempt to strengthen China's strategic presence and influence in the South Asian region. However, these perceptions, not invalid, have not been allowed to resurrect feelings of animosity between India and China. The border dispute between the two countries continues to remain under negotiations without any visible forward movement. At the same time, there have been significant gestures——such as the Chinese recognition of Sikkim as a part of India and the bilateral agreement to resume border trade through the Sikkim sector.

The presence of the Dalai Lama and a large number of Tibetan refugees in the Indian territory and their activities——perceived by Beijing as political behind a religious facade—continue to be a matter of concern to China, but these concerns are no longer articulated in strong language.

China has shown signs of being comfortable with the idea of India emerging as an important power, but it does not seem to be comfortable with the prospect of India emerging as a power on par with China.

This was evident from its strong opposition to India's aspirations of becoming a permanent member of the UN Security Council and its reticence on the question of the Nuclear Suppliers' Group (NSG) relaxing restrictions on the sale of civilian nuclear technology to India, despite India's initiative for separating its civilian nuclear establishments from its military and placing the former under international safeguards. It seems to be opposed to any unilateral concessions to India until such time when such concessions could be made applicable to Pakistan too.

Despite these factors, the trust deficit between India and China has steadily declined. India has been noting with not-openly-articulated concern the steady modernization of the Chinese Armed Forces and the growing Chinese military and economic linkages with the countries of South Asia, but it has not allowed this to come in the way of the steady improvement in the bilateral relations. At the same time, one has also noted the moderating role played by China during the military conflict in 1999 between India and Pakistan following Pakistani military intrusions in the Kargil sector of India's Jammu and Kashmir.

The leaderships of India and China have shown great political maturity in not allowing the continuing differences over the border come in the way of economic and other linkages. Bilateral trade has boomed during the last 10 years—increasing from a total of about US $ two billion to 13 billion. However, it needs to be underlined that this boom has been considerably due to the requirements of raw materials for the rapidly expanding Chinese industries——particularly its steel industry.

Globalization and the consequent networking and interactions between the policy-makers and the business classes of the two countries have contributed to a remarkable resurgence of interest in each other and to a dilution of the mutual threat perceptions. Nobody in India, any longer, talks —at least openly—of China as a threat. In the past, China was viewed mainly as a worrisome power. Now its image is more positive. The remarkable change for the better in Indian threat perceptions of China is evident from the fact that the Indian intelligence and security establishment no longer opposes, as strongly as it used to do in the past, the presence of Chinese companies even in cities such as Bangalore, India's Silicon Valley, where many of India's sensitive defence and other strategic establishments are located.

The steady forward movement of India and China towards a common shared future of prosperity and mutual confidence can be endangered if the leaderships of the two countries do not skilfully manage the misgivings in China over the implications of the growing strategic partnership between the US and India to its aspired pre-eminence in Asia and the world and the likely tensions in Tibet, when the Dalai Lama ceases to be no more and the Chinese attempt to have their say, as they are bound to, in the selection of his successor. The continuously developing military, nuclear and other strategic linkages between China and Pakistan would remain a source of worry to Indian policy-makers and could stand in the way of the bilateral relations developing to their fullest potential.

## INDIA'S PROPAGANDA AGAINST PAKISTAN AND CHINA

Although Indian officials and media have always implicated Pakistan and China on various issues, now with the help of American media, they have started a new phase of propaganda against these two countries in respect of Gilgit-Baltistan. In this respect, Indian writer B. Raman has already been maligning both Beijing and Islamabad, while Selig Harrison, former correspondent of the "Washington Post" in New Delhi has left no stone unturned in this regard.

On August 27, 2010, the "New York Times" carried an article by Selig Harrison who wrote, "While the world focuses on the flood-ravaged Indus River valley, a quiet geopolitical crisis is unfolding in the Himalayan borderlands of northern Pakistan, where Islamabad is handing over de facto control of the strategic Gilgit-Baltistan region in the northwest corner of disputed Kashmir to China. The entire Pakistan-occupied western portion of Kashmir stretching from Gilgit in the north to Azad (Free) Kashmir in the south is closed to the world...but reports from a variety of foreign intelligence sources reveal, "two important new developments in Gilgit-Baltistan: a simmering rebellion against Pakistani rule and the influx of an estimated 7,000 to 11,000 soldiers of the People's Liberation Army."

The report caused considerable sensation in India. The Government of India, while expressing its concern, ordered a verification of it by its agencies. A strong denial of the report came from the Pakistani Embassy in Beijing. "A senior Pakistani official on August 31 denied recent reports that Chinese troops are stationed in the area of Pakistan-controlled Kashmir to build a high-speed rail and road there. Masood Khan, ambassador of Pakistan to China told the Global Times, "The story is not true," and "It is totally fabricated."

Selig Harrison, in his article referred to the Gilgit-Baltistan region as "Pakistan-controlled Kashmir". On the other hand, Chinese Government officials and journalists describe Jammu and Kashmir as "Indian-controlled Kashmir." On the September 1, 2010, the Government-controlled Xinhua news agency disseminated the report: "China rejected reports of the presence of over 11,000 Chinese troops in northern Pakistan, saying that such "groundless reports" were made with "ulterior motives." Chinese Foreign Ministry spokesperson Jiang Yu remarked, "We believe the attempts of some people to fabricate stories to provoke China-Pakistan are doomed to fail." The comment came in response to recent reports of some American and Indian press that China had deployed more than 10,000 troops in the Gilgit-Baltistan region of Pakistan. The next day, during the regular briefing of Bejing-based journalists including some from India, Jiang Yu reportedly used the expression "northern Pakistan" while referring to Gilgit-Baltistan in context of the article of Selig Harrison.

As Pakistan's close neighbour and all-weather friend, China has been helping Pakistan for its severe natural disaster. The Chinese Government has offered several instalments of humanitarian relief supplies worth more than RMB 100 million. An international relief team sent by the Chinese Government has arrived in the hardest-hit southern part of Pakistan and set up a mobile hospital which is in operation now. Beijing has provided sincere and timely assistance to Pakistan without any strings attached. According to reliable sources, China recently refused to grant a visa to Lieutenant General Jaswal, head of Indian Army's Northern Command, and the Indian side said that the refusal was about the Kashmir issue. China's visa policy towards the residents of Indian-held Kashmir is consistent and remains unchanged. Unlike the western countries, Beijing more strongly holds that the Kashmir issue should be properly handled through dialogue and consultation between India and

Pakistan. The fact of the matter is that the Chinese reference to northern Pakistan could have been the result of the use of a similar expression by Selig Harrison who has referred to Gilgit-Baltistan as "Himalayan borderlands of northern Pakistan." Nevertheless, it is evident that the Chinese, while sticking to the decisions to issue stapled visas to residents of Jummu and Kashmir and to assist Pakistan in the development of its infrastructure in Gilgit-Baltistan have irked the Indian eyes—whose high officials and journalists have misperceived the close ties of Beijing with Islamabad.

As regards Beijing's contention that their troops were present in the Gilgit-Baltistan region only for humanitarian relief work, the Chinese have made two humanitarian interventions in the area this year. The first was in January last. On January 4, a landslide created a huge artificial lake in the Hunza area, which subsequently burst submerging a large number of villages in the Gojal Tehsil. About 22 KMs of the Karakoram Highway were submerged under water totally disrupting road communications with Xinjiang in China and with the rest of Gilgit-Baltistan. The Pakistan Army was able to go to the assistance of the affected villages only in the downstream area. It was not able to reach the affected villages in the upstream area for want of helicopters. The Pakistan Government appealed to the Chinese for assistance. Workers of the Chinese Red Cross and engineers of the People's Liberation Army entered the Hunza area for relief.

In that connection, The Xinhua reported: "On January 19, at the request of the Pakistani government, the Chinese side made special arrangements to open the Kunjirap border and facilitate the purchase of relief goods from China and its clearance. The second humanitarian intervention at the request of Islamabad was made after the recent floods.

It is mentionable that during the visit of President Zardari, under Memorandum of Understanding (MoU) officials of the two Governments signed—that China will build the 165-km long Jaglot-Skardu road and the 135-km long Thakot-Sazin road. Under another MoU to be jointly executed by Chinese company Datang and Norwegian company EBT—500 MW electricity would be produced through wind power.

China and Pakistan plan on building a rail link, which would pass through Gilgit-Baltistan near the Karakoram Highway. This has sparked a debate in India. In this regard, Indian Minister of State for Defence M M Pallam Raju said, "It is definitely a matter of concern." Besides, the two leaders of Pakistan and China discussed a host of issues relating to strategic partnership. The most prominent area of this bolstering of ties—especially for the world is the Sino-Pak civilian nuclear deal which is now beginning to see complete formalisation and initiation. It is unfortunate that the US and India have expressed their concerns about this deal, where the main goal is to address the acute power crisis in Pakistan. While rejecting particularly US objections, China has once again clarified that it will supply two nuclear reactors to Pakistan under the old nuclear deal.

It is also regrettable that, until now, we have been denied the same right to civil nuclear technology that India was granted by the US in 2008. It provides the precedent, and in fact, has opened the door for any similar sort of nuclear deal in the future. Indeed, after setting precedent by themselves, both India and the US have no legal and moral grounds to challenge the legality of the Pak-China nuclear deal. In fact, Pakistan's province, Balochistan where China has invested billion of dollars to develop Gwadar seaport that could link Central Asian trade with rest of the world, irritates both Washington and New Delhi. It has even shifted the central gravity of the Great Game to Pakistan. Returning to our earlier discussion, Selig Harrison's information about the presence of Chinese troops in Pakistan has not independently be confirmed as it is part of a new propaganda game against China and Pakistan. —Opinion-Maker

## OBAMA & AMERICA'S CONTINUING AFGHAN MUDDLE

The latest, released earlier this week, is Obama's Wars by Bob Woodward, one of the two journalists who exposed the

Watergate scandal. The earlier one published in May is The Promise by Jonathan Alter, which reviewed the first year of the Obama Presidency. The descriptions in these books – based on briefings by White House officials and interviews including with the President himself – of how decisions on Afghanistan were made last year reveal intense policy rifts and personality clashes within the Administration over the course to follow in what is now America's longest war. They offer instructive insights into the tensions that continue to afflict the US approach. Both books confirm the deep divisions within the US government over how to handle Afghanistan. The most protracted Presidential consideration of a national security decision since the 1962 Cuban missile crisis – which led up to President Barack Obama's announcement of a military surge last December.

Woodward's book focuses on the Afghan war and the internal 'wars' over it by recounting what happened in the strategy discussions. Both books depict Obama as having doubts about investing more deeply in the Afghan conflict and who felt that his military advisers were trying to manoeuvre him into a decision of escalation that he was uneasy with, recognising as he did its risks and the political and economic costs of prosecuting an open-ended war. From the coverage and extracts of Obama's Wars, it seems the US President was deeply conflicted about expanding the war as was his national security team. Obama is left in Woodward's book with the realisation that the policy review process did not yield a clear solution.

Accounts in both books show Vice President Joe Biden advocating a narrow counterterrorism mission in Afghanistan with a lighter footprint and greater reliance on drones and Special Forces and opposing the large-scale counterinsurgency campaign proposed by the military and the Pentagon. "Obama and his senior staff", writes Alter, "believed (Admiral) Mullen and (General) Petraeus were using McChrystal to jam the President, box him, manipulate him, game him" into a policy of extending the war by an unlimited commitment lasting ten years or more.

Woodward's book depicts an exasperated Obama asking his commanders for an exit plan. What he gets instead is military advisers "steering him towards one option and thwarting his search for an exit plan." In response he writes a six-page "terms sheet" that spells out the conditions for the surge so as to prevent any mission creep. Reports of the book cite Obama telling Defence Secretary Robert Gates and Secretary of State Hilary Clinton in an October 2009 meeting: "I'm not doing 10 years – I am not doing long-term nation building – I am not spending a trillion dollars (in Afghanistan)." In confronting the choice between the Biden plan and the one presented by Generals McChrystal and Petraeus, President Obama opts for a middle path, combining elements of both. He gives the military substantially what they wanted but imposes resource and time limits. Most importantly, he announces a date, July 2011, when a withdrawal of American forces would begin from Afghanistan. This surge-and-exit approach was designed to give something to both supporters and opponents of the war. As he tells a senator in Woodward's book: "I can't let this be a war without end and I can't lose the whole Democratic Party."

These anecdotal details about the crafting of Obama's Afghan strategy raise a number of questions. Have the fierce policy differences been reconciled behind an approach that has strategic clarity? Did the "hybrid" plan promote a consensus or leave differences to persist? Has this compromise injected insoluble tensions in US strategy? Does July 2011 reflect a political position rather than a firm deadline in a coherent strategy? Does the date signal a desire to exit but without having a credible exit plan? Answers to these questions go to the very heart of where the US-led mission stands at present and its prospects. While US thinking has evolved since the intense policy battles last year it is not yet clear whether the different elements of its approach have been aligned in terms of timelines, capacity and goals.

Year 2010 has so for been a grim year for coalition forces, with record casualties, falling public support for the war and a Taliban movement that is at its strongest since 2001. There is little consensus between or within coalition countries on how to deal with or even define the approaching Afghan endgame. The strategic flaw in the US policy is that military action continues to define ongoing coalition efforts rather than a political strategy. There is still an aversion to negotiating with the Taliban even though virtually everyone agrees this will have to take place in order to bring an unwinnable war to an end. The belief that a political strategy can or will emerge from a change in the military balance on the battlefield is questionable on many counts but most importantly because it assumes that the surge can bring about a game changing outcome which in turn will strengthen the hand for negotiations later with the Taliban.

The Obama administration's dithering over a decision to shift gear from a military to a political strategy of accommodation with the Taliban may be explained by the compelling consideration to avoid an impression of defeat. But persisting with a failed policy does not address this dilemma. The administration may also want to avoid exposing itself to attacks from the Republicans and the right-wing ahead of critical mid-term Congressional elections in November.

This places the Obama administration in an untenable position where it knows it cannot fight indefinitely but lacks the political courage to negotiate. The only way it can extricate itself from this predicament and pave the way for an orderly withdrawal of Western forces is to pursue a negotiated political settlement and bring Afghanistan's neighbours on board to endorse such a deal. The reluctance to open a dialogue with the Taliban not only delays the inevitable but heightens the risk of a less than tidy or 'dignified' exit. The pursuit of an 'outcome' to avert an impression of defeat can lead to the very mission expansion and goal multiplication that Obama has been rightly determined to avoid.

## SINO-INDIAN RELATIONS: IMPLICATIONS FOR PAKISTAN

Since the beginning of the twentieth century or more precisely the start of World War I, the world has been witnessing an intensive and extensive competition for balancing of power among states. The situation is no different now, although the dynamics of the New World Order have added more variables in the balancing equation. The variables were less natural and more man-made but their outreach and influence have made it beyond the capacity and capability of any State (read human being) to regulate or constrain the unfolding developments. The Cold War was an intense period of international politics and its demise culminated in the emergence of the culture of interdependence – *security and economic*. The Third World states have been the focus of this culture and, further, China and India are two of the six main actors and emerging powers. It is interesting to note that the advent of the unipolar world brought economic interdependence and only two decades later the states are finding themselves intertwined into deep security interdependence as well, making the future of economic prosperity and peace perilous. The China-Pakistan-India trilateral relations have an interesting economic and security interdependence equation. It not only reflects their bilateral misgivings but also how extra-regional states influence is keeping the regional multilateral mechanisms handicapped. China is self-reliant in its security capability but interdependent on the world economies for its economic development. In 2009, the U.S., Japan and India were ranked as first, second and tenth, respectively, top trade partners of China. India, on the other hand, has both economic and security interdependence. For economy it is dependent on China and the U.S. China is India's largest trading partner and the U.S. second-largest. For its security or military capability, India is dependent mainly on Israel, Russia, France and the USA.

Pakistan, at the same time, is also locked into economic and security interdependence. It is mostly dependent on China for security and partially for economy. China is Pakistan's largest defence supplier, but in economic terms, it is the fourth largest trading partner after Europe, the UAE and the USA. Nevertheless, its tilt has always been towards the USA, owing to the superpower's military and diplomatic prowess.

## Diplomatic Support

Pakistan has been a major source of diplomatic support for China in almost every hour of need whether it has been the support for Chinese rights over Tibet, Taiwan and the Xinjiang province or in the world's criticism of alleged Chinese human rights violations. Islamabad has been lending its supportive hand to Beijing at all platforms. Another very important aspect of Pakistan's diplomatic support to China is the facilitation of the American president's groundbreaking visit to Beijing in 1972. China largely owes Pakistan its opening to the world. Acknowledging this support of Pakistan, Prime Minister Wen Jiabao, while addressing Pakistan parliament, said: "At the crucial moments when China sought to break the external blockade, restore its lawful seat at the United Nations and achieve the normalization of relations with the United States, we received valuable help from Pakistan. On those major issues related to Taiwan, Tibet and Xinjiang, we have enjoyed Pakistan's consistent and full support."

## Energy Corridor

Pakistan's strategic location, which links it to the West and Central Asian States, becomes even more significant for China in securing energy routes amid its growing economy: it is the energy corridor which Islamabad has offered to China to pay back its time-tested friend. In 2006, Pakistan developed the Gwadar port as a first step in an elaborate energy corridor proposal that is expected to ship Persian Gulf oil overland from Gwadar to China. Pakistan will expectedly generate US$60 billion a year in transit fees in the next 20 years, and China will secure a cheaper energy route. The Gwadar Port, that has reinvented Pakistan as one of the region's largest energy players, is a highlight of a little-studied dimension of the global quest for depleting oil; the fact is being well gauged by Beijing. China is now the world's second-largest consumer of oil after the US. Its consumption is expected to double by 2025, with 70 per cent coming from the Middle East. Both India and China are competing for finite supplies. Gal Luft, executive director of the Institute for the Analysis of Global Security in Washington, once opined that Gwadar is the closest access point China has to the Persian Gulf. Pakistan is crucial to China's bid for regional influence. China is rapidly diversifying its sources (of oil transportation) by cutting billion-dollar deals from Sudan to Iran and scoping out alternative transport routes through Pakistan, Myanmar, Thailand, and Bangladesh.

## Strategic Partnership

Their strategic partnership is a long-term, win-win commitment between the two nations with the objective to achieve specific goals by maximizing the effectiveness of either side's resources. This relationship is based on integrity, trust, dedication to common goals, and an understanding of each other's expectations and values. When President Pervez Musharraf when visited China in April 2006, Chinese President Hu Jintao proposed a "strategic partnership" with Pakistan to "consolidate and deepen bilateral relations." The proposal indicated the significance in which Pakistan is held by China as its strategic partner. Unfortunately, this partnership has been unable to avail its full potential. In this context, Prime Minister Wen Jiabao, during his December 2010 visit to Islamabad, pointed out, "the international and regional situations at present remain complicated. As all-weather strategic partners, China and Pakistan should communicate and cooperate closely and cope with challenges jointly ... China-Pakistan pragmatic cooperation is a key part of the bilateral strategic partnership and enjoys promising prospects. China expects to take concerted actions with Pakistan to bring more benefits to their people."

## Military Cooperation: The Eye of The Tiger

Sino-Pak military ties can be described as the „eye of the tiger. They continue to flourish amid the Western criticism of Pakistan's nuclear weapons development; China has been Pakistan's largest defence supplier since 1965. Though China is investing heavily in a myriad of economic projects across Pakistan, including power and telecommunication projects in the troubled northern parts of the country, the bilateral military and defence ties surpass every other sector. China's *Sino-Indian relations: implications for Pakistan* 9 unabated military cooperation with Pakistan can be attributed to mutual rivalry with India and the latter's defence and nuclear cooperation with the US. In response to the Indo-US nuclear deal, China has "privately" agreed to follow a "step-by-step" approach to fulfilling Pakistan's aspiration for an expanded nuclear energy programme. In the joint statement issued at the conclusion of Prime Minister Wen Jiabao's visit in December 2010, the two States "reiterated that they will continue to enhance mutual trust and cooperation in the military and security field in line with the principles and spirit of the Treaty of Friendship, Cooperation and Good-neighborly relations ... This is conducive to peace, security and stability of the two countries and the region. ... (They) agreed to step up personnel training, joint exercises, training and cooperation for national defence, science and technology, and collaboration in defence production ... (and) maritime security."

## SINO-INDIAN RELATIONS: A GROWING UNEASE

The dramatic rise of two Asian giants set against the backdrop of a troubled diplomatic history has propelled India and China into a trajectory that will likely prove difficult to navigate in the coming years. With the world riveted by Chinese aggression against Japan and Southeast Asian states in recent months, one country was not surprised: India. After all, New Delhi has been grappling with the challenge of China's rapid rise for some time. Bilateral ties between China and India nosedived so dramatically last year that Indian strategists were even predicting 'the year of the Chinese attack on India'; it was' suggested that China would attack India by 2012 primarily to divert attention from its growing domestic troubles. This suggestion received widespread coverage in the Indian media, which was more interested in sensationalizing the issue than interrogating the claims.

Meanwhile, the official Chinese media picked up the story and gave it another spin. It argued that while a Chinese attack on India is highly unlikely, a conflict between the two neighbours could occur in one scenario: an aggressive Indian policy toward China about their border dispute, forcing China to take military action. The Chinese media went on to speculate that the 'China will attack India' line might just be a pretext for India to deploy more troops to the border areas.

## A Growing Unease

This curious exchange reflects an uneasiness that exists between the two Asian giants as they continue their ascent in the global inter-state hierarchy. Even as they sign loftily worded documents year after year, the distrust between the two is actually growing at an alarming rate. True, economic cooperation and bilateral political, as well as socio-cultural exchanges are at an all time high; China is India's largest trading partner. Yet this cooperation has done little to assuage each country's concerns about the other's intentions.

The two sides are locked in a classic security dilemma, where any action taken by one is immediately interpreted by the other as a threat to its interests. At the global level, the rhetoric is all about cooperation, and indeed the two sides have worked together on climate change, global trade negotiations and demanding a restructuring of global financial institutions in view of the global economy's shifting centre of gravity.

At the bilateral level, however, mounting tensions reached an impasse last year, when China took its territorial dispute with India all the way to the Asian Development Bank. There China blocked India's application for a loan that included money for development projects in the Indian state of Arunachal Pradesh, which China continues to claim as part of its own territory.

Also, the suggestion by the Chinese to the US Pacific fleet commander last year that the Indian Ocean should be recognized as a Chinese sphere of influence has raised hackles in New Delhi. China's lack of support for the US-India civilian nuclear energy cooperation pact, which it tried to block at the Nuclear Suppliers Group (NSG), and its pro-Pakistan position on anti-

India terrorist groups operating on Pakistani soil, including the orchestrators of the November 2008 Mumbai attacks, have further strained ties.

Sino-Indian frictions are growing, and the potential for conflict remains high. Alarm is rising in India because of frequent and strident Chinese claims about the Line of Actual Control in Arunachal Pradesh and Sikkim, where Indians have complained of a dramatic rise in Chinese intrusions into Indian territory over the last few years, most along the border in Arunachal Pradesh, which China refers to as "Southern Tibet". China has recently upped the ante on the border issue. It has been regularly protesting against the Indian prime minister's visit to Arunachal Pradesh, asserting its claims over the territory. What has caught most observers of Sino-Indian ties by surprise, however, is the vehemence with which Beijing has contested recent Indian administrative and political actions in the state, even denying visas to Indian citizens of Arunachal Pradesh.

The recent rounds of boundary negotiations have been a disappointing failure, with a growing perception in India that China is less willing to adhere to earlier political understandings about how to address the boundary dispute. Even the rhetoric has degenerated to such an extent that a Chinese analyst connected to China's Ministry of National Defence claimed in an article last year that China could "dismember the so-called 'Indian Union' with one little move" into as many as 30 states. Pakistan, of course, has always been a crucial foreign policy asset for China, but with India's rise and US-India rapprochement, its role in China's grand strategy is bound to grow even further. Not surprisingly, recent revelations about China's shift away from a three-decades' old cautious approach on Jammu and Kashmir, its increasing military presence in Pakistan, planned infrastructure linking Xinjiang and Gwadar, issuing stapled visas to residents of Jammu and Kashmir and supplying nuclear reactors to Pakistan, all confirm a new intensity behind China's old strategy of using Pakistan to secure its interests in the region.

## INDIA'S FORMIDABLE CHALLENGE

While it has not yet achieved the economic and political profile that China enjoys regionally and globally, India is increasingly bracketed with China as a rising or emerging power-or even a global superpower. Indian elites who have been obsessed with Pakistan for more than 60 years suddenly have found a new object of fascination. India's main security concern now is not the increasingly decrepit state of Pakistan but an ever more assertive China, a shift that is widely viewed inside India as one that can facilitate better strategic planning. India's defeat at Chinese hands in 1962 shaped the Indian elite's perceptions of China, and they are unlikely to alter them anytime soon. China is thus viewed by India as a growing, aggressive nationalistic power whose ambitions are likely to reshape the contours of the regional and global balance of power with deleterious consequences for Indian interests. Indian policymakers, however, continue to believe that Beijing is not a short-term threat to India but needs to be watched over the long-term. However, Indian defence officials are increasingly warning in rather blunt terms about the disparity between the two Asian powers. The Indian naval chief has warned that India neither has "the capability nor the intention to match China force for force" in military terms, while the former Indian air chief has suggested that China posed more of a threat to India than Pakistan.

China's recent hardening toward India could well be a function of its own internal vulnerabilities, but that is hardly a consolation to Indian policymakers who have to respond to an Indian public that increasingly wants the country to assert itself in the region and beyond. India is rather belatedly gearing up to respond with its own diplomatic and military overtures, setting the stage for a Sino-Indian strategic rivalry. Both India and China have a vested interest in stabilizing their relationship by seeking out issues on which their interests converge, but pursuing mutually desirable interests does not inevitably produce satisfactory solutions to strategic problems. A troubled history coupled with the structural uncertainties engendered by their simultaneous rise is propelling the two Asian giants into a trajectory that they might find rather difficult to navigate in the coming years. Sino-Indian ties have entered turbulent times, and they are likely to remain there for the foreseeable future.

## THE INDIAN AND CHINESE EXPERIENCE

One of the cruel ironies of today's world is that India which is applauded as the world's largest democracy has the largest number of poor and destitute in any country, and China which has achieved, a steady rise in people's living standards and has also acquired the status of a world power has failed to develop democratic institutions and practices. It is also interesting to note that despite the absence of liberal democratic freedoms the West has a deep fascination with China which is reflected not only in the tourist inflow to China but also in the flow of foreign investment and government good will. Operation of democratic institutions such as free and fair elections, existence of competitive politics and dissent do not particularly attract either Western tourists or Western capital to India. On the contrary the geopolitics of South Asia has been governed by the US and other Western countries as compared by India's pre-eminent position and therefore they have followed by an large a policy of containment of India vis-a-vis its neighbours. The functioning democratic system of India has had little effect on their policy. The experience of India and China have put the theory of democracy to a severe test. Two old questions need to be asked again about democracy. In addition, two new questions have to be raised. Do formal political institutions and practices constitute democracy or does it involve appropriate socio-economic conditions which enable citizens to exercise their political rights. On this issue India scores poorly with nearly forty per cent of its people below what is statistically called a "poverty line". China has asserted that it is engaged in creating better living conditions for its people after overthrowing semicolonial and semifeudal domination. Today, however, this dichotomy between economic and political conditions of democracy is seriously questioned. Their mutual dependence is emphasised. Therefore both India and China have to achieve yet more conditions of democracy.

The other familiar question relates to equality and freedom. Western liberal democratic theory asserts the priority of freedom over equality even though the radical stream in liberalism stresses that gross inequalities are detrimental to the exercise of freedom. On this criterion pre-Reform China scored higher marks than India. Social inequalities were reduced in China to a very large extent with the abolition of landlordism and formation of cooperatives and Communes and also takeover of the bourgeoisie owned industries by the state. The wage system was directed towards promoting equality and limiting income differences within the six point grade system. In India too there were a number of measures taken in the early decades following independence to curb monopoly in industry, abolish zamindari system and carry out land reforms. In both the countries the stress on equality declined in the 1980s and almost disappeared in the 1990s. In the past decade or so equality has been a low priority in both China and India. The "equalitarianism", "theory of eating from the iron rice bowl" and such ideas of the Cultural Revolution were severely criticised by the Chinese reformers as being obstacles to the development of the productive forces. The perspective of the present day leadership in China is to "allow some people to get rich first" so that the general level of growth is raised steadily. In India the introduction of the Structural Adjustment Programme promoted the ideology of profit and the egalitarian programmes of social transformation took the back seat.

The two new issues arise from the great democratic upsurges of the past few decades, namely the social movements such as the women's movements, the environmental movement, the autonomy movement and the human rights movements. One question posed by them is to concretise freedom as freedom from multiple forms of domination so that freedom to realise the potentialities of the human being is advanced. Patriarchal domination continues substantially in all the countries of the world as evident from the deliberations at the Fourth World Congress of Women in Beijing and as documents in the 1995

*Human Development Report.* China and India have only marginal difference among them. As to ethnic self-determination there has not yet been a scientific measurement. But both the countries have fairly centralised regimes and both have regions manifesting popular discontent. The caste hierarchy and disabilities in India are targets of public attention and social action. There is no comparable social problem in China though new forms of social stratification have emerged in the recent years.

The other issue is response of the modern state to these expanding democratic demands. All ruling elites would like to have an appearance of being popular and responsive to the demands of the various unprivileged groups. And they engage in innumerable measures of legitimation to create a climate of acceptability among the people. Thus the modern state is coercive, responsive and legitimative at the same time. For this purpose it has developed sophisticated systems of management of society, complex methods of propaganda and innovative techniques of manipulation. Today the technology of repression and the vast networks of communication allow the formal democracy to continue while the citizens remain helpless. There is a new authoritarianism in the modern societies including those of the West which make the basic notion of democracy nominal. The tragedy is that while failing on the scores of either political or socio-economic freedom both India and China have fast accumulated the resources of modern authoritarianism. These tools include modern capitalist preoccupation with consumerism promoted through advertisement. Sensate entertainment that commefcialises culture in the global scale on the one hand and building up security forces of all kinds to suppress democratic movements on the other. It is this process which is strengthened by the forces of capitalist globalization. The alliance of Western capitalists and the native elites has intervened to assimilate the rest of the third world into the Western model of capitalist political economy. The alternatives which the socialist revolutions and the anticolonial struggles had presented have been defeated in course of the battles of the recent decades. The socialist experiments adopted the same economic goals as capitalist systems and failed to promote socialist democracy. The anticolonial struggles such as India's which centred on the comprehensive concept of *Swaraj* failed to institutionalise after Independence.

The result was the crisis of the state and crisis of development in the third world to tackle which the elites leaned on the West. Thus today on the one hand there is an expanding demand for multidimensional freedom while on the other hand there is a an advancing tide of global hegemony by the capitalist West. The experiments in India and China are caught in this historical conjuncture. With these comparative notes let us look at the democratic prospects in China.

## SINO-INDIAN CONVERGENCE: BILATERAL AND GLOBAL

Bilateral relations between India and the People's Republic of China (PRC) have indeed come a long way after they touched their nadir in the immediate aftermath of India's nuclear tests in May 1998. China had been singled out as the "number one" security threat for India by India's Defence Minister just before the nuclear tests. After the tests, the Indian Prime Minister wrote to the US President justifying Indian nuclear tests as a response to the threat posed by China. Unsurprisingly, China reacted strongly and diplomatic relations between the two countries plummeted to an all time low.

However, some six years later, the relations between the two countries seem to be on an upswing. The visit of the Indian External Affairs Minister to China in 1999 marked the resumption of high-level dialogue and the two sides declared that they were not threats to each other. A bilateral security dialogue was also initiated that has helped the two countries in openly expressing and sharing their security concerns with each other. India and China also decided to expedite the process of demarcation of the Line of Actual Control (LAC) and the Joint Working Group (JWG) on the boundary question, set up in 1988, has been meeting regularly. As a first step in this direction, the two countries exchanged border maps on the least controversial middle sector of the LAC.

The Indian Prime Minister visited China in June 2003, the first such visit in a decade. The joint declaration signed during the visit stated that China was not a threat to India. The two states appointed special representatives in order to impart momentum to border negotiations that have lasted twenty two years, with the Prime Minister's principal secretary becoming India's political-level negotiator, replacing the India-China JWG. India and China also decided to hold their first joint naval exercise later in the year and discussions on joint air exercise continue. India also acknowledged China's sovereignty over Tibet and pledged not to allow "anti-China" political activities in India. On its part, China has acknowledged India's 1975 annexation of the former monarchy of Sikkim by agreeing to open a trading post along the border with the former kingdom and later rectified official maps to include Sikkim as part of India.

India and China have found substantial convergence of interests at the international level. Both share similar concerns about the growing international dominance of the US, the threat of terrorism disguised as religious and ethnic movements and the need to accord primacy to economic development. India and China have both expressed concern about the US ' use of military power around the world and publicly opposed the war in Iraq. This was merely a continuation of the desire of both states to oppose the US *hyperpuissance* ever since the end of the Cold War.

Like other major powers in the international system, India and China favour a multi-polar world order where US unipolarity remains constrained by the other "poles" in the system. China and India zealously guard their national sovereignty and have been wary of US attempts to interfere in what they see as domestic affairs of other stares, be it Serbia, Kosovo or Iraq. Both took strong exception to the US air strikes on Iraq in 1998, the US-led air campaign against Yugoslavia in 1999, and more recently the US campaign against Saddam

Hussein arguing that these violated the national sovereignty and undermined the authority of the United Nations system.

Both nations also favour more democratic international economic regimes. They have strongly resisted efforts by the US and other developed nations to link global trade to labour and environmental standards, realizing clearly that this would put them at a huge disadvantage vis-a-vis the developed world, thereby hampering their drive towards economic development, a top priority. Both have committed themselves to crafting joint Sino-Indian positions in the World Trade Organization (WTO) and global trade negotiations in the hope that this might provide them greater negotiating leverage over the developed states. They would like to see further liberalization of agricultural trade in the developed countries, tightening of the rules on anti-dumping measures and ensuring that non-trade related issues such as labour and environment are not allowed to come to the WTO.

In recent years, India and China have attempted to build their bilateral relationship on the basis of their larger worldview of international politics. As they have found a distinct convergence of their interests on world stage, they have used it to strengthen their bilateral relations. They have established and maintained regular reciprocal high-level visits between political leaders. There has been a sincere attempt to improve trade relations and to compartmentalize intractable issues that make it difficult for their bilateral relationship to move forward.

India and China have strengthened their bilateral relationship in areas as distinct as cultural and educational exchanges, military exchanges, and science and technology cooperation. Bilateral trade has recorded rapid growth from a trade volume of US $265 million in 1991 to US $3596 million in 2001.

In 2001, bilateral trade saw an increase of 23.4 percent over 2000. It is expected to rise to $10 billion this year. The two nations are even evaluating the possibility of signing a comprehensive economic cooperation agreement and a free trade agreement by the end of this year, thereby building on strong complementarities between the two. Both states are also taking steps to upgrade their military-related cooperation, leading to greater understanding on the bilateral military front, something that would have been unthinkable just a few years ago. As a first step in this direction, the Chinese and Indian navies carried out joint search and rescue operations off the Shanghai coast in November 2003. Both states are also seeking to cooperate on the nuclear front with China planning to import heavy water from India to be utilized in the pressurized heavy water reactors near Shanghai. Many observers have also pointed out a subtle shift in Beijing's stance on Pakistan vis-a-vis India. China's "neutral" position during the Kargil conflict and the intense Indo-Pak crisis following the terrorist attack on the India's Parliament is seen by many as a reflection of China's sincerity in its attempts to improve ties. In keeping with China's attempts to project itself as a responsible regional player, China is seen by some as supporting peace and anti-terrorist efforts in South Asia by cooperating with the US and India. China is also seen as playing a central role in encouraging Pakistan to negotiate with India by using its leverage over Pakistan. After assuming office Prime Minister Manmohan Singh's government made it clear that it favoured closer ties with China and would continue to work towards improving bilateral relations with China. In his first address to the nation, the Prime Minister, Manmohan Singh, also emphasized the carrying forward of the process of further development and diversification of Sino-Indian relations. The late J.N. Dixit, National Security Advisor in the current government, wrote that "the Congress will continue the process of normalizing, strengthening and expanding India's relations with China, which is the most important factor affecting Asian security and stability". One of the first foreign visits of the new Indian foreign minister, Natwar Singh, was to China to attend the Asia Cooperation Dialogue in Qingdao, in East China's Shandong province and apparently had "substantive discussions" with his Chinese counterpart.

All this reflects on India continuing to build its relations with China on the convergence of interests that the two nations have achieved in recent years. Aside from the positive developments, one should not ignore the enormous obstacles that confront this bilateral relationship. There has been a dominant tendency in the Indian foreign policy establishment to focus on the strengths of its bilateral relations with China while pretending that problems confronting the relationship would somehow take care of themselves. The challenges in the Sino-Indian relationship are by no means insignificant nor will China take care of Indian interests. It is for India to recognize them for what they are and evolve a coherent strategy to tackle them.

## REGIONAL NUCLEAR POLITICS: CHINA, INDIA, PAKISTAN

It is quite likely that the development of nuclear weapons by Pakistan would have taken considerably longer without Chinese assistance. Although current assistance is largely in the power sector, in the early years the provision of the design of an implosion bomb was quite crucial. Subsequently, the design was improved upon. That process is still continuing.

The relation of nuclear India with nuclear China differs fundamentally from the relation with nuclear Pakistan. It is, on the one hand, less hostile and free from the kind of tension that makes a Pakistan-India confrontation an ever present possibility. In July 2009 China and India concluded their 13th round of border talks with a wide range of agreements such as the installation of a hot line between the Chinese and Indian capitals, an agreement to celebrate 60 years of diplomatic ties next year, etc. Their mutual trade, which amounted to a whopping $52 billion in 2009, is set to increase to $60 billion in 2010. In comparison, India-Pakistan trade – discounting smuggling and third party trading – amounts to less than $1 billion annually.

On the other hand, India and China are serious competitors for global markets and global prestige. This has fuelled intense nationalism. With competing territorial claims in Arunachal Pradesh and Aksai Chin, the two countries are no closer to resolution today than in 1962. So, once Pakistan firmly resolved to make the Bomb after the Indian test of 1974, China provided key assistance with the aim of creating an offset to India. Thus, even without the equivalent of a Kashmir dispute, regional ambitions are driving China and India towards potential conflict.

The dramatic prediction that China will attack India before 2012, leaving only three years to Indian government for preparationiv. He claims that a desperate Beijing is out to teach India the final lesson, thereby ensuring Chinese supremacy in Asia in this century and it is working towards an end game rooted in the abiding conviction of the communists that the Chinese race is far superior to Nazi Germany. Verma's solution: India must arm itself to the teeth.

This is fear-mongering with a sinister purpose – that of militarizing India. The 1959-1962 conflict is the only recorded war between China and India in the long history of their civilizations. Even this was by no means an all-out war and was limited to the disputed areas. While Verma panders to the right-wing of the establishment, he is not alone in articulating the desire for major arms acquisitions and a blue-water navy.

On August 10, 2009, serving Naval Chief and Chairman of the Chiefs of Staff Committee, Admiral Sureesh Mehta, delivered a major speech on India's National Security Challenges wherein he stated that China will be India's primary challengev. He drew the same corollary: India must arm itself. The recent launch of the nuclear submarine, Arihant is a step in that direction. The US-India nuclear deal – which dealt a stunning blow to arms control globally – purposefully gives India an edge over China. Apart from legitimizing India's nuclear status and giving its nuclear power industry a huge boost, India will be allowed to buy high technology defence equipment from the US but China will not have the option.

In a startling development eleven years after the 1998 test of India's purported hydrogen bomb test, a senior Indian official and technical expert, K. Santanam, has confirmed the long-suspected fact: the Bomb did not do as well as it should have. An irresistible urge to tell the truth or moral unease is scarcely the reason for this dramatic revelation. Santanam's coming clean has the stamp of approval of the most hawkish of Indian nuclear hawks. Among them are P.K. Iyengar, A.N. Prasad, Bharat Karnad, and Brahma Chellaney. By rubbishing the earlier test as a failure, they hope to make the case for more nuclear tests. This would enable India to develop a full-scale thermonuclear arsenal. As is well known, a thermonuclear (or hydrogen) bomb is far more complex than the relatively simple fission weapon first tested by India in 1974, and by Pakistan in 1998. Advanced weapons needs fine tuning to achieve their full destructiveness – France had to test 22 times to achieve perfection.

## RATTLING THE NUCLEAR SABRE

While China was the raison d'etre for India's nuclear weapons, these weapons created new dynamics of hostility in Pakistan-India relations. A fearful Pakistan acquired its own weapons with the obvious formula of balancing Indian nukes with Pakistani nukes. But this was to change very soon in Pakistan.

An enlarged set of objectives appeared even before the nuclear tests. A former director of the Inter-Services Intelligence (ISI), who was later Pakistan's ambassador to Germany put it this way: If, argued General Asad Durrani, we were to make it clear that whatever nuclear deterrence we might have is primarily meant to deter the use of nuclear weapons from the other side, then by so saying we will fail to deter a conventional attack vi. Therefore, he argued, the other side must be led to believe that we are primed, almost desperate to use our nuclear capabilities when our national objectives are threatened, [as] for example, a major crackdown on [the] freedom movement in Kashmir.... vii.

After their successful 1998 nuclear tests, Pakistani generals were quick to see that the calculus of power had changed. Now nuclear weapons could be used for more than just a boring stand-off with India. Drawing a lesson from the NATO-Warsaw Pact experience, they saw a way of equalizing scores with a much larger Indian conventional force. Convinced of an impregnable defence, they embarked on breath-taking adventurism in Kashmir. Just months after the Pakistan had established its nuclear credentials, the Chief of Army Staff, General Pervez Musharraf, sent troops out of uniform along with Islamist militant fighters across the Line of Control. They seized strategic positions in the high mountains of the Kargil area at the beginning of January 1999, setting of a war. This conflict was the direct consequence of Pakistan's nuclearization and almost certainly would not have happened otherwise. The war was to claim about 5000 dead on both sides.

As India counter-attacked, Pakistan stood diplomatically isolatedviii. Gloomy and worried, Prime Minister Nawaz Sharif flew to Washington on 4 July 1999, where he was bluntly told to withdraw Pakistani forces or be prepared for full-scale war with India. Bruce Reidel, Special Assistant to President Clinton, writes that he was present in person when Clinton informed Nawaz Sharif that the Pakistan Army had mobilized its nuclear-tipped missile fleetix. (If this is true, then the preparations for nuclear deployment and possible use could only have been ordered by General Pervez Musharraf at either his own initiative or in consultation with the army leadership.) Unnerved by this revelation and the closeness to disaster, Nawaz Sharif agreed to immediate withdrawal, shedding all earlier pretensions that Pakistan's army had no control over the attackers. This was key in poisoning relations between him and Musharraf, leading to his ouster months later. However, contrary to claims that he made a decade later, Nawaz Sharif had visited forward army posts near the Kargil area where he had given rousing speeches to jihad-shouting soldiersx.

Despite the defeat in the Kargil War, Pakistan political and military leaders insisted that Pakistan had prevailed in the conflict and that its nuclear weapons had deterred India from crossing the Line of Control or the international border. This belief still remains strong in the military, which otherwise would have to concede that its crown jewels were of little utility (that nuclear weapons fuelled the conflict is denied even today by nuclear hawks). With a tense situation threatening to spiral into all out war, western diplomacy went into overdrive. The conflict eventually wound down after Pakistan ordered the withdrawal of its forces. Internationally, Pakistan was branded the aggressor.

But it did not take long to get back to the brink. On 13 December 2001, Islamic militants based in Pakistan struck at the Indian parliament in Delhi, sparking off a crisis that lasted for about seven months. While it is probably true that Musharraf's government did not order or was aware of the planned attack, there is little doubt that a free hand had been given to jihadists in Pakistan controlled Kashmir. Indian tempers soared again. Prime Minister Atal Bihari Vajpayee exhorted his troops in Kashmir to prepare for sacrifices and decisive victory. This set off widespread alarm. It seemed plausible that India was preparing for a limited war to flush out Islamic militant camps in Pakistan administered Kashmir. That nuclear weapons were put on enhanced alert by both sides is a strong possibility, although direct proof has not been made public.

Tensions kept mounting during the stand-off. Sensing a global climate deeply hostile to Islamic militancy after the 11 September 2001 attack on the World Trade Centre, India's ruling BJP echoed the war on terror slogan as a way to garner international support for their military campaign in Kashmir. Although an embattled Musharraf had little to do with the attack on the Indian Parliament, India cut off communications with Pakistan. The Indian ambassador in Islamabad was recalled to Delhi, road and rail links were broken off, and flights by Pakistani airlines over Indian territory were disallowed. Pakistan responded in kind.

Nuclear threats started flying in all directions. In May 2002, as fighter aircraft loudly circled Islamabad, in a public debate with me, General Mirza Aslam Beg, the former chief of Pakistan's army, declared: "We can make a first strike, and a second strike, or even a third." The lethality of nuclear war left him unmoved. You can die crossing the street, he observed, or you could die in a nuclear war. You've got to die some day anyway. Pakistan's ambassador to the UN in Geneva, Munir Akram, sent a threatening message by reiterating Pakistan's refusal of a no-first-use policy.

Indian aggressiveness was also in full display. Defence Minister George Fernandes told the International Herald Tribune India can survive a nuclear attack, but Pakistan cannot. xi Indian Defence Secretary Yogèndra Narain took things a step further in an interview with *Outlook Magazine*: A surgical strike is the answer, adding that if this failed to resolve things, We must be prepared for total mutual destruction.xii Indian security analyst, Brahma Chellaney, claimed "India can hit any nook and corner of Pakistan and is fully prepared to call Pakistan's nuclear bluff." Fortunately, good sense prevailed and international mediation helped wind tensions down after a tense, months-long standoff.

Then came the Mumbai massacre. Carried out by the Pakistan-based Lashkar-e-Tayyaba, it began on 26 November 2008 and lasted 3 days, killing over 200 people and wounding at least 308. Indians describe it as their 911. Even in the first few days, it was fairly obvious that the Pakistani state, embattled as it was by other jihadist groups, could not have ordered the attacks. But Indian temperatures soared when Pakistan vociferously denied that its nationals were involved. The media in both countries poured fuel over the fire, with Indian television anchor persons repeatedly calling for military action against Pakistan.

A personal example from the Pakistani side: just days after the attack, General Hamid Nawaz (Retd), who served as Federal Interior Minister and Defence Secretary of Pakistan, in a widely-watched television program angrily attacked me for suggesting that one of the many Pakistan-based jihad groups could have been involved. Instead he recommended readying Pakistan's nuclear arsenal, and said that a nuclear first-strike should be among Pakistan's preferred optionsxiv. Others on Pakistani television channels were also casual in suggesting the use of nuclear weapons. These could be indicating that deterrence is losing value.

There has, of course, been no actual use of nuclear weapons since Hiroshima and Nagasaki. Although Pakistan and India have viciously clawed at each other, each time they have stepped back from the brink. Doesn't this constitute proof that deterrence works ?

On the face of it, the answer is yes. But there is an important caveat. What has worked a few times may or may not work the next time. And, there are strong indications that a kind of fear-fatigue has set in, reducing the value of deterrence. The efficacy of nuclear deterrence is predicated on the ability of these weapons to induce terror. It presupposes a rational calculus, as well as actors who, at the height of tension, will take decisions based on cold logic rather than emotion. Events in South Asia have put all these assumptions into question. Countries loitering close to the brink may begin to feel that they cannot fall into it.

An example: in early 2002, with a million troops mobilized and leaders in both India and Pakistan threatening nuclear war, world opinion responded fearfully, seeing a fierce and possibly suicidal struggle up ahead. Foreign nationals streamed out of both countries. But even at the peak of the crisis, few Indians or Pakistanis lost much sleep. Stock markets flickered, but there was no run on the banks or panic buying. Schools and colleges, which generally close at the first hint of disturbances, functioned normally. The indifference to nuclear annihilation was simply amazing.

But, on second thought, perhaps it was not quite so amazing. India and Pakistan are still largely traditional, rural societies, albeit rapidly going through a great economic and social transformation. The fundamental belief structures of such societies (which may well be the last things to change), reflect the realities of agricultural economies dependent on rains and good weather – precisely the factors that brought the Rain God and other deities into being. These pre-scientific beliefs encourage surrender to larger, supernatural forces. So conversations and discussions often end with remarks to the effect that fate shall triumph, after which people shrug their shoulders and move on. Risk-taking is natural once unseen forces can be brought to your defence.

There are other reasons for this nonchalance as well. In India and Pakistan, most people lack basic information about nuclear dangers. In India, a November 1999 post-election national opinion poll survey found just over half of the population had not even heard of the May 1998 nuclear tests.xv In the middle of the spring 2002 crisis, the BBC reported the level of awareness of the nuclear risk among the Pakistani public was abysmally low xvi. In India, it found for many, the terror of a nuclear conflict is hard to imagine.

First hand evidence bears out these judgments. Even educated people seem unable to grasp basic nuclear realities. Some physics students (and faculty!) in my department think that a nuclear war would be the end of the world. Others see nuclear weapons as just bigger bombs. Many said it was not their concern, but the army's. Almost none know about the possibility of a nuclear firestorm, about residual radioactivity, or damage to the gene pool.

With each new Pakistan-India crisis, there seems to be a lessening of political restraints and greater nuclear brinksmanship. A key factor is the absence of an informed and organized public opinion able to keep political and military leaders in check and restrain them from brandishing nuclear weapons. In spite of today's vibrant public media, critical discussion of nuclear weapons and nuclear war is not aired in either country. Terror of nuclear weapons was fundamental in moving the Cold War adversaries towards nuclear treaties such as SALT, and the winding down of their aggressive military posturing. But this feeling of terror is not to be found in the Pakistan-India nuclear situation. Instead, oftentimes one finds a casual denial of reality and an almost blasé indifference to what nuclear weapons do.

In the past top Indian and Pakistani political leaders and analysts seem to have deliberately chosen the path of ignorance in nuclear matters. A personal example: two months before the May 1998 nuclear tests by India and Pakistan, a Pugwash delegation met in Delhi with Prime Minister Inderjit Kumar Gujral. As a member of the delegation, I expressed worries about a nuclear catastrophe on the Subcontinent. Gujral repeatedly assured me – both in public and later in private – that Pakistan was not capable of making atomic bombs. The Prime Minister was not alone. Senior Indian defence analysts like P. R. Chari had also published articles before May 1998 arguing this point, as had the former head of the Indian Atomic Energy Agency, Dr. Raja Ramana.

Although Pakistan's nuclear tests shattered this false notion, senior Indian military and political leaders continued to express doubts on the operational capability and usability of the Pakistani arsenal. Shortly after Pakistan's incursion into Kargil, India began to seriously consider making cross-border strikes on militant camps on the Pakistani side of the Line of Control. Proponents of this strategy cast doubt on Pakistan's willingness and ability to use nuclear weapons. This gained wide currency in Indian ruling circles, increasing risks of a misjudgment that could have led to serious miscalculations and an accidental nuclear war.

Many Indian commentators and analysts chose to believe – perhaps some still do – that Pakistan, as a client state of the US, had been forced to put its nuclear weapons under the control of the US. Their assumption was that, in case of extreme crisis, the US would either restrain their use by Pakistan or, if need be, destroy them. At a meeting in Dubai which I attended in January 2002, senior Indian analysts said they were bored with Pakistan's nuclear threats and no longer believed them. K. Subrahmanyam, an influential Indian hawk who has long advocated Indian nuclearization said that India can sleep in peace.

But to fearlessly challenge a nuclear Pakistan in this manner requires an enormous leap of faith. The presumption that United States would have both the political will – and the capability – to destroy Pakistani nukes is simply wrong. The fact is that even tracking a handful of mobile nuclear-armed missiles is extremely difficult. During the Cuban missile crisis, the U.S.

Air Force had aerial photos of the Soviet missile locations and its planes were only minutes away, yet it would not assure that a surprise attack would be more than 90 percent effective. In the first Gulf War, U.S. efforts to destroy Iraqi Scuds had limited success. And, as 2009 moves to a close, the US is extremely reluctant to move on Iran's nuclear weapons – or allow Israel to go for them. No country has ever tried to take out another's nuclear bombs. The consequences of a botched operation cause even the bold to shudder.

## THE QUIET DEATH OF MINIMAL DETERRENCE

In the early days of Indian and Pakistani nuclear development, minimal deterrence or just enough was the mantra of the times. In the 1980's, the late nuclear visionary, General K. Sunderji, would emphasize that India needed only a handful of fission weapons to take out the major Pakistani cities – but should make no more. In my single encounter with him in 1993 at a Carnegie conference in Washington, he hugged me warmly after I introduced myself to him as a Pakistani nuclear physicist. He said that Pakistan too should have a few nuclear weapons because that would make war impossible. I felt it unnecessary to respond that Pakistan was well on its way to having a few at that time, or that his (Sunderji's) initiative, Operation Brasstacks, had nearly brought the two countries to blows in 1987.

But the times kept changing. General Sunderji's ideas died before he did. In August 1999, the Indian Nuclear Draft Doctrine came along. It omitted all mention of a minimum. Instead, after a preamble that nuclear weapons are "the gravest threat to humanity", it went on to say that India needs "sufficient, survivable and operationally prepared nuclear forces" together with "the will to employ nuclear forces and weapons". It spoke of a triad of aircraft, mobile land-based missiles and sea-based assets, and achieving survivability of the forces through a combination of multiple redundant systems, mobility, dispersion and deception. Now there was to be no fixed number of weapons, no restriction on delivery vehicles, and no limits to what flexible response might mean. Tactical nuclear war-fighting, once considered escalatory and way beyond minimal deterrence, is said to have been incorporated into current Indian military doctrine. In fact, the major Indian war game *Poorna Vijay* (Complete Victory) in May 2001, the biggest in over a decade, was reported to centre on training the army and air force to fight in a nuclear conflict.xviii Taken together, Indian military options and Pakistani planning would seem to ensure that that any major India-Pakistan conflict would inexorably lead to the use of nuclear weapons.

## The Race for Nuclear Superiority

Once upon a time, South Asian nuclear proponents were wont to take personal insult upon mention of an arms race, which they debunked as fear mongering. At a 1992 conference in Chicago, the Indian defence strategist K.Subrahmanyan, vehemently asserted that arms racing is a Cold War concept invented by the western powers and totally alien to sub-continental thinking. His Pakistani counterparts happily agreed. In those days nuclear philosophies, like that of Mutually Assured Destruction (MAD), were often attributed to sick western minds which have invented the notion of destroying the world seven times over.

But the expected about-turn did not take long in coming. A full fledged, Cold-War style, nuclear race developed soon after the nuclear tests of 1998. Even a cursory glance at India's subsequent nuclear and conventional spending shows this to be true. More recently, India raised its defence budget in February 2008 by 10% to $26.5 billion for the fiscal year 2008-2009 while its capital defence expenditure of $11.4 billion in 2008 grew 12% over the previous yearxix. It plans to spend between $50 billion and $55 billion between 2009-2014 on various big-ticket items, such as a $10 billion contract for 126 fighter jets being pursued by Boeing Co., Lockheed Martin Corp., BAE Systems PLC and European Aeronautic Defence & Space Co. India was the world's 10th-highest military spender in 2008, according to research by the Stockholm International Peace Research Institute, but plans to head even further upwards. In July 2009, Indian defence minister, A.K. Antony announced that for 2009-2010 India plans to raise its military budget by 50% to a staggering $40 billion, making military expenditure 3% of the annual gross domestic product (GDP)xx. Corporate India and foreign defence suppliers were thrilled.

Marking a quantum escalation, in July 2009, India began sea trials of its 7000-ton nuclear-powered submarine with underwater ballistic missile launch capability. The submarine is the first in a planned fleet of five, and is to be supplemented by a hunter-killer nuclear submarine soon. With an estimated annual budget of $7.8 billion in 2008 – nearly four times lower than India's – Pakistan obviously cannot match India weapon for weapon. Nevertheless, historically every Indian move somehow finds a counter move. Predictably, news of the Indian nuclear submarine was badly received in Pakistan. What should it do? A former diplomat who headed Pakistan's delegation in talks with India on nuclear and conventional CBMs between 2004-2007 gave his answerxxi: follow India into developing nuclear submarines; equip existing conventional submarines with nuclear-tipped cruise missiles; approach the Russians for leasing a nuclear submarine; and make more nuclear weapons by enhancing fissile material production.

In the following, I shall summarize the current Pakistani warhead, missile, and aircraft situation – to the extent that it is known – and then ask what stands in the way of a still larger increase.

## Nuclear Warhead Development

The current size of Pakistan's nuclear arsenal is a secret. Various plausible estimates have placed it in the range of 60-100 warheads in the 5-20 kiloton range. Given that India has chosen not to announce limits upon the size of its nuclear arsenal, one can safely assume that Pakistan has also not set a fixed numerical target. The US-India nuclear deal has essentially removed all possibilities for a fissile material cutoff in the forseeable future. Subject to material and technical constraints, one assumes Pakistan will seek to make as many warheads as possible, as well as make them more powerful and efficient. So what could be the constraints for future expansion of the nuclear arsenal? The maximum number of uranium-based warhead cores that can be produced by Pakistan depends on the quantity of highly enriched uranium produced in centrifuges at the Kahuta enrichment facility, and perhaps at undeclared facilities elsewhere in Pakistan. The initial HEU production was achieved using replicas of the aluminum P-1 centrifuge, brought from Europe by A.Q.Khan in the mid-1970's, which had a capacity of less than 1 separative work unit (SWU). This was the mainstay of the centrifuge program initially, and was supplemented in the late 1980's by the P-2 model which had a throughput of 5 SWU's. Typically, centrifuges are cascaded together in groups of approximately 164.

More advanced centrifuges using faster rotor speeds, made possible by the indigenous development of stronger steels, or possibly by smuggled maraging steel, were subsequently made at the Kahuta Research Laboratory (KRL)xxii. The P-3 was the first of the two later centrifuges. It is a four-tube model with a throughput of just under 12 SWU/yr. According to the reference cited, the P-4, which is still more advanced, may have a throughput of slightly over 20 SWU/yr. Although there is information about the types of these centrifuges in operation, their numbers are not known but are almost certainly in the few thousands by now. One therefore expects that the yearly production rate of HEU is currently several times larger than in the mid 1980's and that it will keep expanding.

The amount of natural uranium mined from presently known deposits, principally in the district of Dera Ghazi Khan, is another constraint. Pakistan has declared to the IAEA that it mines 40 tons of uranium ore yearly. This is distributed between the fuel fabrication for the Karachi Nuclear Power Plant (KANUPP) and for fissile material production.

Pakistan almost certainly has a handful of plutonium-based warheads whose smaller weight makes them more suitable for delivery by missiles over longer ranges. Plutonium-rich spent reactor fuel is produced by the one non-safeguarded 50 MW (thermal) reactor in Khushab which has been functioning since

1998. It produces an estimated 10kg/year of plutonium, which is roughly 2 bombs worth. Recently disclosed satellite imagery shows that there are two similar units that are currently under construction, with the latest unit's construction having been activated in 2007. Reprocessing of the spent fuel, done at the New Labs near Islamabad (and now possibly at the Chashma nuclear complex too) is necessary for chemically extracting the weapons-grade plutonium.

Satellite images obtained in 2009 suggest an increase in plutonium separation capacity, based at the New Labs section of the Pakistan Institute of Science and Technology (PINSTECH) near Islamabad. Earlier, defence analysts in the US had pointed out that a series of commercial satellite images from February 2002 through September 2006 showed the construction of what appeared then to be a second plutonium separation plant adjacent to the original one, suggesting that Pakistan was planning on increasing its plutonium stock. An assessment of fissile stocks in South Asia has been attempted using publicly available information.

The actual number of fission warheads constructed of either type will, in addition to the plutonium available, also depend on the existence of adequate facilities for metallization, explosives, electronics, mechanical component construction, etc. A nuclear weapon has typically about 2000 parts and is a highly complex piece of equipment. Much of the metallization and weapon fabrication work is done in and around the Heavy Mechanical Complex in Taxila, and the adjoining military city of Wah. Many stages of fabrication are involved, the first of which involves conversion of the fissile material in gaseous form into pure metal, then machining it to precise dimensions to make the core. None of this is trivial. But, once a design has been standardized, it becomes easily possible to produce many copies. At the current production rate of a few fissile cores annually, warhead production would most likely follow the same rate and further expansion of warhead production facilities is unlikely to be a major constraint. Although the numbers of Pakistani warheads and delivery vehicles is a closely held secret, a former top official of the CIA is quoted in the September 2009 Bulletin Of The Atomic Scientists as saying It took them roughly 10 years to double the number of nuclear weapons from roughly 50 to 100 xxvi. Pakistan has successfully blocked efforts at the Conference on Disarmament in Geneva to limit fissile materials. It says India's nuclear weapons make this necessary.

Making more powerful nuclear weapons is the next logical step. Boosted nuclear weapons, which use the same fissile materials, are relatively easy to make. A few tens of grams of deuterium or tritium gas are inserted inside the bomb. The additional neutrons released result in more complete fission and can double or even triple the explosive power.

The Khushab reactor is also a source for tritium production. Earlier, the PAEC had attempted to produce it by irradiating lithium. By 1987, the PAEC was able to acquire from West Germany parts for a tritium purification facility. Later, Pakistan attempted to procure from Germany 30 tons of aluminum tubing, used to clad lithium for irradiation in a reactor. In a congressional record of May 1989, Pakistan is said to have acquired from West Germany United States-origin tritium — originally destined for H-bombs – as well as tritium recovery equipment. It also obtained a United States-origin high-power laser, the latter as part of a package of equipment for making nuclear fuel.

Composite core weapons, whose idea is over 60 years old, are another possibility. By combining two materials – a smaller plutonium sphere encased in a shell of highly enriched uranium – Pakistan could make more bombs than if the cores were made of plutonium and uranium separately.

The fusion bomb requires a qualitatively different science. There is little doubt that Pakistan is seeking to make such a weapon, although one has little idea of the progress made so far. A plasma physics group in the Pakistan Atomic Energy Commission (PAEC), established over 20 years ago, is known to be looking into fusion weapon matters. India claims to have already developed a fusion weapon – one of the devices tested on May 11, 1998 was announced to be of this type.

## Missile Capability

Missile development is now part of a burgeoning, increasingly export-oriented, Pakistani arms industry that turns out a large range of weapons from grenades to tanks, night vision devices to laser guided weapons, and small submarines to training aircraft. Dozens of industrial sized units in and around the cities of Taxila and Wah, with subsidiaries elsewhere in the Islamabad-Rawalpindi region, are producing armaments worth hundreds of millions of dollars with export earnings of roughly 300 million dollars yearly in 2008. Much of the production is under license from foreign countries, some from CKD kits, and most machinery for the arms factories is imported from the West or China.

The Pakistani missile series can be categorized into two distinct sets. The Ghauri missile series, based on the North Korean Nodong missile, was developed at the Kahuta Research Laboratories (KRL) while the Shaheen series, based on the Chinese M-9 and M-11 missiles, was developed at the National Defence Complex (NDC A 2007 report says that fewer than 50 four-axled Transporter-Erector-Launcher (TEL) vehicles, needed for deploying the solid-fuelled Ghaznavi (Hatf-III) have been sighted. Most are apparently stored at the Sargodha Weapons Storage Complex adjoining the PAF base. The same report refers to roughly 50 four-axled TELs existing for the Shaheen-I missile. About 15 six-axled TELs, suitable for the Shaheen-II, have been seen in satellite imagery.

Pakistan is also developing a 500km range, nuclear-capable, cruise missile named as Babur. A Pakistani government supported website states that its design capabilities are comparable to the American BGM-109 Tomahawk cruise missile, and that a 1000km version is also being developed. The Babur is advertised as a subsonic, low-level terrain-mapping, terrain-hugging missile that can avoid radar detection and strike with pinpoint accuracy. Rather than being GPS guided – which depends crucially on the integrity of satellite systems being preserved in times of conflict – it is said to use inertial guidance (and possibly laser gyroscopes). Launched from a TEL, it was test-flown on March 21, 2006 with President Gen. Pervez Musharraf in the audience.

According to a spokesman of the Inter Services Public Relations (ISPR), Pakistan is looking into modification that will enable the missile to be launched from its F-16s, Mirage and A-5 air platforms and naval platform such as Agosta 90B attack submarines and its Tariq Class frigates. A test of the Babur on 26 July 2007 was declared successful with a range stated to have been enhanced to 700km.

Pakistan has been surprisingly successful in creating a fairly large and diverse intermediate range missile force in a very short time. How is it possible for any developing country with a weak industrial and scientific infrastructure to do so? Making missiles that can fly over long distances is a highly complex technical task; even today rocket science is sometimes used as a synonym for the most difficult, cutting edge, science.

Making missiles requires acquisition of a broad range of technologies. Some of the key ones are:

- Chemical technology for liquid or solid fuel propellant manufacture, handling, and testing.
- Mechanical technology for rocket motor design, construction, and testing.
- Aerodynamic and structural engineering for design of structures such as missile body, fins, and re-entry cones.
- Special materials manufacturing and molding capability for high-temperature applications as well as for plastics and polymers. Heat shields for re-entry are essential for protecting the warhead from being rendered useless.
- Computational capability and specialized software for various applications including ballistics, navigation, flow rates, dynamic payload balancing, etc.
- Electronics for missile guidance and control, telemetry, and terminal guidance.

These are exacting requirements, but the design challenges are well understood and solutions may be found in specialized textbooks and monographs that are used as texts in graduate level university level courses taught in many countries including the US and China. Component design is no longer essential – the availability of ballistic missile technology, complete subsystems, navigational gyroscopes and GPS equipment, and powerful computers has allowed many third world countries, including Pakistan and India, to leapfrog across major developmental issues.

The details of missile development remains well under the wraps but intense friction between the two main Pakistani organizations, the Kahuta Research Laboratory and the National Defence Complex, headed respectively by Dr. A.Q. Khan and Dr. Samar Mubarikmand, had often led to each organization leaking information to the press in order to get a greater share of the glory. An Urdu newspaper gave a rare account in 1999 in a planted article entitled How the Shaheen was Developed, wherein the achievements of the NDC group are extolled and that of the KRL group minimized.

What conclusions can we draw from this apparently phenomenal progress in missile making? The sophistication of the Babur's propulsion system, a light-weight turbo-fan engine, as well as the complex control systems, electronics, sensors, aerodynamics, etc. places it well outside of any comparable achievements by Pakistani industry or other parts of its technological sector. Much the same can be said of the ballistic missiles in the Hatf series. There can be no doubt that Pakistan received substantial help from China, as well as components smuggled from Europe. North Korean help is an established fact for the Ghauri series, and may well be important for the Babur as well.

While Pakistan officially maintains that its missile fleet comes from indigenous development alone, this is not a tenable claim – or even one that is consistently held. A Pakistani author, evidently commissioned by the Pakistan Atomic Energy Commission to denigrate the achievements of A.Q. Khan and the rival KRL organization, wrote the following in a Pakistani defence journal:

*"When the PAEC concluded an agreement with China to acquire the solid fueled M-11 ballistic missiles from China in*

*1989, A.Q. Khan soon after managed to get the liquid fueled Ghauri, from North Korea, and again hit the public imagination as the man who also gave Pakistan the delivery system for the bomb. The fact was that with the foundations of NDC having being laid in 1990, the PAEC was already on its way to start work on the solid fueled Shaheen ballistic missile, before the Ghauris or the Taepodongs and Nodongs became operational."*

In this effort to bring credit to his parent institution, the PAEC, the author blows away the year after year denials by Pakistan of having obtained M-11 missiles from China, as well as of the Ghauri being indigenous and not of North Korean pedigree.

Nevertheless, to conclude that Pakistan's missiles are mere foreign imports would be wrong. Pakistan has moved on a two-track missile policy. The first track was acquisition of complete missile systems as CKD (completely knocked down) kits. These were brought as commercial cargo, mostly by sea but also through the Khunjarab Pass and down the Silk Route from China. The second track was to understand the systems, then reverse engineer the systems component by component. Once a successful overall system design – say, that of the Tomahawk – is taken as the basic template, the associated subsystems must be built or acquired. For designers and manufacturers in both advanced as well as developing countries, the modular nature of modern technology allows for separate units to be transported and then joined together to form highly complex and effective systems. One only needs to know how the units should be assembled, not very much about the principles on which they work.

Consider, for example, that 30-40 years ago an electronics engineer working on a missile guidance system had to spend years learning how to design extremely intricate circuits using transistors, capacitors, and other components. But now he just needs to be able to follow the manufacturer's instructions for programming a tiny microprocessor chip, available from almost any commercial electronics supplier. Modular technology applies also to rocketry, including engine design and aerodynamic construction. Computer controlled NC machines have made reverse engineering of mechanical parts easy. In this way, countries with negligible other technological achievements, such as North Korea, have been able to create rather advanced missile programs.

In a new development, Pakistan has announced that, in collaboration with Selex Galileo of Italy, it will soon start the manufacture of unmanned aerial vehicles (UAVs, commonly known as drones. The march of technology, spread by the global commercial interests, appears unstoppable.

## Aircraft Capability

The expansion of the army-controlled mobile missile force is being accompanied by expansion of air force capability. Chief of Air Staff, Air Chief Marshal Tanvir Mehmood Ahmed, announced in March 2009 that $9 billion would be spent on upgrading its nuclear status xxxviii. What this means is, however, unclear. Nor does it seem to be an efficient way of increasing nuclear offensive forces.

Fighter-bomber aircraft were once Pakistan's preferred means of delivering nuclear weapons to India, but they have certain definite limitations. First, their ranges do not permit many parts of India to be covered. Moreover they would have to run the gauntlet of an increasingly sophisticated Indian air-defence system. Nevertheless, they have the distinct advantage of being reliable, recallable, and reusable.

Pakistan had a deliverable nuclear weapon by 1987, and plans for aircraft delivery long preceded those for missile delivery. According to an officially inspired account,

*"During the 1983-1990 period, the Wah Group [of the PAEC] went on to design and develop an atomic bomb small enough to be carried on the wing of a small fighter such as the F-16. It worked alongside the PAF to evolve' and perfect delivery techniques of the nuclear bomb including „conventional free-fall, „loft bombing, „toss bombing and „low-level lay-down attack techniques using combat aircraft. Today, the PAF has perfected all four techniques of nuclear weapons delivery using F-16 and*

*Mirage-V combat aircraft indigenously configured to carry nuclear weapons".*

Pakistan started receiving the first of a batch of 36 F-16 C/D block 50/52 fighter aircraft in July 2007, the most modern version currently flown by the US Air Forcexl. It is also receiving assistance for modernizing all 34 of Pakistan's existing F-16 fleet to the same standard. F-16s are still said to be the mainstay for aerial delivery up to a range of about 1600 km, but two squadrons of A-5 Chinese built fighter-bombers are also suitable vehicles. There is, however, a caveat that has been added by the US: the F-16's sold under this deal will be specifically disallowed from carrying nuclear weapons. According to a US official, if Pakistan tried to do so then, we have this extraordinary security plan with United States personnel, we have monitoring, we have leverage to convince them not to do this. The modernized F-16's, however, would presumably be unaffected by this restriction.

The Pakistan Air Force's technical capabilities are mostly limited to aircraft maintenance. The largest units are the Mirage and F-6 rebuilding factories, an avionics and radar maintenance factory at Kamra, and a factory for manufacturing small training aircraft. There is an Air Weapons Complex located near Wah that manufactures a variety of air-delivered weapons. The JF-17 Thunder, of which 150 will eventually be inducted and become the air force's mainstay, is formally a joint China-Pakistan venture but Pakistani technical input into its design is said to be small.

A recent statement by the PAF air chief revealed that an Airborne Warning and Control System (AWACS) was being obtained from Sweden and China, and agreements had been reached with the US to provide electronic warfare system, smart bombs and long-range missile system. He said air-to-air refuellers were being modified. The PAF had almost 550 aircraft, including helicopters and transport aircrafts. The number of fighter planes was around 350, he added. At the moment, he said, there were 46 F-16 aircraft in the PAF, including 14 F-16 aircraft obtained from the US almost free of cost.

## The Skill Deficit

It would be too easy to ascribe Pakistan's success in bomb and missile-making to merely having allocated a large enough amount of money and resources. However, much wealthier Middle Eastern countries – Iraq and Iran in particular – have been less successful. The difference comes from a few hundred scientists and engineers working under the direction of effective and intelligent group leaders, an international buying network, as well as the strong will to do it all. Much of the work was reverse engineering, and there are no declared original applications, devices, or processes that have been declared. Nonetheless, Pakistani weaponeers understood developments in the literature and industry in sufficient detail and clarity. Trained almost entirely in the US, Canada, and Britain under a program initiated in the early 1960's by the Pakistan Atomic Energy Commission, only a few were high-class research scientists, or studied at the best universities. By now, many have retired, or are close to retirement.

The burgeoning demand from the principal defence R&D organizations PAEC, NDC, and KRL has resulted in a skill deficit that is perhaps the most serious constraint in the further development of Pakistan's nuclear and missile programs. Pakistan's public universities are in poor shape, and their graduates are ill equipped to understand modern engineering and technical problems. Manpower is being drawn principally from:

Engineering institutes run by the defence organizations. Examples include the Pakistan Institute of Engineering and Applied Sciences (PIEAS), as well as the Centre for Nuclear Studies (CNS). These institutes offer graduate studies in nuclear engineering, chemical and materials engineering, process engineering, systems engineering, electrical engineering, mechanical engineering, applied mathematics, information technology, etc. They are located on the premises of the Pakistan Institute of Nuclear Science and Technology (PINSTECH) near Islamabad. The NDC is also in the process of creating various institutes and centres on the Quaid-e-Azam University campus.

A handful of engineering colleges of relatively better quality such as the army-run National University of Science and Technology (NUST), Ghulam Ishaq Institute of Technology (GIKI), University of Engineering Technology (UET), etc.

Training of Pakistani missile and weapon designers in Chinese universities and institutes where they undergo short, highly focused, courses on rocket dynamics, navigational techniques, telemetry, etc. These are offered only to employees of government organizations and not general members of the Pakistani public.

Using the 12-fold increase in its budget over the past 5 years, the Higher Education Commission of the government of Pakistan has awarded many scholarships to Pakistanis for studying in Europe, Australia, and the United States. Among the beneficiaries are the employees, or former employees, of various defence organizations.

Academics and engineers in advanced countries can occasionally be interested into solving difficult technical problems for a fee. This follows the widespread global problem of outsourcing technical problems.

# 3

# Sino-Indian War

The Sino-Indian War , was a war between Chinaand India that occurred in 1962.

A disputed Himalayan border was the main pretext for war, but other issues played a role. There had been a series of violent border incidents after the 1959 Tibetan uprising, when India had granted asylum to theDalai Lama.

India initiated a Forward Policy in which it placed outposts along the border, including several north of theMcMahon Line, the eastern portion of a Line of Actual Control proclaimed by Chinese Premier Zhou Enlai in 1959. Unable to reach political accommodation on disputed territory along the 3,225-kilometer-long Himalayan border, the Chinese launched simultaneous offensives in Ladakh and across the McMahon Line on 20 October 1962.

Chinese troops advanced over Indian forces in both theatres, capturing Rezang la in Chushul in the western theatre, as well as Tawang in the eastern theatre. The war ended when the Chinese declared a ceasefire on 20 November 1962, and simultaneously announced its withdrawal from the disputed area. The Sino-Indian War is notable for the harsh mountain conditions under which much of the fighting took place, entailling large-scale combat at altitudes of over 4,000 metres (14,000 feet). The Sino-Indian War was also noted for the non-deployment of the navy or air force by either the Chinese or Indian side.

## LOCATION

China and India shared a long border, sectioned into three stretches by Nepal, Sikkim (then an Indian protectorate), and Bhutan, which follows the Himalayas between Burma and what was then West Pakistan. A number of disputed regions lie along this border. At its western end is the Aksai Chin region, an area the size of Switzerland, that sits between the Chinese autonomous region of Xinjiang and Tibet (which China declared as an autonomous region in 1965). The eastern border, between Burma and Bhutan, comprises the present Indian state of Arunachal Pradesh (formerly the North East Frontier Agency). Both of these regions were overrun by China in the 1962 conflict.

Most combat took place at high altitudes. The Aksai Chin region is a desert of salt flats around 5,000 metres above sea level, and Arunachal Pradesh is mountainous with a number of peaks exceeding 7000 metres. The Chinese Army had possession of one of the highest ridges in the regions. The high altitude and freezing conditions also cause logistical and welfare difficulties; in past, similar conflicts (such as the Italian Campaign of World War I) more casualties have been caused by the harsh conditions than enemy action. The Sino-Indian War was no different, with many troops on both sides dying in the freezing cold.

### Background

The cause of the war was a dispute over the sovereignty of the widely separated Aksai Chin and Arunachal Pradesh border regions. Aksai Chin, claimed by India to belong to Kashmir and by China to be part of Xinjiang, contains an important road link that connects the Chinese regions of Tibet and Xinjiang. China's construction of this road was one of the triggers of the conflict.

## AKSAI CHIN

The western portion of the Sino-Indian boundary originated in 1834, with the Sikh Confederacy's conquest of Ladakh. In

1842, the Sikh Confederacy, which at the time ruled over much of Northern India (including the frontier regions of Jammu and Kashmir), signed a treaty which guaranteed the integrity of its existing borders with its neighbours. The British defeat of the Sikhs in 1846 resulted in transfer of sovereignty over Ladakh, part of the Jammu and Kashmir region, to the British, and British commissioners contacted Chinese officials to negotiate the border. The boundaries at its two extremities, Pangong Lake and Karakoram Pass, were well defined, but the Aksai Chin area in between lay undefined. W. H. Johnson, a civil servant with the Survey of India, proposed the "Johnson Line" in 1865, which put Aksai Chin in Kashmir.

Johnson presented this line to the Maharaja of Kashmir, who then claimed the 18,000 square kilometres contained within. Johnson's work was severely criticized as inaccurate. His boundary line was described as "patently absurd", and extending further north than the Indian claim. Johnson was reprimanded by the British Government for crossing into Khotan without permission and resigned from the Survey. According to Francis Younghusband, who explored the region in the late 1880s, there was only an abandoned fort and not one inhabited house at Shahidulla when he was there - it was just a convenient staging post for the nomadic Kirghiz. The abandoned fort had apparently been built a few years earlier by the Kashmiris. In 1878 the Chinese had reconquered Xinjiang, and by 1890 they already had Shahidulla before the issue was decided. By 1892, China had erected boundary markers at Karakoram Pass.

In 1893, Hung Ta-chen, a senior Chinese official at Kashgar, handed a map of the boundary proposed by China to George Macartney, the British consul-general at Kashgar. This boundary placed the Lingzi Tang plains, which are south of the Laktsang range, in India, and Aksai Chin proper, which is north of the Laktsang range, in China. Macartney agreed with the proposal and forwarded it to the British Indian government.

The British presented this line, known as the Macartney-MacDonald line, to the Chinese in 1899 in a note by SirClaude MacDonald. In 1911 the Xinhai Revolution resulted in power shifts in China, and by the end of World War I, the British officially used the Johnson Line. However they took no steps to establish outposts or assert actual control on the ground. According to Neville Maxwell, the British had used as many as 11 different boundary lines in the region, as their claims shifted with the political situation. From 1917 to 1933, the "Postal Atlas of China", published by the Government of China in Peking had shown the boundary in Aksai Chin as per the Johnson line, which runs along the Kunlun mountains.

Upon independence in 1947, the government of India used the Johnson Line as the basis for its official boundary in the west, which included the Aksai Chin. On 1 July 1954, India's first Prime Minister Jawaharlal Nehru definitively stated the Indian position, claiming that Aksai Chin had been part of the Indian Ladakh region for centuries, and that the border (as defined by the Johnson Line) was non-negotiable. According to George N. Patterson, when the Indian government finally produced a report detailing the alleged proof of India's claims to the disputed area, "the quality of the Indian evidence was very poor, including some very dubious sources indeed". The traditional and customary basis for the border was also presented by the Indian side in the meetings between officials of the governments in 1960. In 1956–57, China constructed a road through Aksai Chin, connecting Xinjiang and Tibet, which ran south of the Johnson Line in many places. Aksai Chin was easily accessible to the Chinese, but access from India, which meant negotiating the Karakoram mountains, was much more difficult. The road came on Chinese maps published in 1958.

## THE MCMAHON LINE

In 1826, British India gained a common border with China after the British wrested control of Manipur and Assam from the Burmese, following the First Anglo-Burmese War of 1824–1826. In 1847, Major J. Jenkins, agent for the North East Frontier, reported that the Tawang was part of Tibet. In 1872, four monastic officials from Tibet arrived in Tawang and supervised a boundary settlement with Major R. Graham, NEFA official, which included the Tawang Tract as part of Tibet. Thus, in the last half of the 19th century, it was clear that the British treated the Tawang Tract as part of Tibet. This boundary was confirmed in a 1 June 1912 note from the British General Staff in India, stating that the "present boundary (demarcated) is south of Tawang, running westwards along the foothills from near Ugalguri to the southern Bhutanese border." A 1908 map of The Province of Eastern Bengal and Assam prepared for the Foreign Department of the Government of India, showed the international boundary from Bhutan continuing to the Baroi River, following the Himalayas foothill alignment.

In 1913, representatives of Great Britain, China and Tibet attended a conference in Simla regarding the borders between Tibet, China and British India. Whilst all three representatives initialed the agreement, Beijing later objected to the proposed boundary between the regions of Outer Tibet and Inner Tibet, and did not ratify it. The details of the Indo-Tibetan boundary was not revealed to China at the time.

The foreign secretary of the British Indian government, Henry McMahon, who had drawn up the proposal, decided to bypass the Chinese (although instructed not to by his superiors) and settle the border bilaterally by negotiating directly with Tibet. According to later Indian claims, this border was intended to run through the highest ridges of the Himalayas, as the areas south of the Himalayas were traditionally Indian. However, the McMahon Line lay south of the boundary India claims. India's government held the view that the Himalayas were the ancient boundaries of the Indian subcontinent, and thus should be the modern boundaries of India, while it is the position of the Chinese government that the disputed area in the Himalayas have been geographically and culturally part of Tibet since ancient times.

Months after the Simla agreement, China set up boundary markers south of the McMahon Line. T. O'Callaghan, an official in the Eastern Sector of the North East Frontier, relocated all these markers to a location slightly south of the McMahon Line, and then visited Rima to confirm with Tibetan officials that there was no Chinese influence in the area. The British-run Government of India initially rejected the Simla Agreement as incompatible with the Anglo-Russian Convention of 1907, which stipulated that neither party was to negotiate with Tibet "except through the intermediary of the Chinese government". The British and Russians cancelled the 1907 agreement by joint consent in 1921. It was not until the late 1930s that the British started to use the McMahon Line on official maps of the region.

China took the position that the Tibetan government should not have been allowed to make a such a treaty, rejecting Tibet's claims of independent rule. For its part, Tibet did not object to any section of the McMahon Line excepting the demarcation of the trading town ofTawang, which the Line placed under British-Indian jurisdiction. However, up until World War II, Tibetan officials were allowed to administer Tawang with complete authority. Due to the increased threat of Japanese and Chinese expansion during this period, British Indian troops secured the town as part of the defence of India's eastern border.

In the 1950s, India began actively patrolling the region. It found that, at multiple locations, the highest ridges actually fell north of the McMahon Line. Given India's historic position that the original intent of the line was to separate the two nations by the highest mountains in the world, in these locations India extended its forward posts northward to the ridges, regarding this move as compliant with the original border proposal, although the Simla Convention did not explicitly state this intention.

## CONTINUATION OF WAR

After Zhou received Nehru's letter (rejecting Zhou's proposal), the fighting resumed on the eastern theatre on 14 November (Nehru's birthday), with an Indian attack on Walong, claimed by China, launched from the defensive position of Se La and inflicting heavy casualties on the Chinese. The Chinese resumed military activity on Aksai Chin and NEFA hours after the Walong battle.

## Eastern Theatre

On the eastern theatre, the PLA attacked Indian forces near Se La and Bomdi La on 17 November. These positions were defended by the Indian 4th Infantry Division. Instead of attacking by road as expected, PLA forces approached via a mountain trail, and their attack cut off a main road and isolated 10,000 Indian troops. Se La occupied high ground, and rather than assault this commanding position, the Chinese captured Thembang, which was a supply route to Se La.

## Western Theatre

On the western theatre, PLA forces launched a heavy infantry attack on 18 November near Chushul. Their attack started at 4:35 am, despite a mist surrounding most of the areas in the region. At 5:45 the Chinese troops advanced to attack 2 platoons of Indian troops atGurung Hill. The Indians did not know what was happening, as communications were dead. As a patrol was sent, China attacked with greater numbers. Indian artillery could not hold off against superior Chinese forces. By 9:00 am, Chinese forces attacked Gurung Hill directly and Indian commanders withdrew from the area and also from the connecting Spangur Gap.

The Chinese had been simultaneously attacking Rezang La which was held by 123 Indian troops. At 5:05 am, Chinese troops launched their attack audaciously. Chinese medium machine gun fire pierced through the Indian tactical defences. At 6:55 am the sun rose and the Chinese attack on the 8th platoon began in waves. Fighting continued for the next hour, until the Chinese signaled that they had destroyed the 7th platoon. Indians tried to use light machine guns on the medium machine guns from the Chinese but after 10 minutes the battle was over.

Logistical inadequacy once again hurt the Indian troops. The Chinese gave the Indian troops a respectful military funeral. The battles also saw the death of Major Shaitan Singh of the Kumaon Regiment, who had been instrumental in the first battle of Rezang La. The Indian troops were forced to withdraw to high mountain positions. Indian sources believed that their troops were just coming to grips with the mountain combat and finally called for more troops. However, the Chinese declared a ceasefire, ending the bloodshed.

Indians suffered heavy casualties, with dead Indian troops' bodies being found in the ice, frozen with weapons in hand. Chinese forces also suffered heavy casualties, especially at Rezang La. This signalled the end of the war in Aksai Chin as China had reached their claim line – many Indian troops were ordered to withdraw from the area. China claimed that the Indian troops wanted to fight on until the bitter end. However, the war ended with their withdrawal, so as to limit the amount of casualties.

The PLA penetrated close to the outskirts of Tezpur, Assam, a major frontier town nearly fifty kilometres from the Assam-North-East Frontier Agency border. The local government ordered the evacuation of the civilians in Tezpur to the south of the Brahmaputra River, all prisons were thrown open, and government officials who stayed behind destroyed Tezpur's currency reserves in anticipation of a Chinese advance.

## Ceasefire

China had reached its claim lines so the PLA did not advance farther, and on 19 November, it declared a unilateral cease-fire. Zhou Enlai declared a unilateral ceasefire to start on midnight, 21 November. Zhou's ceasefire declaration stated,

Beginning from 21 November 1962, the Chinese frontier guards will cease fire along the entire Sino-Indian border. Beginning from 1 December 1962, the Chinese frontier guards will withdraw to positions 20 kilometres behind the line of actual control which existed between China and India on 7 November 1959. In the eastern sector, although the Chinese frontier guards have so far been fighting on Chinese territory north of the traditional customary line, they are prepared to withdraw from their present positions to the north of the illegal McMahon Line, and to withdraw twenty kilometres back from that line. In the middle and western sectors, the Chinese frontier guards will withdraw twenty kilometres from the line of actual control.

Zhou had first given the ceasefire announcement to Indian chargé d'affaires on 19 November (before India's request for United States air support), but New Delhi did not receive it until 24 hours later. The aircraft carrier was ordered back after the ceasefire, and thus, American intervention on India's side in the war was avoided. Retreating Indian troops, who hadn't come into contact with anyone knowing of the ceasefire, and Chinese troops in NEFA and Aksai Chin, were involved in some minor battles, but for the most part, the ceasefire signalled an end to the fighting. The United States Air Force flew in supplies to India in November 1962, but neither side wished to continue hostilities.

Toward the end of the war India increased its support for Tibetan refugees and revolutionaries, some of them having settled in India, as they were fighting the same common enemy in the region. The Nehru administration ordered the raising of an elite Indian-trained "Tibetan Armed Force" composed of Tibetan refugees. The CIA had already begun operations in bringing about change in Tibet.

## TERRITORIAL PROBLEMS BETWEEN SINO-INDIA

In terms of "the rise of China" and its "implications for India", the title of this book, the Sino-Indian territorial dispute represents an immediate arena in which India is having to face the uncomfortable implications from having an increasingly stronger neighbour. For India, the ability of China to deny India's hopes of territorial settlement on India's terms has become ever clearer in the wake of China's rise in military power in and around their disputed territory, which remains the biggest amount of land still in dispute in Asia.

As such, "the 4,056—kilometre (2,520 miles) frontier between India and China, one of the longest inter-state borders in the world, remains ... not defined, let alone demarcated, on maps or delineated on the ground". Here, the judgement over a century ago of Lord Curzon, British Viceroy of India 1898-

1905 still seems relevant; the most urgent work of Foreign Ministers and Ambassadors ... is now the conclusion of Frontier Conventions in which sources of discord are removed by the adjustment of rival interests or ambitions at points where the territorial borders adjoin", for "frontiers are indeed the razor's edge on which hang suspended the modern issues of war or peace, of life or death to nations".

Admittedly, the territorial issue has been officially decoupled from the wider Sino-Indian relationship; as with the PRC rhetoric that "China and India have already reached consensus on the border issue. Before it is completely resolved, both countries will endeavour to maintain peace and stability in the border areas and will not let the border issue affect the general picture of China and India's cooperation". However, in reality their territorial issues do affect their wider relationship, in PRC terms "the existence of immense territorial disputes between China and India".

In dispute terms, this chapter argues that, in International Relations (IR) theory terms, the territorial disputes between India and China involve *classical geopolitics* entwined with *critical geopolitics*. Each strand of geopolitics, in their different ways, both involve the respective "position" that India and China hold for themselves and for each other in their immediate and extended neighbourhood.

Whilst each side argues from history, the chapter argues that in reality the evidence from history is rather ambiguous and inconclusive for both sides' territorial claims. Indeed, history is a sterile area to argue from, as one Indian commentator put it, "can we go beyond history to look at solutions which do not hark back to the past?"

The chapter argues that, from the outside, resolution of the issue seems feasible enough in terms of simple seeming territorial trade offs involving Arunachal Pradesh and Aksai Chin; but is complicated by smaller geographic issues surrounding Tawang, and wider geopolitical issues surrounding Tibet and indeed the balance of power in Asia between India and China.

The two main areas of dispute along this Himalayan frontier are the *Western Sector* (Aksai Chin, around 37,250 square kilometres/ 14,380 square miles); and the *Eastern Sector* (Arunachal Pradesh, around 83,740 square kilometres/ 32,330 square miles). On the one hand, Arunachal Pradesh is inhabited by over a million people, Indian citizens, and includes important Buddhist centres like Tawang. On the other hand, Aksai Chin is a virtually uninhabited bleak barren plateau with no permanent settlements. It is the place "where not a blade of grass grows" as Jawaharlal Nehru once dismissively said; but where China's National Highway 219 runs through Aksai Chin as a key geopolitical infrastructure link for the PRC between its provinces of Tibet and Xinjiang. One further complication is China's occupation of the Shaksgam valley; around 5,180 sq kilometres/1,930 square miles, to which Pakistan relinquished its Baltistan-related claims in 1963, but over which India maintains its own Kashmir-derived claims. Smaller pockets of disputed territory are found, the *Middle Sector* fringes of Himachal Pradesh and Uttar Pradesh. Elsewhere along the Himalayas, lingering uncertainty over China's recognition of Sikkim's incorporation into India in 1975 is entwined with continuing PRC claims to the "Finger Area" in the north of Sikkim, with 71 supposed incidents reported of Chinese troop "incursions" in 2008. Nearby territorial disputes between China and Bhutan around the Chumbi Valley triangulation point with India are of further concern to New Delhi, given the Chumbi Valley's location looking down onto the India's sensitive Siliguri corridor which links India's northeastern states with the rest of India.

Wider nuances arise with India's Foreign Secretary (2004—2006) Shyam Saran, and his comments about *the logic of geography*. In front of one audience, it was a question for Saran of "geopolitical reality" in which "I would like to focus particularly on Asia, where the interests of both India and China intersect. It is said that the logic of geography is unrelenting. Proximity is the most difficult and testing among diplomatic challenges a country faces", where "to those who harbour any skepticism about this fact, it would suffice to remind that we share one of the longest [and disputed] land borders in the world with China.

In front of another audience, it was again a question that "it is said that the logic of geography is unrelenting and proximity is the most difficult and testing among diplomatic challenges a country faces"; with the following gloss that "frontiers with neighbours are where domestic concerns intersect with external relationships. This is where domestic and foreign policies become inextricable and demand sensitive handling", and in which "it is important for us to look at the [disputed] boundary question from the long-term and strategic perspective of India-China relations, rather than as a mere territorial issue.

The territorial issues between India and China form one of the biggest land disputes in Asia, and are of significance not only for the size of area under dispute, but also because the two disputants are the big countries most evidently on the rise in Asia. Alongside this *logic of geography*, there is then what Neville Maxwell called "the logic of power"; a *logic of power* whereby powerful states "in their expansive phases push out their frontiers until they meet the resistance of a strong neighbour or reach a physical barrier which makes a natural point of rest". In geopolitical terms, the current point of rest is along the Himalayas/Karakoram range, but in the long term where exactly is the "natural" point of rest between them? Amidst talk of mutual IR *security dilemma* dynamics, China's strengthening of military forces and related infrastructure in Aksai Chin and Arunachal Pradesh zones is now a spur to India's own more halting augmentation of military forces and related infrastructure. Meanwhile, both countries are seeking to expand their wider strategic space at a time when their immediate mountain borders remain unresolved.

## THE COLLISION OF THE SINO-INDIAN WAR

In many ways, how China and India relate to each other indicates where they see themselves in the international system. Firstly, however, it is necessary to have an understanding of the events leading up to and following the 1962 Sino-Indian

War, as this continues to affect the contemporary Sino-Indian relationship.

The major causes of conflict between China and India – namely, the disputed border and the issue of Tibet, including the fourteenth Dalai Lama's ongoing residency in India – have their roots in the political dealings that went on in the late 1800s and early 1900s between British India, pre-Communist China and feudal Tibet. The major question was whether treaties signed by British India and Tibet demarcating the border – known as the McMahon Line – were valid, given that, according to the Chinese, Tibet was part of China and had no authority to act unilaterally. Disagreements of this nature and the exact location of the border persisted throughout the early twentieth century, further complicated by Indian independence in 1947 (which removed British backing and so altered the balance of power in the region in favour of China) and the Chinese 'liberation' of Tibet in 1950.

1954, marked with a visit to India Chinese by Premier Zhou Enlai in June, and a reciprocal visit by Indian Prime Minister Jawaharlal Nehru to China in October, was a high point in the relationship; it was during the latter visit that the term 'Hindi-Chini bhai-bhai' (Indians and Chinese are brothers) was coined, and denoted a period of rapprochement after decades of strife over the disputed India-Tibet border.

This new-found friendship in theory forged a renewed basis for discussions over the disputed border, though this was tested only two years later. There were (and still are) two contested areas: the north-eastern stretch, which was known under the British as the North-East Frontier Agency (NEFA) and since 1986 has been the Indian state of Arunachal Pradesh (claimed by the Chinese as Southern Tibet), and the western region of Aksai Chin (claimed by the Indians and currently administered by the Chinese), which borders the Indian state of Jammu and Kashmir. Although up until the mid-50s most of the border tensions had existed over the eastern stretch – and specifically the disputed border known as the McMahon Line – the western region became the focus when in 1956 the Chinese constructed a highway from Xinjiang province to Tibet through the Aksai

Chin to allow the rapid movement of troops between the two restive provinces. In spite of disputing the occupation of the territory, India did not actually administer the Aksai Chin in any way, and consequently after the building of the road the region effectively passed into Chinese hands. Nevertheless, the Aksai Chin continued to be a volatile area – not helped by the fact that the rest of Jammu and Kashmir was the subject of an ongoing and often violent dispute between India and Pakistan – and subsequently provided one of the flashpoints for the 1962 Sino-Indian war.

Matters were further complicated with the Lhasa Revolt of March 1959, an uprising of Tibetans which culminated in the fleeing of the fourteenth Dalai Lama (and subsequently thousands of Tibetan refugees) to India and the systematic crushing of the resistance by Chinese forces. In the northern autumn Chinese and Indian troops clashed along the McMahon Line border.

An attempt at resolving the border issue was made during a visit by Premier Zhou Enlai to Delhi from19-25 April 1960, but "the talks...did not resolve the differences that had arisen and the two Prime Ministers decided that officials of the two Governments should examine the factual material in the possession of the two Governments in support of their stands" (Ministry of External Affairs, 1961:1).

The committee met three times throughout 1960, with both sides producing reports of the discussions for their respective governments.

The contents of these reports illustrate how intractable the border problem was and indeed still is, with the two sides unable to agree even on the basic tenor of the talks, such as whether the border had ever been officially delimited (no, according to China; yes, according to India). Consequently no resolution was reached at the 1960 talks which, with hindsight, were really the last opportunity to effect an agreement before relations broke down completely.

The Sino-Indian War began on 8 September 1962 when the Chinese crossed into NEFA (now Arunachal Pradesh) and attacked an Indian border post, alleging that the Indians had already violated the McMahon Line. This was the first time the conflict flared along the McMahon Line, though there had been some fighting around the Aksai Chin region, inflamed by Sino-Pakistani border talks which the Indians alleged were aimed at undermining their position in Kashmir. These skirmishes continued throughout September and into October.

On 20 October the Chinese launched a full-scale offensive all along the frontier, from Ladakh to NEFA, arguing that it was a pre-emptive strike against Indian aggression. This was significant because it moved the conflict beyond the disputed areas and into Indian territory, essentially becoming an invasion of India. The Indian force was fatally under-prepared and crumbled before the Chinese onslaught.

The fighting lasted for just over a month, with the Chinese declaring a unilateral ceasefire on 21 November. Statistics released by the Indian government on 29 October had between 2000 and 2500 Indian soldiers killed during the first week of fighting, with 1102 held prisoner, 291 wounded and 5174 missing and presumed dead.

On 8 November the Chinese proposed a ceasefire agreement whereby both parties would withdraw twenty kilometres behind the positions held on 7 November, 1959. This meant that the Chinese would withdraw back behind the McMahon Line, but they would maintain control of Indian-claimed territory in Ladakh, including the strategically important Aksai Chin road linking Xinjiang and Tibet.

This was initially rejected by the Indians, but after another fortnight of fierce fighting the Chinese surprised everyone by announcing a unilateral ceasefire and the withdrawal of troops from 1 December to the 7 November 1959 positions. The Chinese also added that, provided the Indian government took corresponding measures, the two parties could meet to discuss troop withdrawal and an end to hostilities.

Militarily weakened, and with the rest of the world supporting all measures to solve the conflict, India was in no position to argue.

In December 1962 six non-aligned nations (Ceylon, Burma, Cambodia, Indonesia, the United Arab Republic and Ghana) met in Colombo to try to broker a formal peace deal, but their lack of condemnation of the Chinese invasion incensed India. India nevertheless accepted the Colombo proposals, but China rejected them, insisting on a "unilateral implementation" of its 21 November 1962 statement; consequently the talks broke down and nothing was resolved, even in subsequent bilateral meetings.

Sino-Indian relations did not begin to normalise until the mid-1970s; a turning point was the resumption of ambassadorial relations in 1976. Although the two countries retained non-official diplomatic relations throughout the 1960s (with missions headed by a *charge d'affairs* rather than an ambassador), interaction was minimal. In fact, Gautam Das describes the period between 1962-76 as a period of "cold peace" rather than cold war, and notes that "Sino-Indian relations after 1962 are, in substance if not chronology, Sino-Indian relations after 1976 [because very little of note happened in the intervening period]".

Rapprochement continued after the resumption of diplomatic relations, albeit with a few hiccups, but it wasn't until 1988 that the turning point came with Indian Prime Minister Rajiv Gandhi's visit to Beijing. This made him the first Indian Prime Minister to visit China since Nehru in 1954 and marked the end of the impasse on the border issue which had lasted for most of the 1980s; the two sides agreed to maintain peace and stability along the Line of Actual Control (LAC) in Arunachal Pradesh (roughly equivalent to the McMahon Line), and they also agreed to set up a Joint Working Group (JWG) to help defuse the border issue. In addition, India agreed to curtail the anti-China actions of Tibetans in India. According to Das, "the decade that followed the Rajiv Gandhi visit up to the 1998 Indian nuclear explosions (Pokhran-II) has been the most cordial phase of Sino-Indian relations after 1962".

These warm relations continued during the mid-1990s, and were further consolidated by Chinese President Jiang Zemin's visit to India in 1996, where four mutual cooperation agreements were signed, and it appeared that a breakthrough in the tensions had finally occurred.

Unfortunately, this series of small steps forward was followed by a giant leap backwards in 1998. During a visit of the People's Liberation Army (PLA) Senior General Fu Quanyou to New Delhi, the Indian Defence Minister, George Fernandes, publicly stated that he believed China was continuing to carry out border incursions into Indian territory , and later accused China of being India's number one security threat, greater even than Pakistan. This was immediately followed by India's second ever nuclear tests, known as Pokhran II (ibid). The fact that the tests occurred before Fu had even arrived back in Beijing caused a huge loss of face for the Chinese, because they felt that after a decade of overtures to the Indians they had been callously rebuffed and humiliated.

Nevertheless, the overall Chinese reaction to the tests was initially quite controlled, and might have remained so, had India not justified the tests by claiming they were in response to the 'China threat'. This was articulated in a letter from Indian Prime Minister Vajpayee to US President Bill Clinton, which was printed in the *New York Times* on 13 May (ibid). This was seen as "unwarranted and provocative", and the fact that the issue was given such a public airing caused another immense loss of face for the Chinese; consequently they reacted angrily, cancelling the next meeting of the Joint Working Group on the border issue. This issue of the 'China threat' still permeates relations today, with more than one Chinese interviewee claiming that the Indian military deliberately promotes China as a threat in order to get increased defence spending, and that 1998 was one of the clearest examples of this (Author interviews with Wang Dehua and anonymous interviewee, 2010).

After the low point of the 1998 tests, relations began once again to normalise, in spite of a brief hiccup over Tibet when 14-year-old Ugyen Thinley Dorje, the 17th Karmapa Lama of the Kagyupa sect of Tibetan Buddhism, fled China for Dharamsala in January 2000.

Nevertheless, in February 2000 India and China concluded an agreement for China's accession to the World Trade Organisation ; in March India participated in the first ever Sino-Indian security dialogue in Beijing, and the Joint Working Group sessions resumed in April of the same year.

In 2003 an incursion by Chinese troops into Indian territory occurred in Arunachal Pradesh, shortly after Indian Prime Minister Vajpayee's visit to Beijing; Vajpayee put this down to "differences in perceptions" regarding the Line of Actual Control, but some politicians and analysts took it much more seriously. This incident shows that in spite of another gradual thawing of relations, the border question still remains a highly contentious issue in the Sino-Indian relationship.

Furthermore, in addition to ongoing Indian concerns about the Sino-Pakistani relationship, China is also disturbed about the growing relationship between India and the USA, fearing that such an alliance will upset the balance of power in the region.

Seen in the light of history, the most recent incidents to affect the Sino-Indian relationship – the 2008 Tibet protests and the subsequent disruption of the Olympic torch relay (including in Delhi); and the border skirmishes and associated negative media coverage throughout 2009 – are unlikely to cause permanent damage to the relationship.

They do, however, highlight the fact that the border issue is still unresolved, and most analysts agree that the Sino-Indian relationship will not be able to move forward in any meaningful way until this question is answered. As well as being rooted in political reality, however, a large element of the Sino-Indian conflict also stems from misplaced perceptions, both of each other's motives and of their own place in the world order.

The concept of 'Chindia' is popular at present but it is based on flawed logic. Although the geo-civilisational aspects, where cultural practices flowed freely across what is now Central Asia to India and China and back again, cannot be denied, China and India are also distinct civilisations with their own histories and cultures and to conflate them is to understate the importance of this in shaping their distinctive governments and policies. It also minimises the very real animosity which remains between them and deeply influences not only the Sino-Indian relationship but also how they see themselves and how they relate to the wider international community.

On a political and strategic front, India and China have followed extremely different developmental trajectories with different outcomes and they also have different aims for their status in the international system. These differences in aims, policy and strategic thought can be seen to be playing out in Central Asia at present.

The 'Chindia' concept is for the most part a Western construct developed as a response to the 'China threat' perception and tied into the former US and ASEAN policy of containment, in which India would play an important role. This idea of a mutual rise or equating China and India was seized upon by some in India who were attracted by the idea that India has or will soon have the same type of international economic and political clout as China, even when the present reality suggests otherwise.

In fact, India should not seek to emulate China because it is unlikely that such a course of action would succeed; in any case the two countries' systems are extremely different. Rather, India must forge its own path and decide what kind of a role it wants to play internationally, and how it will achieve this.

It must also in the immediate-term concentrate on domestic development and remember that 'national security' cannot just be about the military but must also include human, food, environmental and other types of security as well as poverty reduction.

This seems to be the path which the Indian government is beginning to take and it is likely to be far more successful than any which frames the question of India's development in relation to China. Regarding China, we need to rethink the way we examine it in terms of international relations theory in order to avoid overlooking the real issues in Chinese strategic thought because of a desire to fit Chinese development into an established international relations model.

Finally, scholarship – both in China and India and further afield – needs to be developed so that more scholars are educated in the practices and policies of both countries, and communication is facilitated between China and India scholars the world over, rather than operating simply in closed 'China studies' or 'India studies' spheres. This would not only prove beneficial to promoting stability in the Sino-Indian relationship, but would also go some way to ensuring that the two countries can be viewed as separate but parallel entities rather than as 'Chindia'.

# 4

# Kashmir Conflict and Territorial Dispute

The Kashmir dispute dates from 1947. The partition of the Indian sub-continent along religious lines led to the formation of India and Pakistan. However, there remained the problem of over 650 states, run by princes, existing within the two newly independent countries. In theory, these princely states had the option of deciding which country to join, or of remaining independent. In practice, the restive population of each province proved decisive.

The people had been fighting for freedom from British rule, and with their struggle about to bear fruit they were not willing to let the princes fill the vacuum. Although many princes wanted to be "independent" (which would have meant hereditary monarchies and no hope for democracy) they had to succumb to their people's protests which turned violent in many provinces.

Because of its location, Kashmir could choose to join either India or Pakistan. Maharaja Hari Singh, the ruler of Kashmir, was Hindu while most of his subjects were Muslim. Unable to decide which nation Kashmir should join, Hari Singh chose to remain neutral. But his hopes of remaining independent were dashed in October 1947, as Pakistan sent in Muslim tribesmen who were knocking at the gates of the capital Srinagar. Hari Singh appealed to the Indian government for military assistance and fled to India. He signed the Instrument of Accession, ceding Kashmir to India on October 26.

Indian and Pakistani forces thus fought their first war over Kashmir in 1947-48. India referred the dispute to the United Nations on 1 January. In a resolution dated August 13, 1948, the UN asked Pakistan to remove its troops, after which India was also to withdraw the bulk of its forces. Once this happened, a "free and fair" plebiscite was to be held to allow the Kashmiri people to decide their future.

India, having taken the issue to the UN, was confident of winning a plebiscite, since the most influential Kashmiri mass leader, Sheikh Abdullah, was firmly on its side. An emergency government was formed on October 30, 1948 with Sheikh Abdullah as the Prime Minister. Pakistan ignored the UN mandate and continued fighting, holding on to the portion of Kashmir under its control. On January 1, 1949, a ceasefire was agreed, with 65 per cent of the territory under Indian control and the remainder with Pakistan.

The ceasefire was intended to be temporary.but the Line of Control remains the de facto border between the two countries. In 1957, Kashmir was formally incorporated into the Indian Union. It was granted a special status under Article 370 of India's constitution, which ensures, among other things, that non-Kashmiri Indians cannot buy property there.

Fighting broke out again in 1965, but a ceasefire was established that September. Indian Prime Minister, Lal Bhadur Shastri, and Pakistani President, M Ayub Khan, signed the Tashkent agreement on January 1, 1966. They resolved to try to end the dispute, but the death of Mr Shastri and the rise of Gen Yahya Khan in Pakistan resulted in stalemate.

In 1971a third war, resulting in the formation of the independent nation of Bangladesh (formerly known as East Pakistan). A war had broken out in East Pakistan in March 1971, and soon India was faced with a million refugees. India declared war on December 3, 1971 after Pakistani Air Force planes struck Indian airfields in the Western sector.

Two weeks later, the Indian army marched into Dhaka and the Pakistanis surrendered. In the Western sector the Indians managed to blockade the port city of Karachi and were 50 km into Pakistani territory when a ceasefire was reached. In 1972 Indira Gandhi, the Indian prime minister, and Zulfikar Ali Bhutto, her Pakistani opposite number (and father of Benazir Bhutto, a later Pakistani premier), signed the Simla Agreement, which reiterated the promises made in Tashkent.

The two sides once again agreed to resolve the issue peacefully, as domestic issues dominated. Both India and Pakistan had other important domestic problems which kept Kashmir on the back-burner. In 1975 Indira Gandhi declared a state of national emergency, but she was defeated in the 1978 general elections.

Zulfikar Ali Bhutto was overthrown and hanged in 1977; Pakistan reverted to military dictatorship under Gen Zia ul Haq. The balance of influence had decisively tilted in Pakistan's favour by the late 1980s, with people's sympathy no longer with the Indian union as it had been in 1947-48 and 1965. Mrs Gandhi's attempts to install puppet governments in state capitals, manipulating the democratic process in the state legislatures, deeply angered the Kashmiris.

The status quo was largely maintained until 1989 when pro-independence and pro-Pakistan guerrillas struck in the Indian Kashmir valley. They established a reign of terror and drove out almost all the Hindus from the valley before the Indian army moved in to flush them out. Meanwhile Indian and Pakistani troops regularly exchanged fire at the border. Whereas in 1948 India took the Kashmir issue to the UN and was all for a plebiscite, by the 1990s it hid behind the Simla agreement and thwarted any attempts at UN or third-party mediation.

Over the decades the plebiscite advocated by India's great statesman Jawaharlal Nehru became a dirty word in New Delhi. These developments have led many to believe that Delhi has squandered the Kashmiri people's trust and allegiance. India and Pakistan both tested nuclear devices in May 1998, and then in April 1999 test-fired missiles in efforts to perfect delivery systems for their nuclear weapons. Pakistan tested its Ghauri II missile four days after India's testing of its long-range (1,250 km) Agni II.

Although Pakistan claims that its missiles are an indigenous effort, in July 1999 Indian customs agents seized components shipped from North Korea which they claim were destined for Pakistan's missile programme. Pakistan's later intermediate-range Ghauri III missile has a range of about 3,000 km. When the Indian Prime Minister, Atal Behari Vajpayee, set out to Lahore by bus on February 20, 1999, inaugurating the four times a week Delhi-Lahore-Delhi bus service, the world felt that such a genuine effort at friendly neighbourhood relations would lower the tension along the Line of Control in Kashmir.

But, all hopes of diplomacy disappeared once the cross-LOC firing in Kargil began during the mid-1990s. The death toll, including both soldiers and civilians, was more than 30,000.

In the first week of August 1998 Indian and Pakistani troops exchanged artillery fire, described by locals as heavier than that of the 1948 and 1965 wars put together. An estimated 50,000 rounds of ammunition were expended and a large number of soldiers and civilians killed. In the summer of 1999 hostility in Kargil went far beyond the now familiar annual exhange of artillery fire.

When India began patrolling the Kargil heights that summer, it found to its horror that many key posts vacated in the winter were occupied by infiltrators. A patrol was ambushed in the first week of May 1999. India belatedly realised the magnitude of the occupation - which was around 10 km deep and spanned almost 100 km of the LOC - and sent MiG fighters into action on May 26.

India contended that the infiltrators were trained and armed by Pakistan, and based in "Azad Kashmir" with the full knowledge of the Pakistani government - and that Afghan and other foreign mercenaries accompanied them. Pakistan insisted that those involved were freedom fighters from Kashmir and that it was giving only moral support. India ordered the jets not to stray into Pakistani territory; but those that did were shot down.

The conflict ended only after Bill Clinton, the US President, and Nawaz Sharif, Pakistan's Prime minister, met in

Washington on July 4, 1999. Meanwhile, the Indian Army had made significant advances, capturing vital territory on July 4. Despite the apparent efforts to mediate, the US maintained that it was not interfering in what India still claims to be a bilateral issue. Pakistan withdrew its forces later that month. However, skirmishing continued, and in August India shot down a Pakistani reconnaissance plane, killing 16.

The official number of Indian troops lost in Kargil was around 500, with almost double that number of "infiltrators" killed. Nevertheless, India did not declare war against Pakistan - instead, Mr Vajpayee ambigously announced a "war-like situation".

Yet this, by all accounts of soldiers and top Indian army officers involved, was a war in which India lost men engaged in hand-to-hand combat with Pakistani soldiers in the heights of Kargil - a war that could be compared with the one of 1948-49, which was limited to Kashmir, with the other border regions remaining peaceful.

Thus in 1999, in a war limited to one sector, India suffered casualities within its own territory. Despite much pressure from the military and the public, the government decided not to cross the LOC. Pakistan too suffered criticism at home for limiting its war to artillery fire across the LOC and shooting down Indian aircraft. The fear of a full-scale war (with nuclear capability adding a deadly dimension), coupled with precarious economies and the knowledge of what international sanctions could do to them, may have prevailed in both countries.

## "TERRITORIAL DISPUTE" IN KASHMIR DISPUTE

It is a "territorial dispute" only in the sense that the State of Jammu and Kashmir is disputed territory and is so recognized internationally. But the expression can be misleading. For it usually suggested contentious claims of two states to a territory, one party basing its claim on the validity of a de facto or de jure boundary demarcation and the other challenging it. That is why territorial disputes are hardly distinguishable from border disputes, amenable to solution through bilateral agreement, judicial determination or, more often, arbitration.

Kashmir is a case qualitatively different from border disputes. Here the territory involved is a whole country, a country larger than many member states of the United Nations, a country larger the major part of which has existed for more than a millennium as a sovereign political entity on its own, a country whose distinct physical environment, history and culture have shaped its people's individuality. Here the matter is not one of placing a few hundred square miles on one side or the other of an international frontier and thus settling a boundary conflict. It is a matter of the disposition of a country through the same process by which the two contestants, the Indian Union and Pakistan themselves emerged as independent states - the process of establishing sovereignties on the basis of popular consent. As long as the Kashmir dispute remains unresolved, the agenda of the independence of the South Asian subcontinent remains unfinished.

If this support had really rested on, and reflected, popular sentiment, then the history of the Kashmir dispute would have been entirely different. In that case, India would have been not merely willing but eager to have the United Nations conduct a plebiscite in Kashmir so that the accession would be speedily ratified and India's position vindicated for good. All that India would have required would have been sufficient safeguards against a breach of the Ceasefire Line or eruption of violence during the period of the plebiscite. These would have been easily obtained. Indeed, they were provided for in the plan drawn by the United Nations Commission for India and Pakistan (UNCIP). With a Plebiscite Administrator appointed by the United Nations and inducted into office, the freedom of the voters from coercion and intimidation would have been assured. Pakistan would have had no means to exert any pressure whatsoever on the voters nor would it have chosen to draw overwhelming international censure for disrupting the plebiscite process. If there has been popular support in Kashmir for joining India, the dispute over Kashmir would have lasted for a year or so at most. It would have dissolved long ago.

Let us here contrast the cases of Hyderabad, Junagarh and Goa - three areas that India annexed through what it called (a phrase reminiscent of Nazi ideology) "police action". In none of these cases did India have to bring in the resounding names of a local political organization or leader to justify the annexations. Yet, leader or no leader, organization or no organization, the overwhelming majority of the people in these areas wished to be part of the Indian nation and, though a certain arrogance on India's part raised some eyebrows, world opinion recognized the fact and the incorporation of the these areas in India met with international acquiescence. Pakistan's complaints in the cases of Hyderabad and Junagarh and the protest of the United States over the invasion of Goa were storms of the teacup variety; the controversies subsided in short time.

The presentation by India of Sheikh Abdullah and his National Conference as the embodiment of mass approval for the entry of Indian troops into Kashmir has itself provided an eloquent commentary on the nature of India's claim to Kashmir. The same Sheikh Abdullah was dismissed as Prime Minister in 1953, kept in prison for years and charged with treason because he insisted on complete autonomy for the State and stressed repeatedly that the accession was provisional. At one time, in 1957, he sent a hand-written letter from jail t the Security Council denouncing the Indian position. The National Conference formed what was called the Plebiscite Front, which demanded that the issue of accession be referred to the people's vote. The fact that later in 1975 Sheikh Abdullah turned a somersault and, signing on the dotted line, became Chief Minister again is an indicator more of his personal character than of the strength or consistency of India's political position in Kashmir.

A glimpse into Kashmir's political history might be apposite here. Kashmir was unique among all the Princely States of India in organizing a political movement on its own in opposition to autocracy.

This took the form of a mass agitation in 1931, which a year later, gave birth to the Muslim Conference. Sheikh Abdullah was undoubtedly the hero the agitation and no one equalled his appeal to huge Kashmiri gatherings. He was at the peak of his popularity from 1931 to 1933. As early as 1934, however, a streak of opportunism in him became visible when he stayed away from an agitation directed by his more steadfast and less theatrical colleague, Ghulam Abbas, against the limitation of the franchise for the legislative assembly and the restriction of the assembly's powers. From that time onwards, although he retained his unsurpassed capacity to arouse the emotions of the masses, his political position zigzagged and his popularity began to wane. When he succeeded in converting the Muslim Conference into the National Conference, he attracted the patronage of Jawaharlal Nehru, enlisted the support of the great propaganda machine run by the Indian Congress, gained some glitter in non-Kashmiri eyes but lost the cohesiveness of his Kashmiri following. Within a short period, the co-architect of the National Conference, Prem Nath Bazaz (Hindu) and the former President of Muslim Conference - both expressed disillusionment about Abdullah's integrity. The former established his own party and the latter revived the Muslim Conference. Non-Muslims regarded Abdullah as a Muslim chauvinist (what is called 'communalist' in India) and Muslims suspected that he had struck some kind of a deal with the Dogra regime despite its practice of open discrimination against the Muslims. Both were right not because Abdullah was taking the middle position but because he easily swung from one extreme to the other.

Two other things affected Abdullah's public standing. First, he betrayed pronounced fascist proclivities and frequently resorted to strong-arm methods in bullying his opponents. This became a scandal in the late 1930s and the early 1940s; he had to suffer physical reprisal for his hooliganism in places like Poonch and Rajauri. Second, while still employing his emotive rhetoric, he veered more and more towards cooperation with the Maharaja's autocratic regime. As if this was not enough, he broke the pledge he had made that he would not side with the Indian Congress against the Muslim League (the two major parties in British India).

In an attempt to recapture his following among Muslims, especially the intelligentsia, Abdullah joined prominently in the jubilant reception accorded to M.A. Jinnah on his visit to Kashmir in 1944. Jinnah tried to reconcile Abdullah and Abbas and put the question squarely to Abdullah. "How much significant support have you obtained from Hindus for the objectives of the National Conference?" When Abdullah could cite only the names of a few individuals, Jinnah queried, "The what is the point of dividing the Muslims into two camps, the Muslim Conference and the National Conference?" Abdullah thought he had a answer to that. "But the National Conference is in reality the Muslim Conference in a better guise," he said. Came back the forthright rebuke, "That means you are committing a fraud on Hindus." This left Abdullah only with one course: vituperative speeches against "outsiders" like Jinnah. (In private remarks, he, however, disowned the speeches.) This was the nadir of Abdullah's position in Kashmir.

When he felt the ground slipping from under his feet, Abdullah sought the counsel of a group of very able communists from Lahore. They drafted the manifesto called 'New Kashmir' for him in 1944 and then produced a most impressive declaration about the sale deed miscalled the Treaty of Amritsar to which the Maharaja owed his title to Kashmir. Armed with this and a stirring slogan, Abdullah launched his 'Quit Kashmir' campaign against the Maharaja in May 1946. He was jailed on a charge of sedition and Jawaharlal Nehru felt impelled to enter the fray. Considerable publicity was generated as a result, but apart from small groups (mostly the cadres of the National Conference, better-trained than those of the Muslim Conference) the masses, both Muslim and Hindu, stood aloof. The Maharaja demonstrated his triumph by arranging to be driven in a spectacular motorcade through the main street of Srinagar on his birthday in September. It was not the respect and sympathy for the Maharaja on the part of the great Muslim majority but the distrust of Sheikh Abdullah that made this possible. The wrong medium had eclipsed the right message.

After the partition of British India in August 1947, Abdullah wrote letters to his friends from jail recommending Kashmir's accession to India, making sure that the letters would be seen by the Maharaja's officials. This reinforced the assurances that the Maharaja had received from the leaders of the Indian Congress, including Mohandas Gandhi, that Abdullah would help him to join India. Abdullah was granted "royal clemency" and released from jail in return for colluding with the Maharaja in maneuvering accession to India. He flew immediately to Delhi to confer with the Indian leaders, as did the Maharaja's courtiers. Abbas, the leader of the Muslim Conference, languished in jail.

At the time, Abdullah's constituency in Kashmir, in the estimate of impartial observers, had shrunk to a few districts of Srinagar. That, in essence, was the reality of the popular backing for India establishing sovereignty over Kashmir. The estimate, of course, was not shared by Jawaharlal Nehru, nor perhaps by Gandhi, but when doubts began to grow in Delhi whether Abdullah's presumed popularity would swing the vote in India's favour, did India begin to wriggle out of its pledge to a plebiscite. The doubts about success turned to certainty of defeat when Abdullah, had to be ousted as Prime Minister and jailed in 1953. From that time, Indian policy was set dead against any ascertainment of the wishes of the people of Kashmir on the accession issue. Nehru did make a promise to the Prime Minister of Pakistan to cooperate in the holding of a plebiscite by April 1954 but, as the ensuing correspondence between the two showed, it was done only to palliate an aroused public opinion in both Kashmir and Pakistan.

No invasion of one country by another encounters an immediate insurrection. There were no popular uprisings in the capitals of Western Europe when they witnessed the victorious march of the Nazi troops. Nor did the Soviet forces when they were triumphant, face mass upheavals and defiance in Eastern Europe. There was no immediate revolt in Kabul against the Soviet invasion of Afghanistan. Resistance against foreign occupation requires organization and takes time to develop.

If in Kashmir, India did succeed in dampening the sentiment of revolt for a number of years by co-opting the section of the people represented by the National Conference which was joined by a whole lot to careerists, it nor more belies the claim of popular loathing of Indian occupation than the existence of the Vichy regime belied French resistance to Nazi occupation. If Sheikh Abdullah who in 1947 supported India taking over Kashmir by force had been at one time the most popular leader in Kashmir, Marshall Petain, who capitulated before Hitler and cooperated with him, had been the most respected war hero of France. All occupation regimes find collaborationists in the occupied countries; there are Quislings and Lavals and Najibs in every society. Kashmir could not be in exception. There were some added circumstances in Kashmir.

First, simultaneously with sending its troops into Kashmir, India made a solemn declaration that the accession of Kashmir was provisional and subject to the people's verdict. She gave this solemn assurance to the people of Kashmir, to Pakistan, to Britain and to "the whole world", in Jawaharlal Nehru's words. This created the reasonable expectation in the mass mind that India's annexation of Kashmir was a temporary affair and would be reversed by a peaceful process. Arzi Ilhaq (temporary accession) became a common expression. A mass uprising seemed unnecessary.

Second, at the time of the entry of Indian troops, the leaders of the Muslim Conference were in jail or in exile from the Vale. The organizing force of resistance was dispersed.

Third, fighting ensued between the Indian army and the Azad Kashmir forces in extensive parts of the State. Though vastly outnumbered, ill equipped and poorly organized, and hence unable to reach Srinagar and Jammu, the two capitals, the Azad forces did hold some ground and, even before Pakistan provided them regular military support, they had prevented India from overrunning the whole State. Newspapers in India itself at the time reported a number of incidents of a few guerrillas holding at bay large companies of Indian troops with all their armour and air support. This along with the proceedings of the Security Council and the dispatch of a United Nations Commission in 1948, created the kind of expectancy that inhibits a people's revolt.

First, it is open to question who in Pakistan count on an insurgency in the Vale of Kashmir at the time. There are different versions, none wholly plausible. However, if anyone in authority did, his thinking must have been at the adolescent level. He must have thought that insurgencies are made like instant coffee; he must have lacked education in rebellions. Uprisings, as distinguished from acts of sabotage, rarely go with inter-state wars; when they do, they end in disaster. Of the first of these two lessons, the Vietnam War provides a good illustration: throughout that war, no uprising took place in Saigon. Of the second, the genuine Shiite uprising in Iraq at the time of the Persian Gulf War in 1991 has been another graphic example. Even when Saddam Hussein's retreating troops, waving white flags, were being bulldozed with the earth, he still had the means to reduce the rebellion to cinders.

If a state at war defeated but not yet admitting defeat, does not make a suitable target for rebellion, far less does an undefeated state. Indian troops would have to be forced by Pakistan's military offensive to begin a retreat from Karachi before a civilian uprising against the remnants of Indian authority and welcoming the entry of Pakistani forces could take place. This had nothing to do with passivity or docility in the Kashmiri character - that myth has been shattered now. It has everything to do with the dynamism of popular uprisings. They need their own impulse and are sustained by their own strategy; they abort if they lack native political guidance. To ignore this principle is to plan for failure.

Second, the situation in Kashmir in 1964-65 has been misrepresented in both Pakistan and India for opposite psychological reasons. India feels the compulsion to prove Kashmiri acquiescence in Indian occupation, Pakistan to account for the miscarriage of its plans. Neither acknowledges the fact that Kashmiris did rise on their own against Indian rule in 1964. When Jawaharlal Nehru sent a senior intelligence official who was his confidant to Srinagar to make a report on the situation, the man returned and candidly said to him, "Prime Minister, from what I have seen, Kashmir is not a part of India." Even Lal Bahadur Shastri, who had not yet become

Prime Minister, remarked significantly after his visit to Kashmir that the situation would have to be resolved ultimately in accordance with the people's wishes. The agitation was intelligently directed by the indigenous Committee of Action set up in Srinagar. There is evidence that Nehru had accepted the need "radical rethinking" about India's policy with regard to both Kashmir and Pakistan. Nehru's death at that delicate point, Sheikh Abdullah's trip abroad during which he met some world leaders, including Zhou En-Lai, his consequent re-imprisonment, Shastri's political inferiority when stepping into Nehru's shoes, the frequent military probing and exchanges across the Ceasefire Line, the worsening of Indian forces by Pakistani troops in the Rann of Kutch (distant from Kashmir), the crescendo of belligerency on both sides, and finally the entry of commandos from Azad Kashmir and Pakistan uncoordinated with a native plan for a guerrilla campaign - all tangled the plot and arrested its denouement.

Nevertheless, besides rendering help to commandos wherever physically possible in August 1965, Kashmiris hardly showed themselves as resigned to Indian occupation since the world media had their attention riveted on the fighting between India and Pakistan, non-military happenings in the Vale of Kashmir itself went rather unnoticed. Still, a number of major western newspapers, including the New York Times carried stories about what was called "the children's revolt": young boys and girls showing defiance of Indian authority. It was then that the slogan (unacceptably abusive but betraying the people's exasperation) "Indian dogs, go home" gained currency in Srinagar and was blazoned by the letters I.D.G.O. painted on walls and pavements. There was not - there could not be, as we have seen - an organized revolt. Nor was there the quiescence that Indians like to believe and Pakistanis prefer to complain about.

It is no more unrealistic that it was to expect Algeria to cease to be a department of France, Namibia to be detached from South Africa or Estonia or Lithuania to become independent of the Soviet Union. France had ruled Algeria, South Africa had held Namibia and the Soviet Union had annexed Estonia and Lithuania for longer periods than the Indian Union has occupied Kashmir. What belongs to a State and cannot be pried loose from it is what feels itself to be part of that State, some discontent notwithstanding. Kashmir never felt itself to be part of India before 1947 and feels even less so after its forcible seizure by the Indian troops. The de-annexation process is inevitable in the post-colonial age. The only question is whether it is accomplished by armed struggle, resulting in a spiral of violence and counter-violence or through negotiation and/or other means of peaceful settlement. The choice always lies with the occupying power. Until now, India has pre-empted negotiation by its adamant assertion that the status of Kashmir is not negotiable.

Is this adamancy an insuperable obstacle, considering that it is backed by the military power of the Indian Union, one of the most formidable in the world? The question invites reflection. Even as recently as the mid-1980s, the idea of the liberation of Estonia and Lithuania was regarded as a pipe dream. So was the institution of majority rule in South Africa. The military and technological arsenal at the disposal of the Soviet Union was mightier than what the Indian Union possesses. The same could be said of the apartheid regime proportionately in the context of the South African subcontinent. Yet military power did not bring political strength to the Soviet Union nor immunize South African because the rest of the world did not bend its knee to it. It is the deference down by the West to India's military power that reinforces India's obduracy. It also weakens the liberal section of Indian opinion that would prefer a sensible and human policy with respect to Kashmir. Unwittingly, the West contributes to the depletion of the already small but the most promising resource in India's political society, the resource of self-criticism, and to the encouragement of that sanctimoniousness which the more thoughtful Indians regard as a bane of their country's attitudes in international affairs.

We have spoken of countries that were liberated from the Soviet Union. Since their release was followed immediately by the collapse of the Soviet Union itself, the suggestion might seem to lurk that Kashmir's freedom is envisaged in the prospective context of the disintegration of the Indian Union. Quite the contrary. It has been brought out elsewhere in these pages that the liberation of Kashmir would strengthen the cohesion and solidity of the Indian Union. It would cure India of what was called "a frontier sore" by Lord Ismay who advised Lord Mountbatten, one of the men chiefly responsible for the invasion of Kashmir by India.

The impression is not groundless but, on a more serious examination, it turns out to be superficial. For some years now, Pakistan's leaders have not displayed qualities or care and sensitivity in certain statements they have made on Kashmir. A couple of these statements, blithely citing the Indian Independence Act passed by the British Parliament in 1947, directly contradict the position clarified by the Founder of Pakistan himself who, besides being the redoubtable constitutionalist that he was, had vetted the Act before it was adopted (the Indian Congress leaders had done the same). In his characteristically straightforward manner, he published his view that the British government or Parliament had "no power or sanction" to restrict the freedom of the Princely States to remain independent, if they so desired. It must be noted, in passing, that he spoke of 'States' not of 'Princes'. The viability of independence, of course, was a separate issue; it could not be judged by legal criteria and it could not be regarded as the same in all cases.

But occasional crude utterances by Pakistan's present-day spokesmen do not affect the validity of Pakistan's traditional position in the Kashmir dispute. The dispute is on the agenda of the world organization as the India-Pakistan question. Pakistan cannot in fairness be expected to relinquish its position as a party to the dispute and assume instead the lesser role of a supporter of Kashmir in the India-Kashmir conflict. The military occupation of Kashmir by India violates not only Kashmir's self-determination but of Pakistan's as well. For Pakistan came into being as the successor state of the British Indian empire comprising Muslim-majority areas as India did comprising Hindu-majority areas. This happened on the basis of a tripartite agreement arrived at by Britain, the Indian

Congress and the Muslim League. It followed from the agreement that, unless the State of Jammu and Kashmir chose to remain independent, its Muslim-majority area would be incorporated in Pakistan exactly as the Muslim-majority area of the province of Punjab was. In fairness and in accordance with the principle of the settlement to which both the Indian Union and Pakistan owe their independence, there were only two options for Muslim-majority Kashmir: either to remain independent or to join Pakistan.

The pre-emption of both these options by India's military action had made Pakistan as much the wronged, aggrieved party as Kashmir itself. In Pakistan's eyes, Kashmir is not just another country whose self-determination is to be promoted in the way Pakistan championed the cause of the freedom of Morocco or Tunisia (in the early 1950s), for example, or of other peoples under colonial rule. Kashmir is potentially a part of Pakistan and its society is intertwined with Pakistan's. If matters had been allowed to take a straight course in 1947, Kashmir would have been one of the provinces of Pakistan (the sentiment for Kashmir's independence at that time was very weak). This is not Pakistan's self-view. Not to speak of all impartial observers, even Lord Mountbatten, who played a crucial role in engineering India's annexation of Kashmir, has conceded that but for a certain "basic mistake" by Pakistan, "Kashmir might well have eventually acceded to Pakistan, either with or without a plebiscite or might conceivably have been peacefully partitioned between India an Pakistan". The "basic mistake" he mentions is questionable but even if it were admitted, neither Pakistan nor Kashmir would merit permanent punishment for it in the form of a an unnatural disposition of the State. Mountbatten's statement recognizes Kashmir's place in Pakistan.

Seen in this light, Pakistan's position would be changed radically were it to come forward as a proponent of independence for Kashmir. It would imply that Pakistan is gratuitously demoting its locus standi and renouncing a claim, which has been made stronger by Pakistan's unquestioned willingness to submit it to the verdict of the people of Kashmir impartially ascertained. Pakistan is acting within its rights and conforming to its obligation in disallowing that kind of a stance for itself.

However, there is a marked difference between not becoming a proponent of Kashmir's independence and becoming an opponent of it. The former is consistent with Pakistan's involvement and interest in the dispute; the latter is entailed by India's standpoint. One would expect persons charged with responsibility for handling delicate issues of law or diplomacy to perceive the difference.

Let us thrash out the question a little. India is asserting a primordial or proprietary right with respect to Kashmir; its rejection of the proposition of independence for Kashmir follows as logically as does its irate reaction to the proposal of a referendum or plebiscite to determine a solution. Pakistan, in contrast, is asserting a claim to Kashmir which, though in justice immeasurably superior to India's, Pakistan is not holding to be self-validated; Pakistan is demanding that both claims - its own and India's - be referred to the democratic decision of the people of Kashmir. The demand was originally accepted by India and the common ground of both parties was the basis of the plan of settlement laid down in the resolutions of the United Nations. This aspect of the issue has been fully brought out in the voluminous debates at the United Nations. What still needs to be made clear is that neither Pakistan's demand nor its original acceptance by India nor its endorsement by the United Nations encompasses the whole area of the right involved. For overriding the contesting claims of India and Pakistan and the putative right of one or the other is the right of the people of Kashmir to decide the issue according to their own will. That the two claims of India and Pakistan be submitted to the people of Kashmir makes them subjects of legitimate consideration but it does not exclude the exercise of a different option by the people of Kashmir. The exclusion is inherent in India's position, not in Pakistan's. Enlightened opinion in Pakistan fully appreciates the point and is far ahead of the country's official spokesmen.

The statement that "Kashmir has been historically a part of India" is true precisely in the same sense as the statement, for example, that Belgium or Norway has been historically a part of Europe. All through the ages, the word "India" has been like Europe, the name of a region, a subcontinent, not of a state. It has been a geographical, not a political, term. The great empires of the past - the Maurya (3rd century BC), the Mughal (16th to 18th century) - which more or less unified the subcontinent did not have uniform boundaries; the included variously what today are the states of Afghanistan, Pakistan, India, Nepal, Bangladesh and Myanmar, as well as Kashmir. Even under the British, "India" was not a compact political entity: there was what was called "British India" and "Indian or Princely India".

In the sense currently employed, India is as much a new state as Pakistan; both were established in August 1947; both came into existence on the basis of the agreed two-fold principle that (a) Hindu-majority areas in British India would constitute India and Muslim-majority areas form Pakistan and (b) the territories not directly administered by British (i.e. Princely India) would be incorporated in one of the other (i.e. India or Pakistan) according to geographical contiguity and the composition of the population or they could remain independent, if their people so wished.

Kashmir was the largest of the territories not directly ruled by the British. It is a Muslim-majority area, contiguous to Pakistan, sharing the largest part of its border with Pakistan. Its territorial highways led into Pakistan or Central Asia; its rivers flow into Pakistan; its commerce was conducted through what is now Pakistan; from 14th century onwards, it drew its cultural stimulus exactly from the same sources as Pakistan. Politically, it has maintained an independent, sovereign existence through the preponderant part of its history.

From whatever standpoint one looks at it - geographical, historical, cultural or economic - Kashmir's inclusion in India is as irrational as it has been shown to be contrary to its popular will. The mere circumstance that the state, which has its capital in Delhi, appropriated the name of a region to itself

- a gigantic advertising gimmick - does not provide it with an historical claim or entitlement to Kashmir. Incidentally, India's native name inscribed in its constitution is Bharat but it fights shy of using that expression; indeed, it has uses a word which does not exist in any of its dozen main languages. It is the only country in the world which has borrowed its own name from others. As historically "India" meant the land of the Indus, it is Pakistan that has a title to the description, not the state that has arrogated it.

All movements of resistance against foreign occupation which embrace a whole society draw in all its elements - the extremists, religious or secular, at one end and the criminal-minded, at the other, with sincere freedom fighters in the middle, constituting the bulk. The resistance in France against Nazi occupation had the active participation of communists; could it on that account be regarded as a communist movement? No insurgency - particularly against a regime, which has become incapable of civilized administration - remains uncontaminated by extremism, crime of corruption: this had been historically true even in the most sophisticated societies. Such contamination, however, does not affect the purity of its object viz. liberation from an alien, brutal regime; restoration of human rights and assertion of the popular will. This holds in the case of Kashmir as it would in all similar cases.

Speaking of fundamentalism, there is a marked difference between Pakistan and India. The extremist religious forces in Pakistan have never been able to muster popular electoral support and they operate to the extent that they do and meet with resistance within Muslim society itself. In India, in contrast, the fundamentalist frenzy is directed against the Muslim population. The barbarities inflicted on the Muslims of Kashmir are to a great extent actuated by Hindu hatred against Muslims. Communal hatred and intolerance. No attempt is underway to establish a theocratic state in Kashmir. However, it is only natural that, under the unbearable stress of the kind faced by Kashmiris, people should try to draw spiritual strength and sustenance from the faith they follow. A powerful ingredient of the Kashmiri psyche in both normalcy and crisis is the consciousness of their Islamic affiliation. But the fact is writ large on Kashmir's history since the 14th century that this consciousness has harmonized with amity between Muslims and Hindus.

The mass exodus of Kashmiri Pandits from the Vale of Kashmir has been cited as a glaring example of the extremism of the Resistance movement. Any impartial investigation will show that the exodus was encouraged and facilitated by the Government of India, represented at the time in the person of the notorious Governor, Jagmohan, to clear the field for the actions that had been planned against the Kashmiri Muslims. The total breakdown of the administration in Kashmir was also an important contributing factor. When there is anarchy, people flee. In any uprising, those who collaborate with the oppressors become targets. However, more Kashmiri Muslims have been targeted than Pandits. It is not a question of religion: it is a question of what side you are on? The popular uprising or the imposed regime?

Moreover, if the international community continues to look the other way while Kashmir burns and a repulsive military machine massacres its people, then desperation will set in. In such an environment, fundamentalism becomes the face of frustration. Extreme repression, accompanied by little relief and meager sympathy from the supporters of human freedom, can so traumatize a people as to pervert their psychology and disfigure their movement.

India's uses the pejorative term "fundamentalist" in order to exploit the fear and prejudice associated with this phenomenon, real or perceived, and thus undermine support for the cause of Kashmir's freedom. India's use of the label "terrorist" is similarly motivated. The aim is to divert the sympathy and compassion that would be felt at the plight of the Kashmiri people to concerns felt in other contexts.

## KASHMIR CONFLICT : ISSUE AND FIGHT

The bitterness was palpable among the young fighters squatting on the floor of a dingy, cold room in their hideout outside Muzaffarabad. Some of them had just returned from a guerrilla operation on the other side of the Line of Control, dividing the disputed state. They looked frustrated and exhausted with their dishevelled beards and dirty clothes. Some of them were quiet while others talked about their future plans.

It was the most testing of times for the veterans of the 14-year-long guerrilla war after Musharraf had assured India that Pakistani territory would not be used for cross-border operations. Most of them were visibly frustrated and resigned to the fact that their jihad might well be coming to an end. 'We have no choice but to return to our homes,' said 30-year-old Mohammed Ashfaque, in a voice choked with emotion. A resident of Srinagar in Indian-controlled Kashmir, he had left his home and joined the guerrilla struggle some ten years ago after his brother was killed by Indian forces. However, others sounded more defiant and vowed not to lay down their weapons.

Meeting on the sidelines of the South Asian Regional summit in Islamabad, in January 2004, Musharraf and Indian Prime Minister Atal Bihari Vajpayee, had agreed to start a peace process to resolve all outstanding issues, including the Kashmir dispute, through bilateral negotiations. Musharraf was more categorical this time in his pledge to switch off the tap for Kashmiri militants. He had promised to curb the jihadists before, but in the past he had hedged his bets, ordering only a temporary halt, in the hope that India would reciprocate by sitting down for talks.

With India back to the negotiating table and after two assassination attempts on him involving jihadist groups, Musharraf had more reason than ever to crack down on his home-grown militants. He could not allow the militants to take over the country. His tone became increasingly conciliatory towards India and he hinted that he was willing to drop Pakistan's long-standing demand that a plebiscite be held in Kashmir under the 1948 UN resolution to determine its status as long as India was equally forthcoming.

Musharraf's peace overtures had angered the militants, who accused him of having conceded too much ground to India by reversing Pakistan's long-standing aggressive Kashmir policy. The jihadists saw the war in ideological and civilizational terms. Any concession to the 'enemy' was therefore a very serious matter. Many Islamist leaders described the peace process as the beginning of the end of the Kashmir jihad.

Islamabad's policy shift was also driven by external factors. Musharraf's change of tack had also placed him on the horns of a serious dilemma. Islamabad's new role as a key US ally in the war on terror was no longer compatible with Pakistan's use of those proxies, which underscored its Kashmir policy. Yet, while Musharraf was quick to abandon support for the Taliban, he was reluctant to break ties with the militants waging 'a holy war' in Kashmir.

In fact, Musharraf had sought to use his country's broad cooperation with the United States to gain some leeway for continuing Pakistan's proxy war in the disputed Himalayan state. He tried to draw a fine line between what he described as 'freedom fighters' and terrorists. But America was not interested in such distinctions.

For more than half a century, the Kashmir cause had been almost the raison d'e^tre for Pakistan's existence – not to mention for the role of the armed forces in the politics of the state. Musharraf's assumption of power had alarmed India at the time, as he was known for his aggressive stance on Kashmir. Once in power, however, Musharraf displayed the pragmatic tendencies which would later cause him to disappoint fighters like Mohammed Ashfaque so bitterly. The first sign of a thaw came in June 2001, when the two countries agreed to a ceasefire along the 1,000-kilometre Line of Control, dividing the Indian and Pakistani sides of the disputed territory. That helped to ease tensions and cleared the way for the first high level government contact between the two countries. In July 2001, the Indian Prime Minister, Atal Bihari Vajpayee, invited Musharraf for talks after dropping his precondition that Pakistan should first put an end to the infiltration of militants into Kashmir. That put the onus on Musharraf to come up with some offer to defuse tensions.

Musharraf was under tremendous strain when he proceeded to Delhi for talks with the Indian leader. Closely watched by both hardliners and peaceniks, often with contrary agendas, General Musharraf walked a political tightrope. He was under scrutiny, not only by the conservative, militant Islamic groups, but also by the hardline generals. The Jamaat-i-Islami and Islamic militant groups had warned him not to deviate from a single point of the Kashmir agenda. His own future was at stake, and dependent on the outcome of the most crucial diplomatic mission he had ever undertaken. His hardline generals were opposed to any concession on Kashmir. The officers, a number of whom had served in the ISI, argued that it was the 'success of jihad' that had forced India to come to the negotiating table. They wanted Musharraf to continue supporting the Islamic militants fighting the Indian forces.

Although he had appeared stronger with his ascension to the presidency, Musharraf continued to face growing domestic opposition to the perpetuation of military rule. The pressure on Musharraf not to let the talks fail was enormous, as Pakistani leaders had constantly been calling for a negotiated settlement of disputes with India. However, any room to manoeuvre was restricted by the long-standing, thorny Kashmir issue, which was the major cause for the festering conflict in the region.

While the summit was made possible largely because of strong international pressure, it had created its own dynamics. There were strong internal pressures forcing both countries to start a dialogue. For Musharraf, in order to prevent Pakistan from economic collapse, it was important to ease tension with India. A few weeks before his departure to India, in an interview on Pakistan state television, he had declared that Pakistan's economy was not compatible with its defence capability. A de-escalation was necessary, to win the support of the international community and to restart the flow of foreign aid.

On the very first evening of the summit, Musharraf gave a speech which seemed to push all the right buttons: 'The legacy of the past years was not a happy one ... blood has been spilt, precious lives have been lost.we must not allow the past to dictate the future,' he declared in his speech at the Indian President's dinner. Musharraf's call for peace changed the atmosphere and set a positive tone for the summit. The General seemed to have established a good rapport with the ageing Indian Prime Minister. Unlike any other summit, the Agra summit had no prior agreed-upon agenda and most of the meetings were one-on-one. Inevitably though, the summit ended in a stalemate on 16 July 2001, with the two leaders unable to agree on the wording of the declaration. The deadlock did not come as a surprise. The final breakdown came when India refused to accept the centrality of the Kashmir issue and insisted on including the question of 'cross-border terrorism' in the declaration. Pakistan also showed its reservations over the reference to the Agra process as a continuation of the Simla and Lahore declarations. Both sides blamed each other of intransigence, but the reality was that neither leader was prepared to resist pressure from their respective hardliners.

Musharraf's position certainly didn't leave much room for compromise in negotiations. Never before had a Pakistani leader brought Kashmir to the centre of the summit table as forcefully as he did. His blunt talk with the Indian media editors on 16 July, which was televised by several networks, was also used by the Indian hardliners to obstruct an accord. The mood on the Indian side turned visibly bitter when Musharraf declared there should not be any illusion that the main issue confronting the two countries was Kashmir. 'I will keep saying it whether anyone likes it or not,' he said.

All was not lost, however. Musharraf and Vajpayee bade each other goodbye with a promise to meet again and pick up the threads from there. Despite the acrimony and bitterness that marked its closure, the Agra summit had broken the ice and revived the process of dialogue which had frozen after the Kargil conflict in the summer of 1999. The Indian Prime Minister accepted Pakistan's invitation for a return visit to Islamabad. It was also agreed to hold summit meetings between the Indian and Pakistani leaders once a year, and biannual talks at the foreign ministerial level to discuss issues relating to peace, security, confidence-building measures, Kashmir, narcotics and terrorism.

Not surprisingly, the stalemate at Agra was hailed by extremists in both India and Pakistan, who hoped to thrive in an atmosphere of tension. Islamic militant groups like LeT intensified suicide attacks in Kashmir and vowed to extend attacks inside India. Musharraf had provoked the ire of Islamic fundamentalists when he warned them against religious terrorism and militancy and tried to restrict the activities of militant groups, many of whom were fighting in Kashmir. Even more disturbing was the resumption of the exchange of artillery fire along the Line of Control, breaking the eight-month-old ceasefire. With the intensification of guerrilla attacks, India stepped up efforts to get Pakistan branded as a terrorist state. But this attempt to isolate Pakistan received a setback, as Musharraf's decision to support the US-led war in Afghanistan, improved Islamabad's international standing.

The 11 September terrorist attacks and their aftermath had changed the entire regional security scenario and triggered a rapid downslide in India-Pakistan relations. Worried with Pakistan's role as a key US strategic ally, India lost no time in urging Washington not to forget its sufferings from 'Pakistani-backed cross-border terrorism'. New Delhi tried to use the 'war on terror' to its advantage. It portrayed the Kashmir problem purely as a matter of combating terrorism and made the case that it also had the right to pursue militants from Pakistani-controlled Kashmir, exactly as the USA hunted down al-Qaeda and the Taliban in Afghanistan.

The tension mounted further in October 2001, following the LeT suicide attack by militants on the Kashmir assembly building in Srinagar which claimed 36 lives. The incident occurred as US forces were in the last stages of preparation to launch an attack on Afghanistan. Indian leaders and military commanders warned of 'hot pursuit', sending troops into Pakistani-controlled Azad Kashmir to destroy militant camps there. Musharraf denounced the attack as an act of terrorism, but that failed to pacify India. Both countries traded accusations, backed by an 'ominous troop build-up' along the border. The situation raised serious concerns in Washington. Fearing that a fire could break out at any time in the base camp of its anti-terror campaign, the USA rushed its Secretary of State, Colin Powell, to India and Pakistan. The Bush administration, which had initially chosen to distance itself from the Kashmir conflict, showed greater enthusiasm to defuse tensions. Powell succeeded in persuading India and Pakistan to exercise restraint, but it was only a matter of time before the situation flared up again. A terrorist attack on the Indian Parliament on 13 December renewed the threat of war.

India quickly blamed two Pakistani-based Islamic militant groups, JeM and LeT, for the attack. This audacious raid on the symbol of Indian power brought the two newly nuclear-powered nations once again to the brink of war. India retaliated by severing diplomatic relations and cut rail and air communications and put Pakistan on notice to rein in the militant groups or face the consequences of war. The gravity of the terrorist attack and the post-9/11 global security environment provided India the excuse to consider military action, to stop what it described, as cross-border terrorism. Meanwhile, India demanded that Pakistan hand over 20 'most wanted terrorists', including Masood Azhar, Ahmed Omar Saeed Sheikh and five other men involved in the December 1999 hijacking of an Indian Airlines plane. The new Bush doctrine of pre-emptive strikes against the source of terrorism and the changes in the international rules of engagement afforded India the chance to engage Pakistan in brinkmanship.

In the third week of December, India launched 'Operation Parakaram' (Valour), which constituted the heaviest Indian troop mobilization since the 1971 war. It was a deliberate move by New Delhi, amidst the war on terror, to threaten Pakistan with military strikes if Islamabad did not stop sponsoring cross-border terrorism. There was every indication that India would not shy away from going to war. With Pakistan's counter-mobilization, nearly one million troops sat eyeball to eyeball across the India-Pakistan border. Both countries moved ballistic missiles and troops close to their shared border. There was a considerable risk of nuclear escalation.

The threat of war, coupled with US pressure, forced Pakistan to take action against the Islamic militant groups. On 12 January 2002, Musharraf banned LeT and JeM, which were blamed by India for the 13 December attack. He promised not to let Pakistani territory be used for cross-border terrorism. Some two thousand activists of banned extremist groups were detained in a nationwide crackdown. Musharraf, however, made it very clear that the measures against the Islamic extremist groups did not change his position on Kashmir. 'Kashmir runs in our blood. No Pakistani can afford to severe links with Kashmir. We will continue to give all diplomatic, political and moral support to the Kashmiris,' he declared.

India reacted positively to Musharraf's 12 January speech and subsequent moves to curb the militants. Nevertheless, it kept its military on high alert and in forward positions. The Indian leaders wanted to see whether Musharraf's pledge was translated into practice. They refused to resume negotiations and normalize relations with Pakistan until all their conditions were met, including their extradition demands. Musharraf's 12 January speech drew domestic as well international, support. But the measures taken by his government were insufficient against the activities of the jihadist groups. The ban was not applied to Pakistani-controlled Kashmir, or the semi-autonomous tribal areas bordering Afghanistan, which enabled militant organizations to shift their infrastructure and cadres to these regions. Hundreds of Islamic militants, returning from Afghanistan after the collapse of the Taliban regime in December 2001, had moved to the Pakistani part of Kashmir and were ready to join the armed struggle on the other side of the border. Most of these militants belonged to the three outlawed Islamic groups.

It became apparent that, while promising to curb Islamic extremism and sectarianism, Musharraf was still not willing to completely de- link Islamabad's connection with the Kashmiri militants. Meanwhile, India's refusal to pull back troops from advance positions and resume negotiations with Pakistan also tied his hands. Cross-border infiltration of militants into Indian-controlled Kashmir slowed down, but never completely stopped. Most of the militants detained following the 12 January declaration, were released. On 20 March 2002, the CIA chief, George Tenet, told the United States Senate Armed Services Committee that the chances of war in the region were the highest since 1971. In the midst of the military stand-off with India, Musharraf decided to hold a referendum to extend his term in the office of President. In his address to the nation in March 2001, Musharraf declared his intent to enter politics and stay at the helm, a far cry from the 'reluctant coup- maker' of October 1999.

With a feeling of de´ja' vu in the air, Musharraf announced that he was seeking public approval for an extension of his tenure in office, for an additional five years beyond the three-yearperiod stipulated by the Supreme Court. The General also announced plans to introduce a new political formula, which he claimed was in conformity with the country's requirement for progress and stability. He declared that the military would continue to play a dominant role in the new political system, which was to emerge after the parliamentary elections scheduled for October 2002. Predictably, Musharraf received more than 90 per cent of the votes in a highly rigged referendum held in April 2002. The dubious polls not only dented Musharraf's credibility, but also sharpened the political polarization as the country braced for a possible war.

A series of suicide attacks by militants on a bus and in the residential quarters of an Indian army camp in Kaluchak in Kashmir on 14 May 2002 killed 35 people, mainly women and children, and brought the region closer to the nuclear precipice. Free of Islamabad's control, the militants had tried to push the two countries towards a military conflict. India quickly moved its forces to forward positions on war alert. It also expelled Pakistan's ambassador, closing the last line of direct communication with Islamabad. With missiles and heavy weapons in place, an Indian attack appeared imminent between

29 and 31 May. Nuclear signalling from both sides reminded the world of the gravity of the situation. Some Pakistani leaders openly warned of using nuclear weapons to counter India's overwhelming conventional military superiority. In the third week of May, Pakistan tested a series of nuclear-capable ballistic missiles and stepped up its nuclear weapons programme.

As the world faced perhaps its tensest nuclear stand-off since the Cuban missile crisis in 1962, the USA and Britain launched frantic diplomatic efforts to defuse the situation. President Bush and Colin Powell called the Indian and Pakistani leaders several times, urging them to pull back. On 28 May, the British Foreign Secretary, Jack Straw, visited Islamabad and asked Musharraf to take tougher measures to counter cross-border terrorism. He reminded Pakistan that as a UN member it had the responsibility to bear down 'effectively and consistently on all forms of terrorism, including cross-border terrorism'. In Delhi the next day, Straw called on the Indian leaders to exercise restraint. He also told them that Musharraf had promised to close down 'terrorist camps' operating in Pakistani-administered Kashmir and curb infiltration into India. Serious strains had emerged in relations between Washington and Islamabad after reports that the ISI was still linked with the militant groups. On 31 May, Colin Powell publicly accused Pakistan of continuing infiltration across the Line of Control, despite Musharraf's assurance that it would be halted. The following day, Musharraf told the BBC that he had issued instructions to end the crossing and stop all militant activities. But the statement did not satisfy the Bush administration which had demanded that Pakistan shut down cross- border infiltration permanently. 'When and if, it does stop, it must also stop permanently,' Colin Powell retorted. International patience was clearly running out with Musharraf's game of deception.

Musharraf was firmly wedged between a rock and a hard place. He sincerely wanted to prevent a war, but at the same time did not want to be seen as the leader who gave up his country's 'sacred' cause: Kashmir. He badly needed a face-saving device if he was to take further steps backward to meet the expectations of the international community. Musharraf tried desperately to maintain his balancing act. His 'blow hot, blow cold' posture accurately reflected the difficulties he faced at home, where he was, once again, taking a controversial position on a sensitive issue.

On 1 June, the USA, Britain, France, Canada, Japan, Australia and some other countries, issued travel advisories asking their citizens to leave India immediately and warning others against travelling to the country. Pakistan was already on the 'travel advisory' list after 9/11. The warning led to the exodus of thousands of businessmen, visitors, tourists and diplomatic personnel from India. This threatened the closure of foreign and multinational companies and caused much annoyance in Delhi, which perceived the advisory as an attempt to pressure it against launching an attack on Pakistan.

Once again, intensive US intervention was the key to walking both sides back from the brink. On 6 June, the US Deputy Secretary of State, Richard Armitage, arrived in Islamabad to build on Straw's visit and hammer out a deal between India and Pakistan. A former wrestler and a veteran diplomat, Armitage was known for his blunt talking. He had met Musharraf several times in the past and appeared to have developed a good rapport with the Pakistani military leader. Armitage had one critical objective when he arrived for talks at the sprawling presidential secretariat at the Margala foothills on the afternoon of 6 June: to extract an assurance from Musharraf that would satisfy India and remove the threat of a potential nuclear war.

Musharraf had previously pledged to stop the infiltration of Islamic militants into Kashmir, but Armitage wanted him to go one step further. The talks between the two men had stretched to two hours, when Armitage put the critical question: 'What can I tell the Indians?' he asked. He wanted to know whether Musharraf would agree to a 'permanent end' to the cross-border terrorist activity long accepted by Pakistan. 'Yes,' Musharraf replied. An elated Armitage flew to Delhi the next morning to brief the Indian leaders on his talks with Musharraf.

Musharraf's agreement to the word 'permanent', backed by US assurances to India that he would keep his word, immediately led to the easing of tension. It was a hugely significant foreign policy victory for India, which, for more than a decade, had sought an end to the cross-border terrorist attacks. Indeed, Musharraf had no other option, as his refusal to concede would have had disastrous consequences. 'If Pakistan had not agreed to end infiltration, and America had not conveyed that guarantee to India, then war could not have been averted,' Vajpayee told an Indian newspaper a week later.

The Musharraf-Armitage agreement was a turning point in Pakistan's long-standing policy of using militancy as an instrument for its proxy war in Kashmir and paved the way for a new relationship between two nations long divided by a bloody, tense history. In return for his concession, Musharraf received private assurances from US officials that they would stay involved. On 5 June, President Bush had called Musharraf and gave his firm commitment that his administration would remain engaged to resolve the Kashmir conflict. Musharraf told Armitage that he expected an early and substantial response from the Indian side to make his action sustainable.

Within days of Armitage's departure, a thaw was evident. India responded to Musharraf's steps to curb cross-border terrorism by moving its naval fleet back to its base and allowed commercial overflights. It also announced the revival of diplomatic relations with Pakistan. That effectively ended the longest military stand-off between the two countries. Pakistan's military and the ISI had always kept a fairly tight control on their militant clients and the restrictions resulted in an immediate drop in the infiltration of militants into Kashmir. But it never completely stopped. Some militant groups were not prepared to toe the new Pakistani line and continued to send their men into Kashmir. Pakistani officials argued that it was impossible to completely seal the LoC. For Musharraf, the major challenge was how to rein in the powerful militant groups. Predictably, his decision to stop cross-border infiltration, evoked angry reactions from the militant groups who, for more than a decade, had fought Pakistan's proxy war. The atmosphere in the room was grim. A sense of unease gripped the two dozen guerrilla commanders, who had come to meet with a senior ISI officer at an army base in Muzaffarabad in the last week of May. The capital of Pakistani-controlled Azad Kashmir had long been the headquarters of more than a dozen Kashmiri militant groups. Some two hundred kilometres from Islamabad, the city was at an equal distance from Srinagar, the capital of Indian-administered Kashmir. 'We don't have a choice given the tremendous pressure on Pakistan,'

Major-General-Khalid Mahmood told them. 'So, you have to stop all cross-border operations.' Several of the guerrilla commanders leapt to their feet, shouting that Pakistan should not surrender to Indian and American pressure. 'After ditching the Taliban, Musharraf has now betrayed the Kashmiri cause,' said a senior commander belonging to HuM, one of the largest Islamic militant groups involved in the separatist war in Kashmir. 'How can we accept this?' The commanders were bitter and vengeful, and left the meeting declining the officer's invitation to join him for lunch.

This outburst of anger towards Musharraf and his policies appeared logical. Thousands of militants had perished fighting Pakistan's war in Kashmir. Islamic militant leaders, who had depended for over a decade on the active support of Pakistan's army for their cross- border guerrilla actions, viewed Islamabad's move as a betrayal of the Kashmiri freedom struggle. 'We have lost so many friends, brothers and relatives in the Kashmir struggle. What was that for?' asked Amiruddin, a veteran Kashmiri guerrilla fighter. He reflected the sentiments of thousands of jihadist cadres trained and armed by the Pakistani military establishment. 'We are not going to sit quietly.'

The orders came as hundreds of fresh guerrillas were waiting at their base camps in Azad Kashmir to cross the border. It was generally at that time of the year that infiltration took place. 'The volunteers are becoming increasingly upset over the delay. They have not been informed about Pakistan's ban,' said the commander. He complained that the communication link between the guerrilla fighters inside Indian Kashmir and their base on the Pakistani side had been cut off and that training centres inside Azad Kashmir had been closed down. 'Many of our colleagues are stuck across the border without reinforcements and supplies,' he said.

Pakistan's decision to withdraw support had caused a setback to the militancy, but did not bring it to an end. The militant infrastructure remained intact and outlawed groups continued working, either under new banners, or merged into others. Hundreds of Pakistani fighters who were inside Kashmir at that point had continued their jihad, ignoring Pakistan's policy shift. Most militant leaders hoped that the restrictions were temporary and still had faith in the army. 'The army will always be our ally,' a senior militant commander told me. Facing down the jihadists was not going to be an easy task for Musharraf. Since an indigenous insurrection against Indian domination broke out in Kashmir in 1989, some 10,000 fighters had crossed the border to help their Kashmiri brethren.

They were not prepared to give up the cause on Islamabad's orders. As an inevitable consequence of Pakistan's policy of using jihad as an instrument of covert war, some elements within the intelligence agencies had been radicalized by the Islamists. The handlers had become coloured by the ideology of the militants. They were unhappy with Musharraf's decision to support America's war on Afghanistan's Islamic regime, which they had helped install. But even deeper was the resentment on the reversal in Kashmir. There was a strong anti-American feeling in the military ranks. Many officers believed that western countries, particularly the USA, had not come to Pakistan's support when it faced the threat of war from its nuclear rival.

Once again Musharraf was walking a tightrope. His position had become even more tenuous after he ordered his troops to stop the infiltration. He had come to the conclusion that there was now a conflict of interest between the militants and the military. But it was not clear whether other army officers agreed with him. There was a strong feeling in the army that

India was trying to humiliate them by dictating terms for peace.

Some hardline retired generals, who had been responsible for organizing the Kashmiri 'jihad', warned Musharraf that there was a limit to how far the army would go along with a policy of using force against those who were seen as fighting for Pakistan's interest in Kashmir. Lt.-General Hamid Gul, a former ISI chief and a fiercely anti-American former commander, accused Musharraf of 'going too far in appeasing the west' and taking a 'step back' on the Kashmir issue. 'By calling those attacking the Indian forces, terrorists, General Musharraf is only echoing the Indian position,' he declared. Despite military de-escalation, there was a wide gap between what the Indian leaders demanded and what Musharraf could deliver. India's mistrust of the Pakistani military leadership had thwarted all moves by the international community to bring the two sides to the negotiating table. It was only after the relatively peaceful polls for the Kashmir state assembly in October 2002, that Delhi and Islamabad opened secret back-channel diplomacy. Beginning in April 2003, Vajpayee's Principal Secretary, Brajesh Mishra, and Musharraf's top aide, Tariq Aziz, held several meetings in London, Dubai and Bangkok exploring avenues to begin a peace process.

A seasoned bureaucrat, Tariq Aziz was a college-mate of Musharraf's and had worked as his principal secretary after the military takeover. A former income tax officer, he was more into political wheeling and dealing and had no experience of diplomacy. However, being Musharraf's closest aide, he was considered the best man for this secret and extremely delicate job. Even the foreign ministry was kept out of the loop. Facilitated by the USA, this was the first senior official contact between the two countries for nearly two years.

Tariq Aziz was later appointed secretary of the National Security Council. In April 2003, the Indian Prime Minister extended a 'hand of friendship' to Pakistan during a public address in Srinagar. Pakistan's Prime Minister, Zafarullah Khan Jamali, responded by speaking to Vajpayee and invited him to visit Islamabad. In yet another highly symbolic gesture, India announced the resumption of bus links with Pakistan. The twice-weekly coach service between Delhi and Lahore had been abruptly suspended 18 months earlier, after Islamic militants had attacked the Indian Parliament in Delhi. The bus service, which started in February 1999, had significant symbolic value. Vajpayee had travelled to Lahore by the inaugural coach for his historic meeting with Pakistan's then Prime Minister, Nawaz Sharif. Given their deep-rooted mistrust of each other, the process remained a slow diplomatic dance, with the two governments circling one another warily, each making tentative offers. The efforts at that stage were largely aimed at de-escalation and the restoration of the situation that existed prior to the military stand-off, rather than any great leap forward.

Pakistan moved very cautiously, given its traditional suspicion of its much bigger, and militarily powerful, neighbour. It was reluctant to open its airspace to Indian planes and remove all trade barriers. Pakistan feared that lifting the overflight ban could provide India with an opportunity to establish close trade links with, and consolidate its influence in, Afghanistan. There were strong apprehensions in Islamabad that the emerging process could prove to be another false start if India raised the size of the table, rather than picking up the thread from previous talks.

Kashmir remained the thorniest issue as the two countries moved towards a rapprochement. The events of May and June a year before had indicated how quickly the situation could escalate into a fully fledged conflagration, with both countries appearing all too willing to engage in nuclear sabre-rattling. There was no sign of flexibility yet on the Kashmir issue on either side. While India was eager to demonstrate that the Kashmir violence was totally Pakistani sponsored, Pakistan appeared equally adamant to keep up the pressure on Delhi.

Although Musharraf had agreed to clamp down on militant groups, the situation on the ground did not change much. Pakistan's promise of a complete halt to support for the Islamic militants did not seem credible at that stage. Pakistani military officials contend that a total turnaround in Pakistan's policy could not be possible without some reciprocity from India, for example, reduction of troops and an end to human rights violations in the state. 'We will lose all leverage if we just pull out our support to the Kashmiris without any show of flexibility by India,' said a senior Pakistani official. 'In the absence of any light at the end of the Kashmiri tunnel, it would be hard for the government to sell any proposal for peace with India to its own people.' It was quite apparent that the military-backed administration was not ready to put the Kashmir issue on the backburner.

The military officers, who stood by Musharraf when he moved away from Pakistan's long-standing policy of supporting the conservative Taliban regime in Afghanistan and joined the US-led coalition against terrorism, were not likely to maintain their loyalty towards him if he had decided to make a radical shift on the Kashmir issue.

With India agreeing to resume peace talks, Pakistan faced increasing pressure to come down hard on Islamic guerrilla groups and destroy militant infrastructure. A serious international concern was that Pakistan's inability to contain militancy could continue to be a significant obstacle to the normalization of relations between the two countries. While acknowledging that there had been a decrease in infiltration and that the level of violence in Kashmir had declined, Washington was not fully satisfied with the situation.

The situation then took a most dramatic turn in January 2004, when Vajpayee came to Islamabad to attend the seven-nation South Asian regional summit. Few had expected any breakthrough when the aged Indian Prime Minister went to pay a 'courtesy call' on Musharraf at the imposing presidential palace on 5 January. Although there had been hints of a possible meeting, nobody was sure until it actually happened.

The outcome of the 65-minute parley between the two leaders went beyond anybody's expectations. Not only were some significant decisions taken to move the process of normalization forward, but a road map for further interaction was also clearly stated.

Most importantly, Musharraf pledged to prevent the use of the territory under Pakistan's control 'to support terrorism in any manner'. It was the first direct commitment of this nature since the Pakistani- backed armed insurgency in Kashmir began in 1989. The joint statement also declared that both leaders were 'confident' of reaching a peaceful settlement of all bilateral issues, including Kashmir. It was a great leap forward in the relations between the two countries, which had been on the brink of nuclear war just a year before.

The outcome of the Islamabad meeting was not the result of a sudden surge of goodwill. The script was prepared after intensive back-channel diplomacy between Brajesh Mishra and Tariq Aziz. From 1 to 4 January, the two officials were in regular contact. Mishra also met with the ISI chief, Lt.-General Ehsan ul-Haq.

Those interactions remained secret, even from Pakistani foreign ministry officials. Only the President's Chief of Army Staff, General Hamid, and Tariq Aziz were involved in the preparation of the joint communique´. Foreign Secretary, Riaz Khokar, was handed a copy just a few hours before the summit meeting. Musharraf's change of course on the Kashmir policy indicated that the Pakistani military establishment had finally acknowledged that support for militancy could not dislodge India from the disputed land. But there had also been concern that, in the absence of such pressure, India would not agree to a negotiated settlement of the Kashmir dispute. Vajpayee's agreement on a composite dialogue on all bilateral issues, including Kashmir, gave Musharraf some leeway to convince his generals of the need for peace with India.

Musharraf went one step further when he declared his readiness to consider all possible alternatives for the Kashmir solution. In November 2004, he outlined a step-by-step approach towards resolving the decades-old dispute, which involved making some parts of the disputed territory independent or placing them under joint Indian-Pakistani control. Indeed, the suggestion to identify the region, demilitarize it and change its status, signified a radical shift in Pakistan's Kashmir policy.

Though premature, the proposal indicated a significant come-down from Pakistan's traditional hardline position of holding a plebiscite, under the 1948 UN resolution that required Kashmiris alone to decide their political future. For the first time, a Pakistani leader had suggested making the territory a joint protectorate. Finding a solution acceptable to both sides had always been a difficult task, even in the best of circumstances, as Kashmir has been so deeply intertwined with India and Pakistan's perceptions of national security and identity.

Domestic political compulsions had made the issue more complex. What had made securing peace even more difficult was the past baggage of mistrust and suspicion the two nations continued to carry. It had been such an accident-prone relationship that any incident could derail the whole process.

Musharraf's turnaround divided the separatist movement in Indian- administered Kashmir. The moderate elements supported his peace initiatives. For them, militancy could not provide the solution to the festering problem and it was time for the political parties to play their roles for a negotiated settlement of the issue. Once dismissed by the Pakistani military establishment as 'weak links', the moderate Kashmiri leaders became Musharraf's new allies.

Mirwaiz Umar Farooq, a charismatic young Kashmiri leader, remembered his first meeting with Musharraf in New York in September 2001, when the Pakistani military leader accused him of being 'cowardly' for suggesting a non-militant course towards the solution of the Kashmir problem. 'The meeting ended on a bitter note,' Mirwaiz recalled when I met him in his heavily guarded house in Srinagar in April 2005.

The mood had completely changed when the two met again in Holland three years later, following the Indo-Pak rapprochement. 'It was I this time asking him to go slow on the peace process. Musharraf sounded too enthusiastic about the prospect of reaching a settlement,' Mirwaiz said.

The Kashmiri leader was thrown into separatist politics as a teenager after the death of his father, Mirwaiz Maulvi Farooq, in 1989. As a prayer leader at Srinagar's Jamia Masjid, he wielded considerable spiritual and political influence in the disputed state. He led the moderate faction of the All Parties Hurriyat (Freedom) Conference (APHC), a loose coalition of more than 32 organizations, that wanted militancy to give way to political struggle. 'Militancy has played an important role in drawing international attention to the Kashmir issue, but now we should concentrate on a political struggle,' he declared. The moderates were also concerned about the struggle falling into the hands of the extremists.

The resumption of the Indo-Pak talks was fully backed by the moderates, though Musharraf's change of tack shocked the hardliners who had been fighting for the annexation of the entire disputed state with Pakistan. Their bitterness was palpable when the bus service between Srinagar and Muzaffarabad was restored on 7 April 2005, after a 57-year hiatus. It was a momentous occasion when the new Indian Prime Minister, Manmohan Singh, waved off the first bus with its 19 passengers. Described as the mother of all confidence-building measures between India and Pakistan, the bus link reunited divided Kashmiri families. But for the militants it was a betrayal of their cause. In an attempt to derail the peace process, the militants attacked the Tourist Reception Centre in Srinagar, where the passengers of the inaugural bus were kept under strict security.

'This is not what we have sacrificed thousands of lives for,' Syed Ali Shah Geelani, the head of his own faction of APHC, told me when we met at his Srinagar residence, a day after the bus had left for Muzaffarabad.

The 70-year-old, white-bearded Geelani was the chief of Jamaat-i-Islami in Kashmir, and had close links with the Islamic militants fighting Pakistan's proxy war. For his ardent support for Pakistan, he was often described as an ISI agent until Musharraf's turnaround. With Pakistan now betting on the moderates, Geelani felt isolated. But his loyalty to Pakistan was unquestionable. 'Musharraf is destroying Pakistan. Things will change once he is gone,' he said.

## KEY ASPECTS OF KASHMIR DISPUTE

Before we discuss the various proposed options, it is important to first understand the nature of the dispute between India and Pakistan, which provides the backdrop to the official statements and positions taken by both governments in the post-1947-48 period, when India first took the Kashmir case to the United Nations. The following are the key aspects of this long-standing dispute.

*Legacy of the Partition of the Sub-continent in 1947:* The sub-continent was partitioned on the agreed principle that contiguous Muslim majority areas were to be separated from the contiguous non-Muslim majority areas, to form the two independent states of Pakistan and India. There were about 562 Princely States, which existed under the overall paramountcy of the British Crown. The Cabinet Mission, in its statement of May 16, 1946, clarified that 'Paramountcy could neither be retained by the British Crown nor transferred to the new Government'. Also, in Section 7 of the Indian Independence Act, 1947, it was stated that ' the suzerainty of His Majesty over the Indian States lapses.' Thus, legally the Princely States became independent. However, the last British Viceroy Lord Mountbatten, during his address to the Chamber of Princes on July 25, 1947, asserted that 'the rulers were technically at liberty to link with either of the dominion (India or Pakistan)'. As regards the criteria to be followed, he held that 'normally geographical situation and communal interests and so forth will be the factors to be considered.' On various occasions between June and July 1947, Quaid-e-Azam, the Governor General-designate of the new State of Pakistan, stated, 'The legal position is that with the lapse of Paramountcy on the transfer of power by the British all Indian States would automatically regain their full sovereign and independent status. They are, therefore, free to join either of the two Dominions or to remain independent. The Muslim League recognises the right of each State to choose its destiny. It has no intention of coercing any State into adopting any particular course of action.' By August 15, 1947, the majority of the Princely States, owing to their geographical contiguity and Hindu population, joined India while only ten joined Pakistan. However, disputes over independence arose with India in the case of three Princely States, namely Junagadh, Hyderabad and Jammu and Kashmir.

Junagadh, a maritime state in Kathiawar, with a Muslim ruler and a Hindu majority population, decided to accede to Pakistan on August 15, 1947. By middle of September 1947 Pakistan accepted the accession. India reacted by criticising Pakistan's acceptance as ' in utter violation of the principles on which Pakistan was agreed upon and effected.' On September 17, India deployed troops around Junagadh and by November 1947 India had militarily annexed the State, as its first expansionist act after the partition of 1947. It is to be noted that this happened when Pakistan had no defence structure of any sort. Pakistan's complaint, claiming Junagadh as its territory, is still pending before the Security Council. Similarly, Hyderabad, also with a Muslim ruler and a majority Hindu population, despite Indian pressures, decided to remain independent and in fact executed a Standstill Agreement with India in November 1947, which India duly signed. However, India continued to increase pressure on Hyderabad and by the middle of 1948 had imposed an economic blockade as well as carried out border raids. During a parliamentary debate, on July 30, 1948, the then British Prime Minister, Winston Churchill referred to a speech by Pandit Nehru made in the last week of July, 1947, in which he had declared, 'If and when we consider it necessary we will start military operations against Hyderabad.' Commenting on this remark, Winston Churchill said 'It seems to me that this is the sort of thing which might have been said by Hitler before the devouring of Austria.' On August 24, 1948, Hyderabad filed a complaint before the Security Council, but before the case was heard before the Council, Hyderabad was militarily annexed by India on **September 13, 1948.**

While India laid claim on the other two Princely States on the basis of them being Hindu majority areas, as well as geographically contiguous to India, and that the partition of the sub-continent was agreed to on these principles, it did not apply the same principle to the Jammu and Kashmir State, which had a Muslim majority population, under a Hindu ruler who was in favour of remaining independent. During the previous hundred years, the subjects of the Jammu and Kashmir State had been in a state of ongoing series of revolts against the Dogra rulers.

When Partition took place, the Muslim majority population of Jammu and Kashmir was in favour of joining Pakistan, whereas the Hindu Maharaja was reluctant, hoping that he would retain his independence. Internally, there were already tensions due to repressive measures of the Maharaja against the Muslims. The situation further deteriorated when, towards the end of July 1947, the Maharaja ordered the Muslims to surrender their arms to the police, and communal violence erupted.

In the Jammu province, hundreds of Muslims were massacred by the Hindus and Sikhs, who attacked Muslim villages. The massacre was one of the first attempts of ethnic cleansing, which, in fact, had begun even before independence, with the connivance of the local administration comprising units of the Maharaja's Army and Police. In August 1947, on the eve of Partition, Poonch revolted against the Maharaja's rule and in September 1947, the Muslim population liberated the area from the State Police. According to some estimates, between August-October 1947, in the State of Jammu and Kashmir out of the Muslim population of 500,000 about 200,000 just disappeared, presumably were killed, and many Muslims from among the rest fled to the neighbouring West Pakistan (now Pakistan).

## SIGNIFICANT DEVELOPMENT

Another significant development of the time was that on August 12, 1947, the then Prime Minister of Jammu and

Kashmir, Janak Singh, proposed a 'Standstill Agreement' to both India and Pakistan. This was agreed to and signed by Pakistan on August 15, but India was reluctant and suggested further discussions, keeping matters pending. Eventually no discussion took place and, thus, the 'Standstill Agreement' was never signed by the Indian government with the Maharaja of Kashmir even though it had signed a Standstill Agreement on November 29, 1947, with Hyderabad, since Prime Minister Nehru had other plans to annex the State of Jammu and Kashmir.

In October 1947, there was a revolt by the Muslim population against the Maharaja. He fled from the capital Srinagar to Jammu on October 26, 1947, and appealed to India for help. India claims that the Maharaja signed the 'Instrument of Accession' on October 26, following which the Indian forces landed in the State supposedly on October 27, 1947.

Regarding the signing of the Instrument of Accession, its timing, terms and conditions, and the timing of the landing of Indian troops, are all controversial. The study of historical events shows that initially the Maharaja sent the Deputy Prime Minister, R. L. Batra, to New Delhi, on October 24, with a 'letter of accession to India' which could not be signed. Mr. Batra, in New Delhi, held discussions with 'who would listen to him; but his mission was fruitless.' According to British historian, Alastair Lamb, this was 'certainly no blanket unconditional Instrument of Accession but rather a statement of the terms upon which an association between the State of Jammu and Kashmir and the Indian Dominion might be negotiated in return for military assistance. The Indian side have been careful to avoid specific reference to this particular document in their descriptions of the State of Jammu and Kashmir's plea for assistance. It is probable that it involved no more than a token diminution of the State's sovereignty. It certainly did not provide for an administration in the State of Jammu and Kashmir presided over by Sheikh Abdullah.'

Moreover, research also shows that Indian leaders were not in favour of signing the Instrument of Accession before any military help was provided to the Maharaja. The Maharaja was not in favour of unconditional surrender of sovereignty. Pandit Nehru, however, was of the view that what was required was *'not so much the formalities of accession as some pragmatic arrangement whereby the Maharaja's government might be obliged to collaborate politically with Sheikh Abdullah and his National Conference, bolstered in power by Indian arms.'* Also, during the Indian Defence Committee meeting on October 25, 1947, which discussed the situation in Jammu and Kashmir, V. P. Menon stressed, *'it would technically be quite proper for India to send its forces to the State of Jammu and Kashmir without its prior accession to India, be it definitive or provisional.'*

Subsequent research has also thrown doubts on the official Indian version, which claims that its intervention was legal, basing it on the signing of the so-called 'Instrument of Accession' signed by Maharaja Hari Singh. According to the British historian Alastair Lamb, the Maharaja was forced to sign a conditional Instrument of Accession *after* the Indian troops had landed at Srinagar. As the International Law expert Dr. Ijaz Hussain points out, article 49 of the Vienna Convention on the Law of Treaties states, 'A treaty is invalid if its conclusion is procured by the threat or use of force in violation of the principles of the Charter of the United Nations.' Therefore, the fact that the Instrument of Accession was signed under duress in the presence of Indian troops 'points to the use of force in obtaining consent of the Maharaja to the said Instrument. This makes it patently defective.'

## THE INSURGENCY AND POLITICAL SYSTEM

Contrary to the popular view that the insurgents picked up their guns in response to an undemocratic political system, in no way was the movement fighting for greater democratic rights. In fact, as already shown, they had already picked up their guns prior to the election. Their cause was religiously and ideologically fuelled. In many ways, the ruling National Conference party had encouraged this atmosphere through a range of propaganda campaigns. Even as far back as the 1984 election, Farooq Abdullah and the National Conference deliberately tried to create revulsion against India for their own political ends. These Propaganda ads tried to demonstrate that India's iron fist was bleeding Kashmir. There is little evidence of Indian repression in this period, and it seems likely that the National Conference was trying to use this as a way to hide the poor and corrupt performance of the State Government. Indeed, perhaps if India had done more to intervene in State affairs, it could have abated the insurgency that followed.

## The Role of Pakistan

Having failed to take Kashmir by force, and unable to win the hearts of the Kashmiris by offering them a democracy when they themselves had a military dictatorship, Pakistan had to woo the Kashmiris by its ideology of communalism.

Before the insurgency in Kashmir began, there was an insurgency movement in neighboring Punjab, which had also been split between India and Pakistan in 1947. That died out by the late 1980s, when the Sikhs that had taken up arms against India had realized they were being used by their Pakistani sponsors and gave up arms. And so Pakistan's attention turned to Kashmir. One major reason Pakistan needed to sponsor insurgency in India was to gain intelligence on India, and its army. After suffering three consecutive defeats, each time after attacking India unprovoked and by surprise, Pakistan was fearful India would be tempted to launch a pre-emptive strike against Pakistan to destroy its army to ensure Pakistan never again attempted to invade India.

The Pakistani view is that they are providing moral support to the Kashmiri People in their fight for freedom against the brutal Indian Army who commit excessive humans rights abuses on the oppressed Muslims living in India, a non-Muslim country. The Indian perspective is that they are dealing with a proxy war by Pakistan who have never accepted the Kashmiri's democratic reaffirmation of their accession to India. The Kashmiris themselves are split between supporting Pakistan,

India and independence. But while the Pakistanis and Indians live in relative peace, it is the Kashmiri who suffers the most while the issue remains unresolved.

The slogans: "Pakistan se kya rishta? La ilaha ilallah" (What is the relation with Pakistan? There is no God but God.) followed by "Azaadi ka matlab kya? La ilaha ilallah" (What is the meaning of freedom? There is no God but God.) indicate that Pakistan for Kashmiris meant Islam, and freedom for Kashmiris meant Pakistan. Those who coined and floated these slogans went on to form the Jammu Kashmir Liberation Force (JKLF). The JKLF wanted to liberate Kashmir. In fact its founder, Hashim Qureshi, later fled to Western Europe for asylum after the Pakistanis hijacked his organization and used its members to fight India as part of a religious struggle rather than for the independence he had desired.

In 1990 a report showed that almost a thousand of the elite Kashmiri Muslims were on the payroll of the ISI. In 1993, with pro-independence insurgents separating from the pro-Pakistan factions, Pakistani border troops shot and killed some thirty Kashmiri youth on their way to POK for training. Slowly but surely the ties between Pakistan and the Kashmiri youth were being severed.

## Republic Day

In addition to the Afghan War, local Kashmiris also watched on TV as mass movements against authoritarianism arose in East Europe and Central Asia. The most significant of these was in Romania, where on Christmas Day 1989, dictator Nicolae Ceausescu was executed. Less than a month later was to be Kashmir's turn.

Perhaps the most significant event was the insurgents successful kidnapping of India's Home Minister. In December 1989, there was a change in the Federal Government in India, with Rajiv Gandhi losing to VP Singh's Government. Singh's deputy, the Home Minister, was Mufti Mohammed Sayeed, the current Chief Minister of Jammu & Kashmir. Just weeks after being sworn in, his daughter was kidnapped near Srinagar by insurgents who demanded the release of their colleagues from prison. Mufti, holding the third highest office in India behind the President and Prime Minister, broke India's policy of non-negotiation with terrorists and released the captured insurgents and his daughter was released. The whole episode has subsequently been referred to by insurgents as a key moment when they were able to show their Kashmiri people that India could be brought to its knees.

These incidents gave the Kashmiris fighting for independence a great deal of confidence, unlike the early years when dreams of independence were always viewed as a practical impossibility. Many Kashmiris felt that independence was imminent after the fall of the communist era, and some locals remarked that they thought the reality of independence was only a matter of weeks away.

## Kashmiri Independence Day

January 20, 1990 was to be Kashmiri Independence Day. This date was chosen a few weeks prior as the day the masses would take to the streets and take power from India, effectively their army, for the Kashmiri people (and they would subsequently become a Republic and/or join Pakistan). Most Kashmiris were convinced that this would occur, and in fact the largest exodus of Kashmiri Pandits occurred on January 19. Despite the fact that the masses were limited to Srinagar, and not regions of the State such as Ladakh and Jammu did not mean it was not a very real threat. There were reportedly between January 1 and January 19, 1990, 319 violent acts - 21 armed attacks, 114 bomb blasts, 112 arsons, and 72 incidents of mob violence. In fact the Indian Government was so desperate they sent Jagmohan, the former Governor of the State, on the night of 18th January to make a last ditch effort to save the Kashmir Valley. He was able to organize a last minute blockade that stopped people from leaving their local neighborhoods so they could not reach the main streets and mobilize into a large crowd. The momentum of the masses was soon lost, and such a mass protest was never attempted again.

## Exodus of Pandits

One reason why Kashmiris were uncomfortable in joining Pakistan was its large non-Muslim minority, who would have no place in Islamic Pakistan. Hence by resorting to the systematic killings of Hindus, as well as spreading fear amongst them through newspaper ads and pamphlets ordering them to leave or face death, Pakistan was able to overcome this major obstacle.

With most of the Hindus gone by January 1990, and the secular minded Muslims powerless to help them return, Pakistan was able to strengthen its claim on Kashmir. There was religious indoctrination, by misusing mosques and other available platforms, in a bid to frighten the secular Muslims.

## Kashmiri Pandits

The crimes against humanity perpetrated against the Kashmiri Pandits were tragic. While genocide occurred on a small scale, it is more likely that the objective was to drive them away rather than wipe them out. The dozens of killings and rapes were always followed by warnings for Pandits to get out, which suggest that the attacks were more as a statement rather than intent for mass genocide. But what was most surprising to Pandits was how there were large demonstrations in several Kashmiri cities by common Kashmiris with the slogan: "Asi gachi Pakistan, batni rosin batta gatssin." In Kashmiri this means: We will become a part of Pakistan, Pandit women can stay with us but Pandit men must leave." They could understand why the extremists wanted them to leave, but were shocked when the masses joined in.

## The Momentum Dies

The list of innocent persons who fell prey to the bullets of terrorists is again illustrative of the Islamization drive. The victims included prominent educationists and subscribers to secular ideals. Not only Pandits, but Muslims such as Professor Mushir-ul-Haq, Vice Chancellor, Kashmir University, and Maulana Mohammad Syed Masoodi, a renowned Muslim scholar were among such victims at the hands of the terrorists. Libraries of Universities were destroyed for having unislamic books, and freedom of speech was suspended. It was clear the movement was not against India,. but all things unislamic in their eyes.

While comparisons to Nazi Germany are fraught with danger, it does seem the population were caught in a mass hysteria that they now admit was a mistake. I have heard many anecdotal stories from others who have met with Kashmiri Muslims in Kashmir who have shown much resentment in not doing anything to stop the fundamentalists. It is difficult to determine if they genuinely wanted an Islamic State of Kashmir, or if they merely followed the trend as if it were a fad.

## IMPACT OF CONFLICT ON WOMEN IN KASHMIR

The most superficial study of current day Kashmir would reveal deep and widespread impact on the entire society and especially women. The experience and impact of violence and trauma in Kashmir is ever-present in its patterns. Drawing upon our experience, the first point I would like to emphasize is that there are gaps and the situation requires a systematic and integrated response – particularly in mitigating and address the needs of women affected by violence and trauma. Another point I would like to make, again drawing upon our experience, is that taking an integrated approach is effective – our hope is that this today's conclave would lead to: 1) a community dedicated to taking a comprehensive study of the effects of conflict on women in Kashmir, 2) a stream of coordinated efforts to address their needs and recovery process, and 3) efforts to empower the voice of victims of conflict to advocate against and to prevent a repetition of the repeating cycle of tragedy in Kashmir.

The Help Foundation experience has truly focused on responding in a comprehensive way to the needs of women affected by the violence and trauma of conflict – perhaps what we can contribute to this discourse is our body of experiences that has clearly taught us that the response needs to be multi-disciplinary. Since 1997, Help Foundation J&K has been responding to the devastations of conflict in Kashmir, particularly focused on women and children – from relief work to rehabilitation (including psychosocial counseling) to education and economic empowerment. Within this multi-faceted response, a key area of concern for us has also been addressing the gaps in the healthcare system vis-à-vis psychosocial healing and support and facilitating care to the underprivileged. In the course of our work, we have seen the deep impact that, that violence and conflict has had on Kashmiri women and we have had the privilege of partnering with women who have been direct and indirect victims of violence and trauma to become champions in their own recovery and rehabilitation. For thousands of families' whose heads are now conflict widows, we have seen women emerging from deep shock to take charge of their lives. Indeed, in our economic empowerment work with widows, in combination with psychological counseling, we have found that by equipping these women with new vocational skills and small livelihood grants we are able to not only economically empower them but also help them rediscover their own sense of agency. 90% of such beneficiaries have not only succeeded in rehabilitating their own family, but some of them employed other people in their business.

But a key challenge for us is to ensure that women to do not remain isolated from the broader community and that we find ways to increase awareness and build capacities at the community-level that will foster great sustainability of our interventions. There is certainly a need to engage key community members – doctors, nurses, teachers, relief and development workers, imams – in such an effort. Certainly, the only way to address gaps regarding violence against women at the level of other institutions – whether legal or political – would be a broad-basing of today's discussions to include the entire community followed by informed public advocacy.

We would like to now shed some light on the health scenario in Kashmir and share some of the work HELP has been doing in the health sector, with the hope that some of our response strategies and experiences might inform today's dialogue aimed at chalk out a way forward.

## THE KARGIL WAR AND ITS COLLISION ON INDO-PAK RELATIONS

The euphoria that followed the February Lahore Declarations by India and Pakistan abruptly dissipated when nearly 1500 Pakistan-backed Muslim militants known miles into the India-held Kargil region of North Kashmir. The militants who were mostly Afghanis together with Pakistani regulars, occupied more than 30 well-fortified positions located atop the most inhospitable frigidly cold ridges, at 16,000 and 18,000 feet above sea level, in the Great Himalayan range facing Dras, Kargil, Batalik, and the Mushko Valley sectors stretching covering over 30 miles.

Indian army patrols, between May 8 and 15 detected and came in contact with the militants and on May 26, India launched air attacks known as Operation Vijay (victory) against the bunkers from which the intruders had been firing upon the Indian troops below the ridges. On May 27, two MIG aircrafts were shot down. One pilot was taken prisoner of war (POW) and the other killed.

On May 28, a MI-17 helicopter was shot down and the four-man crew killed. As the battle raged on between May 31 and June 11, Indian troops were able to clear up some pockets of resistance and to cut off the supply lines to the intruders by outflanking them. They also launched a major offensive in the Kargil Drass sector accompanied by air strikes on June 6, in order to protect the only highway linking Srinagar to Leh in Ladakh region from Pakistani threat.

On June 10, Pakistan returned seven severely mutilated bodies of soldiers to New Delhi outraging India. In the face of India's fury, on June 12, Pakistan's foreign Minister Sartaj Aziz visited New Delhi to talk to Jaswant Singh. But the talks failed. India identified Pakistan as an aggressor that had violated the LOC, while Aziz surprisingly questioned the validity of the line, which was based on the 1972 Simla Agreement signed by both countries. He also called for a joint working group to help settle India's claim of the Kargil, which Singh angrily rejected. Before he visited New Delhi, Aziz had visited

China, a Pakistan ally, China, seeking its support, but was coming visit to China was designed to garner. This was especially important to India, since it was the first time Singh visited China after the Pokhram II nuclear tests.

As the battle turned bloodier and more intense, the Clinton administration intervened to help defuse the crisis. In the second week of June, Bruce Reidel, Special Assistant to President Clinton, in a briefing at the Foreign Press Center, asserted the inviolability of the LOC by stating the following: "we think the Line of Control has demarcated the area over the years. The two parties have not previously had significant differences about where the LOC is," and the "forces which have crossed the line should withdraw to where they came from." He noted that the President in his recent letters to both Prime Ministers had stressed that point. On June 15, in separate telephonic conversations, Mr. Clinton told Sharif to withdraw the infiltrators from across the LOC, and Vajpayee that he appreciated his display of restraint in the conflict. To Pakistan's further sense of isolation, the G-8 members, at their annual meeting in Cologne, Germany, June 19-20, came out strongly in support of India's contention that the Kargil crisis was precipitated by mercenaries backed by Pakistani troops. Mr. Brajesh Mishra, the Principal Secretary to Vajpayee, who had taken Vajpayee's letter to Mr. Clinton at the G-8 in Cologne, also took the opportunity to explain the situation to the rest of the G-8 leaders. Following that meeting, a communiqué was issued on June 20 by the G-8, which condemned in unequivocal terms the violation of the LOC and dubbed Pakistan's military action as "irresponsible" in its attempt to change the status quo at the LOC, and called on it to end the intrusion. The communiqué also urged the two countries to resolve the Kashmir dispute with "dialogue". This position was also supported by China. by Gen. Anthony Zinni, Commander-in-Chief of the US Central command. The delegation also included Gibson Lampher, the Deputy Assistant Secretary of State for South Asia, and Karl F. Inderfurth. On behalf of the President Zinni asked Sharif to withdraw the troops from across the LOC and Lampher traveled to New Delhi to brief Brajesh Mishra on the details of their visit to Pakistan. On June 28, a day after Zinni's visit, Sharif rushed to Beijing to seek Chinese diplomatic support of the conflict. The Chinese, however, told him that he could not count on their support, and he cut short his six-day visit and returned home disappointed. Meanwhile, on June 20, Indian troops, after a fierce battle and the loss of 50 lives, recaptured Tololing Rill in the Drass sector, and on July 4, recaptured Tiger Hill, which is considered to be the most strategic point in Drass sector as it overlooks the Srinagar-Leh highway.

As the Indian troops steadily recaptured one hill or ridge after another, and Pakistan's isolation in the world community increased (only Saudi Arabia and the United Emirates supported Pakistan), it desperately sought a face-saving formula to extricate itself from its miscalculated adventure. For instance on June 27, former Foreign Secretary Niaz Naik, a person known to be close to Sharif as well as to the Americans, secretly went to New Delhi, met with Vajpayee and his Principal Secretary Mishra, and slipped back to Pakistan. Although Pakistan's foreign office insisted that it was "Naik's private visit and had nothing to do with Pakistan's foreign policy," it was speculated that he presented a set of "face-saving" proposals to Sharif that would allow Pakistan to escape from the Kargil imbroglio as gracefully as possible. On July 3, Sharif requested a meeting with Clinton on "an urgent basis" and met with him on July 4, in Washington.

The statement indicated that the forces needed to be returned to the Pakistani side. This was followed by the White House statement which stated that the President shared with Sharif the view that the current fighting "contains the seeds of wider conflict" and that "it was vital for the peace of South Asia that the LOC in Kashmir be respected by both parties in accordance with their 1972 Simla accord," and that "bilateral dialogue begun in Lahore in February provides the best approach for resolving all issues dividing India and Pakistan, including Kashmir," and that the President would take a "personal interest in encouraging an expeditious resumption and intensification of those bilateral efforts once the sanctity of the LOC has been fully restored." Mr. Clinton also indicated that he would visit

South Asia soon. As the meeting with Sharif progressed, Mr. Clinton frequently called Mr. Vajpayee in order to "keep him fully appraised of the discussion," as the latter had declined the invitation to go to Washington. On July 12, the Congress also turned up the heat on Islamabad when it passed House Resolution 227 "expressing the sense of the Congress in opposition to the Government of Pakistan's support for armed incursion into Jammu and Kashmir, India." Further declaring that Pakistan was culpable in sending armed insurgents into the Indian territory, while stressing that India and Pakistan "resolve all of their differences within the framework of the Simla agreement in order to preserve peace and security in South Asia." It also suggested that the administration block loans to Pakistan from international financial institutions.

Following this agreement, beginning on July 11, the infiltrators began retreating from Kargil as India set July 16 as the deadline for the total withdrawal. On July 12, in Clinton as well as his request to the intruders to withdraw from Indian Territory. He also defended his Kargil policy as something designed to draw the attention of the international community to Kashmir issue. In the war, more than 400 Indian soldiers, 679 intruders, and 30 Pakistani regulars were killed excluding those who were wounded. Sharif's agreement to withdraw intruders upset the military so much that on October 12, he was ousted from power in a bloodless coup. When Musharraf, who is rumored to have been the architect of the Kargil war and who is called Mr. Kargil in India, heard on his return from Sri Lanka that he was being replaced by Sharif's confidant, Lt. General Khowaja Ziauddin, he had his generals remove Sharif on charges of hijacking and treason. Musharraf declared himself the Chief Executive, the Chief of Army, and later as President. Sharif, who was convicted and given a life sentence by a military court, was subsequently exiled to Saudi Arabia in December 1999.

The coup upset India and got Pakistan suspended from the Commonwealth Conference. Tensions between them escalated. Artillery fires across the LOC intensified and on December 24, a New Delhi-bound plane, carrying 178 passengers from

Katmandu, Nepal, was hijacked to Kandahar, Afghanistan by the Pakistan-based Harakat ul-Mujahideen terrorists. They demanded a release from jails of 35 Kashmiri militants including the Pakistani cleric, Maulana Masood Azhar, in exchange with the passengers. When India's government refused to concede their demands, they killed a newlywed husband who was on his honeymoon with his wife. Pressured by the passengers' relatives, on December 31, India exchanged the passengers with three hardcore militants including Azhar. This was humiliating to India. India implicated Pakistan in this avail. Unlike his predecessors, Musharraf came out openly in support of terrorists by declaring that "Islam does not recognize political boundaries, and Jihad is a concept of God."

Emboldened by the successful results of their hijacking, the militants escalated their assaults and suicide bombings against innocent bystanders and the security forces. Realizing that negotiations with militants and the APHC leaders were essential to resolve this conflict, in November 2000, on the eve of the beginning of Ramadan (month of Muslim fasting) the Vajpayee government declared a unilateral cease-fire and invited them for talks. It also agreed to talk to Pakistan if the latter ceased supporting cross-border terrorism. The APHC leaders including its chairman Abdul Ghani Bhat at that time welcomed the initiative. They sought visas from the government to visit Pakistan to talk to the militant leaders living there. But they were denied visas because they wanted the Pro-Pakistani leader Syed Ali Shah Geelani of the Jamaat-I-Islami included in the team. The Musharraf government refused to cease supporting cross-border terrorism but agreed to abide by the cease-fire declaration along the LOC.

However, some of the Pakistani-based militant groups such as the Lashkar-e-Toiba, Hizbul-Mujahideen, Jash-e-Mohammed, founded later by cleric Azhas, and Al-Umar-Mujhideen rejected the cease-fire declaration as a sham and vowed to liberate Kashmir with a Jihad directed against pagan India. They escalated terrorism not only in Kashmir, but also in other locations like New Delhi. Their belief being that they will go to Paradise if they die as martyrs fighting pagan India.

Hoping to persuade the APHC leaders to talk to his government, Vajpayee appointed a noted politician and former Congress cabinet minister K. C. Pant as leaders, but also to other politicians from Kashmir who were committed to a peaceful resolution of the conflict. The APHC leaders rejected the invitation on the grounds that Pakistan was not included.

However, on April 30, one of its leaders, Shabir Ahmad Shah, the chairman of the Democratic Freedom Party (DFP), agreed to talk to Pant, even though he had earlier insisted on Pakistan's inclusion in the talks. When it became clear that India's unilateral declaration had only helped the militants to escalate their terrorism, and that the APHC leaders rejected negotiations the Vajpayee government ended the six month cease-fire on May 25, 2001, and invited Musharraf for talks without any pre-established conditions – which he accepted. The talks were held on July 14 – 16, 2001 in Agra, near New Delhi, but they failed because General Musharraf insisted that the Kashmir dispute be the core issue of the talks, which Vajpayee rejected. Although both leaders had agreed to meet again during the November UN General Assembly meetings, it did not take place as India was angered by the suicide bomb attack of the Jammu and Kashmir State Assembly building on October 1, in which forty innocent civilians and the three terrorists who had caused the blast were killed. The Pakistani Cleric Maulana Masood Azher, leader of the Jaish-e-Mohammed, which is linked to Osama Bin Laden's Al Qaeda, took credit for the bombing. Vajpayee took a tough stance indicating that he would not talk to Musharraf unless he ceased supporting cross border terrorism. Moreover, India's foreign minister, Jaswant Singh, cancelled his scheduled trip to Pakistan to talk to his counterpart. Relations between the two countries again turned tense and resulted in an intense exchange of fire along the LOC. The Bush administration called on India to show restraint as it did not want to jeopardize its Al Qaeda that Pakistan had supported in the past. In January and June 2002 the tensions between India and Pakistan increased along with the threat of another war.

## FUTURE OPTIONS FOR DECLARATION OF THE DISPUTE

Over the past fifty years, besides the UN resolutions, observers and intellectuals have proposed various other options for resolving the Kashmir dispute time and again at the UN fora and at the bilateral India-Pakistan levels. These proposals are examined below.

### UN Resolutions: The Plebiscite Option

The UN Security Council resolutions of August 13, 1948 and January 5, 1949, proposed the plebiscite option for resolving the Kashmir dispute. However, it is important to note that the Government of India itself accepted *plebiscite* or *referendum* as a right of the Kashmiri people, when it filed the initial complaint against Pakistan before the United Nations on January 1, 1948, as pointed out in Part I of this paper. Beginning with Governor General Mountbatten, Indian leaders like Prime Minister Nehru also repeatedly made the commitment to 'the will of the Kashmiri people'.

After India filed its initial complaint, the UN Security Council passed the two important resolutions of August 13, 1948 and January 5, 1949. These resolutions laid down the principles and procedures for a free and impartial plebiscite under UN auspices. Broadly, the resolution of January 5, 1949, stated: '(a) the question of the accession of the State of Jammu and Kashmir to India and Pakistan, would be decided through the democratic method of a free and impartial plebiscite after the cease-fire and truce agreement provided for in the Resolution of August 13 had been carried out; (b) the Secretary General of the UN would nominate a Plebiscite Administrator, who would be appointed by the government of Jammu and Kashmir and given powers which he considers necessary for holding a free and impartial plebiscite; (c) on implementation of the ceasefire and the truce agreement, the Commission and the Plebiscite Administrator would determine, in consultation with the Government of India, the final disposal of Indian and State Armed Forces, as well as the Forces in Azad Kashmir (in consultation with the local authorities); (d) persons who had entered the State since August 15, 1947 would be required to leave the State, and citizens of the State who had left the State on account of disturbances would be allowed to return.'

Both India and Pakistan accepted the above UN Resolutions. However, later, differences arose over the interpretation of various clauses of the resolutions, especially on the issues of demilitarisation and disbandment/disarming of the 'Azad Kashmir' forces. India gave its own interpretation to the agreement and suggested that the Azad Kashmir forces be disbanded and the defence and administrative responsibility of the region be given to India and Indian Kashmiri authorities. Pakistan, on the other hand, was in favour of a complete and simultaneous withdrawal of armed forces personnel by both the countries. On this issue, the President of the Security Council, General McNaughton, in his proposal of December 22, 1949, in para 2, clarified that the Resolutions of 1948 and 1949 called for demilitarisation of the whole State of Jammu and Kashmir and not merely Azad Kashmir: that 'demilitarisation should include the withdrawal from the State of Jammu and Kashmir of the regular forces of Pakistan; and the withdrawal of the regular forces of India not required for purposes of security or for the maintenance of local law and order.' The UN Security Council passed Resolution 80 on March 14, 1950, which called upon the Governments of India and Pakistan 'to prepare and execute within a period of five months from the date of this resolution a programme of demilitarisation on the basis of the principles of paragraph 2 of General McNaughton's proposal, or of such modifications of those principles as may be mutually agreed.' Pakistan accepted that Resolution as well, but India maintained its position as regards the demilitarisation issue.

The UN Security Council passed Resolution 98, in December 1952. The UNSC Resolution, regarding demilitarisation issue clarified that: (Article 4) 'the Governments of India and Pakistan to enter into immediate negotiations under the auspices of the United Nations representative for India and Pakistan in order to reach agreement on the specific number of forces to remain on each side of the cease-fire line at the end of the period of demilitarisation, this number to be between 3,000 and 6,000 armed forces remaining on the Pakistan side of the cease-fire line and between 12,000 and 18,000 armed forces remaining on the India side of the cease-fire line.' Though during the discussions Pakistan's representative to the UN, Mr. Zafrulla Khan, pointed out that the number of forces proposed was not fair, yet he said that Pakistan 'is prepared to go forward on the basis of this resolution.' The Indian representative, Mrs. Pandit, in her speech, however, categorically said, 'I should like to repeat that we reject the proposal in it and we are not prepared to enter into any talks on the basis suggested.'

Regarding the question of plebiscite, Pakistan was in favour of giving complete authority to the UN for holding, organising and supervising the plebiscite. India, on the other hand, only wanted the non-binding advice of the UN. Various UN mediators were appointed to resolve this issue, but no one was successful in convincing India on a compromise. Sir Owen Dixon, the UN mediator, in his report submitted in 1950, wrote: 'In the end I became convinced that India's agreement would never be obtained to demilitarisation in any such form, or to provisions governing the period of plebiscite of any such character, as would in my opinion, permit of the plebiscite being conducted in conditions sufficiently guarding against intimidation and other forms of influence and abuse by which the freedom and fairness of the plebiscite might be imperilled.' Dr. Frank P. Graham, appointed UN representative for India and Pakistan in 1951, submitted five reports, up to March 1953, but his efforts at mediation also proved to be unsuccessful as India would not agree on the size of the forces to be left on either side of the cease-fire line after demilitarisation. India, therefore, consistently refused to take recourse to all proposals of various statesmen and UN representatives for the holding of a plebiscite in Jammu and Kashmir. On the other hand, it is on record that Pakistan supported all such international mediation and UN efforts.

Defending the Indian position on plebiscite, Sisir Gupta, an Indian scholar, wrote: 'it became obvious even at the early stages of the Kashmir dispute that a plebiscite -an "ideal" solution according to some – because of the complexities in Kashmir was difficult to accomplish. Even as a democratic solution, it had loopholes. Kashmir, clearly, is not composed of one people: in religion, it has three major groups; in language, four. If there is a section which wants to secede from India, there are others who do not.' However, the fact of the matter is that, right from the beginning, India feared that if a plebiscite was held it would lose what it had already occupied. According to a Kashmiri activist, Prof. Mrs. Shamim Shawl, 'plebiscite is the most plausible solution of the problem. This has been accepted in the Resolutions of August 48 and January 1949. It is these resolutions, which confirm the disputed character of the problem and negate the Indian position that says Kashmir is an irrevocable part of India. India is in fact challenging the rightful and legal authenticity of the United Nations by delaying the implementation of UN resolutions.'

Keeping in view the basic genesis and nature of the dispute, the option incorporated in the then UN resolutions is still valid. The UN resolutions are not time-barred, as observed in 1956, by the UN Secretary General, Dag Hammarskjold, who clarified the important principle that 'the UN decision is valid until it has been invalidated by the organ which took it.'

## The UN Trusteeship Option

Generally, this option proposes that Kashmir should be placed under UN Trusteeship and then plebiscite may be held for the final resolution of the dispute. It is argued that this will provide a face-saving for India, and will also give Kashmiris, on both sides of the Line of Control, enough time to come up with a joint option. The JKLF Chairman, Ammanullah Khan in December 1993, proposed: (1) complete, simultaneous withdrawal of Indian and Pakistani troops and civil administration, non-Kashmiri personnel from Jammu and Kashmir; (2) the reunification of Indian and Pakistani-controlled parts of Kashmir; (3) placement of the State under UN control for five to ten years; and (4) holding of a plebiscite. Well-known Pakistani economist, the late Dr. Mahbubul Haq, in an interview he gave to an Urdu Weekly *Hurmat,* in 1994, proposed that only the Kashmir Valley be placed under UN Trusteeship for ten years and then plebiscite be held in the Kashmir Valley.

As India regards Occupied Kashmir as its integral part, it is obvious that it will never voluntarily agree to the placing of the State, or the Kashmir Valley under UN trusteeship. *Secondly,* both the above trusteeship options support the plebiscite option under the UN auspices, an option that has been rejected by India even though in the early years of the dispute India committed itself to holding of the plebiscite.

As regards Pakistan and the Kashmiris, since the above proposals support a UN role and the option of plebiscite, in view of the already existing UN resolutions which provide the plebiscite option under UN auspices, the above proposal would mean unnecessarily prolonging the solution beyond five or ten years. Moreover, according to Article 76 of Chapter XII of the UN Charter one of the basic objectives of the trusteeship system is 'to promote the political, economic, social, and educational advancement of the inhabitants of the trust territories, and their progressive development towards self-government or independence, as may be appropriate to the particular circumstances of each territory and its peoples...' The case of Jammu and Kashmir does not require placement under UN trusteeship as the Kashmiris have, over the years, demonstrated their political will by waging an indigenous movement in Occupied Kashmir for their right of self-determination, underscoring the fact that their preferred option is self-determination.

## The Partition Option

Regarding the option of the partition of Jammu and Kashmir, this has largely been an academic debate and various scholars have suggested different proposals. The *first* is a division-related option for Jammu and Kashmir, based on the holding of regional plebiscites. This proposal was first given by UN Representative, Sir Owen Dixon, in his report of 1950-51.

Called the 'Dixon Report', it proposed the idea of holding regional plebiscites, instead of a general plebiscite as proposed in the UN resolutions. The Owen Dixon Plan proposed the division of the State of Jammu and Kashmir into four main regions: Jammu, Ladakh, the Vale of Kashmir including Muzaffarabad, and Gilgit-Baltistan. According to his plan the district of Poonch was to remain with Pakistan. He proposed that of the four regions, Jammu and Ladakh should go uncontested to India and the Northern Areas to Pakistan. He concluded that in the Valley a plebiscite might be held to decide about its future. Pakistan, did not outrightly reject the proposal, but was in favour of a general plebiscite in the whole of Jammu and Kashmir. India on the other hand regarded Jammu and Kashmir as a unit of the Indian Federation and thus was not in favour of any regional plebiscite.

*The second* partition proposal is an option based on a 'Trieste-type' solution. The Trieste issue, between Italy and Yugoslavia, arose as a result of the two World Wars. After World War I, Trieste and the adjoining areas, including the whole valley of the Adige river and Istria, went to Italy, but in 1945 it was claimed by Yugoslavia on the grounds that Italy was guilty of aggression against Yugoslavia. However, Trieste and its environs and the Gorzia region to the northwest (Zone A) remained under Anglo-American control and the southern portion (Zone B) was under the control of the Yugoslav troops. Finally, in 1954, Italy and Yugoslavia agreed to a partition and Zone A (including Trieste) was given to Italy and Zone B to Yugoslavia. Italy agreed to maintain a free port at Trieste. Later, the agreement was given a *de jure* status by the 1975 Treaty of Osimo between Italy and Yugoslavia.

The 'Trieste'-type option for Jammu and Kashmir proposes that the Valley along with some adjoining parts of Jammu and the Pakistani side of Kashmir (Azad Kashmir), be made an autonomous units, under India and Pakistan, respectively. The LoC would be a soft border between the two autonomous units. The remaining areas on both sides of the LoC may be merged with India and Pakistan, respectively. India and Pakistan would be required to withdraw their forces under UN supervision.

Again, this proposal lacks viability, as it does not address either the genesis of the dispute, nor the complexities that have accumulated since then to date. The struggle in Jammu and Kashmir is not for autonomy of any one region but for the right of self-determination to be expressed by the Kashmiris, as granted to them under UN resolutions. Also, India and Pakistan being parties to the dispute will continue to have a clash of interests in the proposed autonomous regions; therefore, this would certainly not result in any stability in the region. Moreover, the option implies that the existing Line of Control (LoC) may serve as the line of division. The LoC remains the UN-recognised ceasefire line (CFL) and was not drawn with any basis for serving as a permanent border, but with the intention of bringing about cessation of military hostilities.

*The third* partition proposal considers the conversion of the Line of Control (LoC) into an international border. This means maintenance of the prevailing *status quo*. This option is in principle supported by India. If it were accepted, India would take additional advantage by then propagating that it had conceded Indian territory to Pakistan and would try to emerge as a peacemaker in the region. As assessed by Robert Wirsing, 'by asserting the primacy of actual military *control* over punitive legal *entitlement*, it tacitly acknowledges India's dominant political standing in the region. By requiring Pakistan to relinquish its claim of the coveted Valley of Kashmir and the Kashmiri separatists their claim of independence, while at the same time entailing little or no detachment from India of territories now in its possession, it leaves existing political and economic arrangements essentially undisturbed. Thus, of the several conceivable forms of partition, it is clearly among the most generous to India.'

However, the 'the LoC as a border' option has to take into account the fact that the LoC is merely a ceasefire line, as well as take stock of the struggle for the right of self-determination that is going on in the Indian-held Kashmir. Moreover, Kashmiris do not recognise the LoC. Prof. Mrs. Shamim Shawl, a Kashmiri scholar from Srinagar, has argued that 'the proposal of division is in contravention of the basic principle that Jammu and Kashmir is an indivisible entity. It also violates the fundamental fact that the Kashmir problem is basically the problem of the people of Jammu and Kashmir. It is not a bilateral problem between India and Pakistan. Nor is it a territorial dispute.' Secondly, the present LoC is an altered ceasefire line, whereby India acquired territory through military aggression in 1971. Therefore, accepting LoC would mean legitimising Indian military aggression. Thirdly, the LoC as accepted by both Pakistan and India at Simla in 1972 does not exist anymore. Indian incursion into Siachen in 1984 has destroyed the sanctity of the ceasefire line.

*Fourthly,* some Western scholars have proposed the partition of Kashmir along ethnic/cultural, religious, and linguistic lines. For example the *Kashmir Study Group*, a US-based group comprising academics and diplomats from various countries as members, has made various proposals along these lines in its report entitled, *Kashmir: A Way Forward* (September 1999). The proposals suggested are as follows:

*Two hypothetical sovereign entities, self-governing in all aspects, established on both sides of the Line of Control on cultural and linguistic grounds.* According to the study, 'On the Indian side of the LOC every tahsil in Kashmir proper and in Doda district in Jammu, and Gool Gulab Ghar tahsil in Udhampur district in Jammu would seek incorporation in the proposed state. All these areas are imbued with "Kashmiriyat" or interact with Kashmiri speaking people. On the Pakistani side it is conceivable that the whole of Azad Kashmir would opt to have a sovereign status. This is predominantly Punjabi-speaking, wholly Muslim area';

*A new sovereign state on the Indian side of LoC with no territorial exchange between India and Pakistan.* The state would include 'within its maximum potential area the whole of Kashmir proper as well as adjoining areas in which Kashmiri is either the majority language or that of a plurality of the population';

*Desirable territorial changes along and beyond the Line of Control in Jammu and Kashmir.*

Viewing that 'LoC is dysfunctional and has been violated innumerable times', it proposes that a new state be created with territorial exchanges between India and Pakistan. However, it proposes that Pakistan gives almost twice as much area (7,366 sq. km) to India, than India ceding territory (4,501 sq. km) to Pakistan. The rationale given for such an exchange is 'overall, the territorial adjustments should not be excessively disruptive of the established order and yet should appear significant and be of such a nature as to allow all parties to claim a victory.'

The above proposals are again not viable solutions, as they tend to complicate the situation in Jammu and Kashmir and result in a further division of the region, rather than leading to a stable solution. Moreover, the 'Kashmir Study Group's' proposals make no provision for the right of self-determination of the people of Kashmir to which presently a military struggle is underway by the Kashmiris in Indian-occupied Kashmir.

## The Independence Option

An option gradually evolved as a result of the impasse on the Kashmir issue is that of independence, generally known as the 'Third Option'. Under this option, the pre-Partition status of the Jammu and Kashmir State is to be restored and an independent state established. The proposal is mainly advocated by the JKLF. Its Chairman, Amanullah Khan, in one of his articles says, 'the future independent Kashmir is to be neutral, like Switzerland, with friendly and trade relations with all its neighbours.' According to Amanullah Khan's proposal, 'Independent Kashmir is to consist of five federating units: Kashmir Valley, Jammu province, Ladakh, Azad Kashmir and Gilgit-Baltistan, each enjoying considerable internal autonomy, having its own elected provincial government. At the centre there will be a bicameral parliament.' He further says, 'the re-unification and independence of the state can be brought about without making any drastic changes in the existing socio-economic, political and administrative structures of any of the present three units i.e. Indian occupied areas, Azad Kashmir and Gilgit-Baltistan.'

According to Indian scholars 'independence, either for part or all of J&K, is equally unrealistic. They maintain that although an artificial product of war, the Line of Control does follow a rough and ready ethno-cultural divide in some measure. Further, "self-determination" within the two parts of J&K could result in the Balkanisation of a mosaic put together by history, with every new 'self-determined' minority being assailed for a newly-created majoritarianism, which lesser minorities refuse to accept. Such an unravelling would be a recipe for strife, insecurity, and destabilisation of the region.'

The option for an independent Jammu and Kashmir state does not seem to be a viable solution, as the State would be land-locked and, therefore, permanently dependent on its neighbours. For India the proposition would be unacceptable because it could lead to a similar unravelling in other areas where separatist movements are going on in India.

As regards Pakistan, the 'third option' can be advantageous. An independent Jammu and Kashmir state would have a preference for good relations with a neighbour that has consistently extended its support to the principles of self-determination. Pakistan's position on the 'third option' has been that it should not confound the existent problems further, and, therefore, it stresses the need to address the issue in the light of the Security Council Resolutions, as a first step in the resolution of the dispute.

## The Irish Model

Recently, various scholars have suggested the Irish model, based on the 'Good Friday Agreement' signed in April 1998 between the Governments of the United Kingdom of Great Britain and Northern Ireland and the Government of Ireland, as a possible option for resolving the Kashmir dispute between India and Pakistan.

The main features of the 'Good Friday Agreement' are: (a) it recognises the consent principle: that change in the status of Northern Ireland can only come about with the consent of the majority of its people. It acknowledges that while a substantial minority in the North and a majority on the island want a united Ireland, the majority in the North currently wishes to maintain the Union. However, it says that if that situation changes, there is a binding obligation on both governments to give effect to whatever wish the people of the North express; (b) it recognises 'the birthright of all the people of Northern Ireland' to identify themselves and be accepted as Irish, British or both; (c) it proposes concrete legislative and constitutional changes; such as, the Government of Ireland Act, claiming British jurisdiction over all of Ireland is to be replaced, future polls in the North on its status are to be held on the order of the Secretary of State for Northern Ireland. Such polls must be at least seven years apart; (d) it proposes a 108-member Assembly elected by proportional representation; (e) it establishes a North-South Ministerial Council under legislation at Westminister and the Oireachtas, to bring together ministers from the North and the Republic; (f) it establishes a British-Irish Council consisting of representatives of the British and Irish Governments, devolved in situations in Northern Ireland, Scotland and Wales, the Isle of Man and the Channel Islands; (g) it establishes a new British-Irish Conference; (h) reaffirms commitment to the total disarmament of all paramilitary organisations, and confirms intention to work constructively with the Independent Commission on Decommissioning; and, (i) establishes an independent commission to make recommendations for future policing arrangements in the North.

Based on the Irish model, some Indian scholars have made suggestions supporting autonomy for various regions of Jammu and Kashmir. For example, Amit A. Pandya, an Indian scholar, has proposed the following steps: (1) An India-Pakistan commission to discuss boundary issues in Jammu and Kashmir, and to engage in joint monitoring of the LOC; (2) Phased demilitarisation at the LOC, contingent first on substantial cessation of 'cross-border' terrorism; (3) Three-way (Indian, Pakistani, Kashmiri) commission on internal law and order. Kashmiris to be chosen from Pakistan-occupied Azad Kashmir and all Indian-occupied segments—Valley, Jammu and Ladakh. (4) Indian and Pakistani commitments to proceed with a scheme of local government reform and strengthening of local institutions and local autonomy in respective areas of Kashmir. (5) Issue-specific consultative bodies (water, power, tourism, finance) comprising such local units, and Indian Jammu & Kashmir State and Azad Kashmir governments. (6) Regularly scheduled and publicity-free consultative mechanism for Indian government's talks with all parties, and with non-party civil society institutions, within Indian Kashmir on political issues. (7) Corresponding mechanism for Azad Kashmir. (8) Consultative mechanism for talks among all parties on ethnic and religious minority protections. (9) Consultative mechanism for dialogue between these processes on the Indian and Pakistani side of the LOC. (10) Indian commitment to allow free access, consistent with security requirements, to independent and credible Indian human rights monitoring organizations, and to Indian, and Pakistani press. Corresponding commitment by Pakistan for Azad Kashmir.

Another Indian scholar, Professor Sumantra Bose, basing his suggestions on the Irish model proposes three dimensions. *Dimension one: the New Delhi-Islamabad axis*, involving the 'establishment of a permanent India-Pakistan Intergovernmental Conference to promote the harmonious and mutually beneficial development of the totality of relationships between the two countries.' As suggested by Professor Bose, this body is to be chaired by the respective prime ministers, and its twice-yearly meetings to be rotated between Indian and Pakistani cities. *Dimension two: the New Delhi-Srinagar and Islamabad-Muzaffarabad axis,* here the 'objective in Kashmir would be the gradual, incremental normalisation of politics within Kashmir in both Indian-and Pakistani-controlled zones, and the devising and implementation of political frameworks which can foster a working degree of internal accommodation and cooperation between the representatives of communities holding radically different basic political allegiances.' *Dimension three: the Srinagar-Muzaffarabad axis,* proposes 'along with the progressive normalisation of the overall framework of India-Pakistan relations and the gradual normalisation of life and politics in both sides of the Kashmir border', that there is greater need to make the border porous. He further suggests 'the establishment of a cross-border Jammu and Kashmir Council for Cooperation, with representatives from inclusive, elected and autonomous governments from both sides of the line of control.'

These Indian proposals, selectively use the Irish model, but basically support autonomy for the regions of Jammu and Kashmir under the supervision of India and Pakistan. The central aspects focusing on self-determination and total disarmament after implementation of the agreement are ignored. The Indian proposals are similar to the idea of a condominium with dominant Indian influence. Also, the LoC has been proposed as the dividing line and a soft border. This is against the genesis of the Kashmir dispute, which is not for greater autonomy or 'self-government', as proposed, but for the right of self-determination to be expressed by the Kashmiris. However, as Dr. Mazari has suggested, it is the central aspects of the Irish model, which are relevant in case of the Kashmir dispute and could be used as guiding principles for a resolution of the conflict. For instance the underlying principle is *recognition of the right of the people as of Northern Ireland* to choose their political future through a referendum. Also, the principle of deweaponisation is linked to it, as following the implementation of the Agreement.

# 5

# Indo-Pakistani Wars

## HISTORY OF INDO-PAKISTANI WAR OF 1947

After rumours that the Maharaja supported the annexation of Kashmir by India, militant Muslim revolutionaries from western Kashmir and Pakistani tribesmen made rapid advances into the Baramulla sector. Maharaja Hari Singh of Kashmir asked the government of India to intervene. However, India and Pakistan had signed an agreement of non-intervention. Although tribal fighters from Pakistan had entered Jammu and Kashmir, there was no iron-clad legal evidence to unequivocally prove that Pakistan was officially involved. It would have been illegal for India to unilaterally intervene in an open, official capacity unless Jammu and Kashmir officially joined the Union of India, at which point it would be possible to send in its forces and occupy the remaining parts.

The Maharaja desperately needed military assistance when the Pakistani tribals reached the outskirts of Srinagar. Before their arrival into Srinagar, India argued that the Maharaja must complete negotiations for ceding Jammu and Kashmir to India in exchange for receiving military aid. The agreement which ceded Jammu and Kashmir to India was signed by the Maharaja and Lord Mountbatten of Burma. In Jammu and Kashmir, National Conference volunteers worked with the Indian Army to drive out the Pakistanis.

The resulting war over Kashmir, the First Kashmir War, lasted until 1948, when India moved the issue to the UN

Security Council. Sheikh Abdullah was not in favour of India seeking UN intervention because he was sure the Indian Army could free the entire State of invaders. The UN had previously passed resolutions for setting up monitoring of the conflict in Kashmir. Following the set-up of the United Nations Military Observer Group in India and Pakistan (UNCIP), the UN Security Council passed Resolution 47 on 21 April 1948. The resolution imposed an immediate cease-fire and called on the Government of Pakistan 'to secure the withdrawal from the state of Jammu and Kashmir of tribesmen and Pakistani nationals not normally resident therein who have entered the state for the purpose of fighting.' It also asked Government of India to reduce its forces to the minimum strength, after which the circumstances for holding a plebiscite should be put into effect 'on the question of Accession of the state to India or Pakistan.' However, both India and Pakistan failed to arrive at a Truce agreement due to differences in interpretation of the procedure for and extent of demilitarisation one of them being whether the Azad Kashmiri army is to be disbanded during the truce stage or the Plebiscite stage.

In November 1948, The Indian and Pakistani governments agreed to hold the plebiscite, but Pakistan did not withdraw its troops from Kashmir, thus violating the conditions for holding the plebiscite. In addition, the Indian Government distanced itself from its commitment to hold a plebiscite. India proposed that Pakistan withdraw all its troops first, calling it a precondition for a plebiscite. Pakistan rejected on the grounds that the Kashmiris may not vote freely given the presence of Indian army and Sheikh Abdullah's friendship with the Indian Prime Minister, Jawaharlal Nehru. However, Pakistan proposed simultaneous withdrawal of all troops followed by a plebiscite under international auspices, which India rejected. Hence Pakistan didn't withdraw its forces unilaterally In addition, the Indian Government distanced itself from its commitment to hold a plebiscite. Over the next several years, the UN Security Council passed four new resolutions, revising the terms of Resolution 47 to include a synchronous withdrawal of both Indian and Pakistani troops from the region, per the recommendations of General Andrew McNaughton. To this end, UN arbitrators put forward 11 different proposals for the demilitarization of the region. All of these were accepted by Pakistan, but rejected by the Indian government. The resolutions were passed by United Nations Security Council under Chapter VI of the United Nations Charter. Resolutions passed under Chapter VI of the UN charter are considered non-binding and have no mandatory enforceability, as opposed to the resolutions passed under Chapter VII.

### Sino-Indian War

In 1962, troops from the People's Republic of China and India clashed in territory claimed by both. China won a swift victory in the war, resulting in the Chinese annexation of the region called Aksai Chin, which has continued since then. Another smaller area, the Trans-Karakoram, was demarcated as the Line of Control (LOC) between China and Pakistan, although some of the territory on the Chinese side is claimed by India to be part of Kashmir. The line that separates India from China in this region is known as the "Line of Actual Control".

### 1965 and 1971 Wars

In 1965 and 1971, heavy fighting broke out again between India and Pakistan. The Indo-Pakistani War of 1971 resulted in the defeat of Pakistan and the Pakistani military's surrender in East Pakistan, leading to the creation of Bangladesh. The Simla Agreement was signed in 1972 between India and Pakistan. By this treaty, both countries agreed to settle all issues by peaceful means using mutual discussion in the framework of the UN Charter.

## THE SUBSEQUENT KASHMIR WAR (SEPTEMBER 1965)

Pakistan became frustrated with India's increasing attempts to integrate Kashmir into its fold. Embolded by a presumed victory against India in the Rann of Kutch in April 1965, Pakistan made plans for "Operation Gibraltar" to recover

Kashmir. As it did in 1947, it first sent Pakistani guerrillas into the Valley in August 1965 hoping that the Kashmiri Muslims would rise in rebellion against India. Instead, the guerrillas were apprehended and handed over to the Indian authorities. The situation worsened rapidly. On September 1, when Indian troops crossed the international border, Pakistan launched an attack on Jammu. In response, India launched a series of attacks through the state of Punjab toward Lahore, Pakistan, and battled the Pakistani army. As the clashes continued, the UN Security Council, supported by the United States, Britain, and the USSR, called for an immediate cease-fire, which India and Pakistan accepted on September 6. Although the war was brief, it was a bitter one. Neither country was a winner. In January of 1966, at the invitation of Soviet Premier Alexsei Kosygin, both Shastri and Khan met in the city of Tashkent (Republic of Uzbesistan) and signed the agreement known as the Tashkent Declaration. On January 10, the agreement was formalized and the hostilities ended followed by the withdrawal of the Indo-Pakistani forces to the previous cease-fire lines. Shastri died of a heart attack in Tashkent right Pakistan fought a third war over Bangladesh's Independence in which the Kashmir dispute was only a peripheral issue.

On July 2, 1972, Mrs. Gandhi signed the Simla agreement with Mr. Zulfikar Ali Bhutto, the first President and later Prime Minister of Pakistan who had succeeded the military dictator General Yahya Khan in 1971. Under this agreement, India and Pakistan, among others, committed themselves to "settling their differences through bilateral negotiations or by any other peaceful means mutually agreed upon between them," and that the "basic issues and causes which bedeviled the relations between the two countries for the last 25 years shall be resolved by peaceful means." They also agreed that in "Jammu and Kashmir, the Line of Control (LOC) resulting from the cease-fire of December 17, 1971, shall be respected by both sides without prejudice to the recognized position of either side." The agreement became the basis for the renewal of official relations between the two countries both at political and economic levels, thus ending any role for either the UN or outside powers including the US. On July 24, 1973, they both signed another agreement in New Delhi agreeing to repatriate all POW's except for 195 who were held to be tried but were later released without trial.

While it demanded a plebiscite in the Indian-part of Kashmir, Pakistan unilaterally detached Gilgit Agency and Baltistan from Azad Kashmir in 1974, and integrated them into Pakistan. This move ignored the UN Security Council's longstanding resolutions in the same fashion that India did when it had integrated Kashmir into her union in 1956. Pakistan and India also renewed diplomatic recognitions in 1976.

In 1968, following the end of the third Indo-Pakistani war, India released Sheikh Abdullah and his colleague, Mirza Afzal Beg, from jail unconditionally. Abdullah became reconciled to accepting Kashmir's accession to India as final. For example, on March 10, 1972, in an interview with *The Times* (London), he said, "our dispute with the government of India is not accession but it is the quantum of autonomy" for Kashmir. In June of the same year, the state government headed by Side Mir Passim lifted the ban on Abdullah's entry into Kashmir as he dropped the demand for a plebiscite. Beginning in 1974, he and Beg joined India in a series of negotiations. The negotiations between Mrs. Gandhi's special representative G. Parthasarathi and Beg resulted in a six-point accord called the Kashmir Accord signed by Abdullah on February 12, 1975. Abdullah agreed to Kashmir's status as a part of India while being allowed to enjoy special provisions for the state under Article 370. On February 25, 1975, Abdullah became the Chief Minister of the state replacing Qasim of the Congress Party. In July 1975, his party, the National Conference finally came into existence again. He governed the state until he died on September 21, 1982. His son, Dr. Farooq Abdullah, succeeded him. But Farooq joined by the influential Cleric Maulvi Farooq of the Awami Action Committee demanded autonomy, the kind that had been promised in the 1952 Delhi Agreement to his father. During the 1983 legislative elections despite Mrs. Gandhi's anger and her manipulation of the elections, he stressed this theme and won the election. Upset by his demand for autonomy, Mrs. Gandhi intervened in the domestic politics of the state and dismissed Abdullah's government in 1984, by engineering defections from his party led by his brother-in-law, G. M. Shah. She brought the state under central control (Presidential violence increased under his leadership, in the Valley and Jammu, between Muslims and Hindus allegedly encouraged by him, he was dismissed in 1986. In the same year, in a surprisingly *volte face*, perhaps, as a matter of expediency, Abdullah signed a deal with Mr. Rajiv Gandhi, the new Prime Minister, who had succeeded his mother following her assassination in June 1984. In June 1986, a coalition of National Conference and Congress was formed. This coalition won a landslide victory in the March 1987 elections but it did not help Abdullah to keep power for long. The election of 1990 resulted in Abdullah downfall following the outbreak of a Muslim uprising in 1989.

## INDO-PAKISTANI WAR OF 1965

The Indo-Pakistani War of 1965 was a culmination of skirmishes that took place between April 1965 and September 1965 between India and Pakistan. This conflict became known as the Second Kashmir War fought by India and Pakistan over the disputed region of Kashmir, the first having been fought in 1947. The war began following the failure of Pakistan's Operation Gibraltar, which was designed to infiltrate forces into Jammu and Kashmir to precipitate an insurgency against rule by India. The five-week war caused thousands of casualties on both sides. It ended in a United Nations (UN) mandated ceasefire and the subsequent issuance of the Tashkent Declaration.

Much of the war was fought by the countries' land forces in Kashmir and along the International Border between India and Pakistan. This war saw the largest amassing of troops in Kashmir since the Partition of India in 1947, a number that was overshadowed only during the 2001-2002 military standoff between India and Pakistan. Most of the battles were fought by opposing infantry and armored units, with substantial backing from air forces. Many details of this war, like those of other Indo-Pakistani Wars, remain unclear and many media reports have been riddled with media biases.

## PRE-WAR ESCALATION

Since Partition of India in 1947, Pakistan and India remained in contention over several issues. Although the Kashmir conflict was the predominant issue dividing the nations, other border disputes existed, most notably over the Rann of Kutch, a barren region in the Indian state of Gujarat. When Junagadh, a former princely state, had been integrated into India, whose muslim prince wanted to join Pakistan. On March 20, 1965, and again in April 1965, fighting broke out between India and Pakistan in the Rann of Kutch. Initially involving border police from both nations, the disputed area soon witnessed intermittent skirmishes between the countries' armed forces.

In June 1965, British Prime Minister Harold Wilson successfully persuaded both countries to end hostilities and set up a tribunal to resolve the dispute. The verdict, which came later in 1968, saw Pakistan awarded 350 square miles (900 $km^2$) of the Rann of Kutch, as against its original claim of 3500 square miles. After its success in the Rann of Kutch, Pakistan, under the leadership of General Ayub Khan, believed the Indian Army would be unable to defend itself against a quick military campaign in the disputed territory of Kashmir as the Indian military had suffered a loss to China in 1962.

Pakistan believed that the population of Kashmir was generally discontented with Indian rule and that a resistance movement could be ignited by a few infiltrating saboteurs. Pakistan attempted to ignite the resistance movement by means of a covert infiltration, codenamed Operation Gibraltar. The Pakistani infiltrators were soon discovered, however, their presence reported by local Kashmiris, and the operation ended in a complete failure.

Pakistan claimed to have been concerned by attempts of India to absorb Kashmir - a state claimed by Pakistan as "disputed", into the Indian Union. The basis for this claim was the application of Articles 356 and 357 of the Indian Constitution that allow the President of India to declare President's Rule in the State.

## THE WAR

On August 15, 1965, Indian forces crossed the ceasefire line and launched an attack on the region referred to by the disputants as either "Azad Kashmir" or "Pakistan-occupied Kashmir". Pakistani reports cite this attack as unprovoked, while Indian reports cite the attack as a response to massive armed infiltrations of Kashmir by Pakistan. Initially, the Indian Army met with considerable success, capturing three important mountain positions after a prolonged artillery barrage. By the end of August, however, both sides had experienced successes; Pakistan had made progress in areas such as Tithwal, Uri and Punch and India had captured the Haji Pir Pass, eight kilometers inside Pakistani-occuppied territory.

On September 1, 1965, Pakistan launched a counterattack, called "Operation Grand Slam", with the objective to capture the vital town of Akhnoor in Jammu, which would sever communications and cut off supply routes to Indian troops. Attacking with an overwhelming ratio of troops and technically superior tanks, Pakistan initially progressed against Indian forces, who were caught unprepared and suffered heavy losses. India responded by calling in its air force to blunt the Pakistani attack. The next day, Pakistan retaliated, its air force attacked Indian forces and air bases in both Kashmir and Punjab. Although Operation Grand Slam ultimately failed, as the Pakistan Army was unable to capture Akhnoor, it became one of the turning points in the war when India decided to relieve pressure on its troops in Kashmir by attacking Pakistan further south.

India crossed the International Border on the Western front on September 6, marking an official beginning of the war. On September 6, the 15th Infantry Division of the Indian Army, under World War II veteran Major General Prasad, battled a massive counterattack by Pakistan near the west bank of the Ichogil Canal (BRB Canal), which was a *de facto* border of India and Pakistan. The General's entourage itself was ambushed and he was forced to flee his vehicle. A second, this time successful, attempt to cross the Ichhogil Canal was made over the bridge in the village of Barki, just east of Lahore. These developments brought the Indian Army within the range of Lahore International Airport. As a result, the United States requested a temporary ceasefire to allow it to evacuate its citizens in Lahore.However,the Pakistani counter attack took Khem Karan from Indian forces which tried to divert the attention of Pakistanis from Khem Karan by an attack on Bedian and the adjacent villages.As said by Indian Lt. General Kaul,

"The C-in-C(Indian) got cold feet and decided, while the battle of Khem Karan was still in progress to take up an alternate position, several miles in the rear which would have meant giving up some well known and vital places and areas." (Kaul op. Cit. P478)

The thrust against Lahore consisted of the 1st Infantry Division supported by the three tank regiments of the 2nd Independent Armoured Brigade: they quickly advanced across the border, reaching the Ichhogil (BRB) Canal by 6 September. The Pakistani Army held the bridges over the canal or blew up those it could not hold, effectively stalling any further advance by the Indians on Lahore.One unit of the Jat Regiment, 3 Jat, had also crossed the Ichogil canal and captured the town of Batapore (Jallo Mur to Pakistan) on the west side of the canal. The same day, a counter offensive consisting of an armored division and infantry division supported by Pakistan Air Force Sabres forced the Indian 15th Division to withdraw to its starting point. Although 3 Jat suffered minimal casualties, the bulk of the damage being taken by ammunition and stores vehicles, the higher commanders had no information of 3 Jat's capture of Batapore and misleading information led to the command to withdraw from Batapore and Dograi to Ghosal-Dial. This move brought extreme disappointment to Lt-Col Desmond Hayde, CO of 3 Jat. Dograi was eventually recaptured by 3 Jat on 21 September, for the second time but after a much harder battle due to Pakistani reinforcements.

On the days following September 9, both nations' premiere formations were routed in unequal battles. India's 1st Armored Division, labelled the "pride of the Indian Army", launched an offensive towards Sialkot. The Division divided itself into two prongs, was forced back by the 6th armoured division(an understrength formation of few armoured regiments) at Chawinda and was forced to withdraw after suffering heavy losses of nearly 100 tanks. Similarly, Pakistan's pride, the 1st Armored Division, pushed an offensive towards Khemkaran, with the intent to capture Amritsar (a major city in Punjab, India) and the bridge on River Beas to Jalandhar. The Pakistani 1st Armored Division never made it past Khem Karan, however, and by the end of September 10 lay disintegrated by the defences of the Indian 4th Mountain Division at what is now known as the Battle of *Asal Uttar* (lit. meaning - "Real Answer", or more appropriate English equivalent - "Fitting Response"). The area became known as 'Patton Nagar' (Patton Town) as Pakistan lost or abandoned nearly 100 mostly US-made Patton tanks.The Pakistani 1st Armoured Division less 5th Armoured Brigade was next sent to Sialkot sector behind Pakistani 6th Armoured Division where it didnt see action as 6th Armoured Division was already in process of routing Indian 1st Armoured Division which was superior to it in strength.

The war was heading for a stalemate, with both nations holding territory of the other. The Indian army suffered 3,000 battlefield deaths, while Pakistan suffered no less than 3,800. The Indian army was in possession of 710 mile$^2$ (1,840 km$^2$) of Pakistani territory and the Pakistan army held 210 mile$^2$ (545 km$^2$) of Indian territory. The territory occupied by India was mainly in the fertile Sialkot, Lahore and Kashmir sectors, while Pakistani land gains were primarily in deserts opposite Sindh and in Chumb, in the northern sector.

## Aerial Warfare

The war saw the Indian Air Force and the Pakistani Air Force engaged in full scale combat for the first time since independence. Though the two forces had previously faced off in the First Kashmir War during the late 1940s, that engagement was limited in scale compared to the 1965 conflict. The two countries have made contradictory claims of combat losses during the war and hardly any neutral sources have verified the claims of either country. The Pakistan Air Force (PAF) claimed it shot down 104 IAF planes, losing only 19 in the process. The Indian Air Force (IAF) claimed it shot down 24 PAF planes, losing only 75 itself.[18] India also pointed out that, despite PAF claims of losing only a squadron of combat craft, Pakistan sought to acquire additional aircraft from Indonesia, Iraq, Iran, Turkey and China within 10 days of the beginning war.

Pakistan's strike force comprised the U.S. made F-86 Sabre jets, which claimed a fair share of Indian planes, though remaining vulnerable to the diminutive Folland Gnat, nicknamed "Sabre Slayer".[19] The F-104 Starfighter of the PAF was by far the fastest fighter plane operating in the subcontinent at that time. Unlike the PAF, whose planes largely consisted of American craft, the IAF flew an assortment of planes, from Vampires to Hawker Hunters, many of which were outdated in comparison to PAF planes.

## Tank Battles

The 1965 war witnessed some of the largest tank battles since World War II. At the beginning of the war, the Pakistani Army had both a numerical advantage in tanks, as well as better equipment overall. Pakistani armour was largely American-made; it consisted mainly of Patton M-47 and M-48 tanks, but also included many M4 Sherman tanks, some M24 Chaffee light tanks and M36 Jackson tank destroyers, equipped with 90 mm guns. The bulk of India's tank fleet were older M4 Sherman tanks; some were up-gunned with the French high velocity CN 75 50 guns and could hold their own, whilst some older models were still equipped with the inferior 75 mm M3 L/40 gun. Besides the M4 tanks, India fielded the British-made Centurion Tank Mk 7, with the 105 mm Royal Ordnance L7 gun, and the AMX-13, PT-76, and M3 Stuart light tanks.

Pakistan fielded a greater number and more modern artillery; its guns out-ranged those of the Indian artillery, according to Pakistan's Major General T.H. Malik.

At the outbreak of war in 1965, Pakistan had about 15 armoured cavalry regiments, each with about 45 tanks in three squadrons. Besides the Pattons, there were about 200 M4 Shermans re-armed with 76mm guns, 150 M24 Chaffee light tank and a few independent squadrons of M36B1 tank destroyers. Most of these regiments served in Pakistan's two armoured divisions, the 1st and 6th Armoured divisions - the latter being in the process of formation. The Indian Army of the time possessed 17 cavalry regiments, and in the 1950s had begun modernizing them by the acquisition of 164 AMX-13 light tanks and 188 Centurions. The remainder of the cavalry units were equipped with M4 Shermans and a small number of M3A3 Stuart light tanks. India had only a single armoured division, the 1st 'Black Elephant' Armoured Division, also called 'Fakhr I Hind' ('Pride of India'), which consisted of the 17th cavalry Poona Horse, the 4th Hodson's Horse, the 16th 'Black Elephant' Cavalry, the 7th Light Cavalry, the 2nd Royal Lancers, the 18th Cavalry and the 62nd Cavalry, the two first named being equipped with Centurions,. There was also the 2nd Independent Armoured Brigade, one of whose three regiments, the 3rd Cavalry, was also equipped with Centurions.

Despite the qualitative and numerical superiority of Pakistani armour, Pakistan was outfought on the battlefield by India, which made progress into the Lahore-Sialkot sector, whilst halting Pakistan's counteroffensive on Amritsar they were sometimes employed in a faulty manner, such as charging prepared defenses during the defeat of Pakistan's 1st Armored Division at Assal Uttar.

India's tank formations experienced same results. India's attack at the Battle of Chawinda, led by its 1st Armored Division and supporting units, was brought to a grinding halt by newly raised 6th Armoured Division(ex-100th indepedant brigade group) in the Chawinda sector. The Pakistanis pushed the Indians back farther after the Battle of Chawinda with Operation

Windup. One true winner to emerge was India's Centurion battle tank, with its 105 mm gun and heavy armor, which proved superior to the overly complex Pattons and their exaggerated reputations..However, in the Sialkot sector outnumbered Pattons performed exceedingly well in the hands of the 25th Cavalry and other regiments of the 6th Armoured Division, which exacted a disproportionately heavy toll of Centurions from the Poona Horse and Hodson's Horse.

The Indian Army has made much of the fact that some of its Centurions survived repeated hits; yet have failed to point out that the majority of tanks in the Sialkot sector were Shermans whose guns were inadequate even in 1944. Neither the Indian nor Pakistani Army showed any great facility in the use of armoured formations in offensive operations, whether the Pakistani 1st Armoured Division at Asal Uttar or the Indian 1st Armoured Division at Chawinda. In contrast, both proved adept with smaller forces in a defensive role such a the 2nd Armoured Brigade at Asal Uttar and the 25th Cavalry at Chawinda, where they defeated their better equipped but clumsier foes

## Naval Hostilities

The navies of India and Pakistan did not play a prominent role in the war of 1965, although Pakistani accounts dispute this. On September 7, a flotilla of the Pakistani Navy carried out a small scale bombardment of the Indian coastal town and radar station of Dwarka, which was 200 miles (300 km) south of the Pakistani port of Karachi. Codenamed Operation Dwarka, it did not fulfill its primary objective of disabling the radar station and there was no immediate retaliatory response from India. Later, some of the Indian fleet sailed from Bombay to Dwarka to patrol the area and deter further bombardment. Foreign authors have noted that the "insignificant bombardment" of the town was a "limited engagement, with no strategic value."

According to some Pakistani sources, one submarine, PNS Ghazi, kept the Indian Navy's aircraft carrier INS Vikrant besieged in Bombay throughout the war. Indian sources claim that it was not their intention to get into a naval conflict with Pakistan, and wished to restrict the war to a land-based conflict. Moreover, they note that the Vikrant was in dry dock in the process of refitting. Some Pakistani defence writers have also discounted claims that the Indian Navy was bottled up in Bombay by a single submarine, instead stating that 75% of the Indian Navy was under maintenance in harbour. There were, however, unconfirmed reports of underwater attacks near Bombay by the Indian Navy against what they suspected were American-supplied Pakistani submarines.

## Covert Operations

The Pakistan Army launched a number of covert operations to infiltrate and sabotage Indian airbases.[30] On September 7, 1965, the Special Services Group (SSG) commandos were parachuted into enemy territory. According to Chief of Army Staff General Musa Khan, about 135 commandos were airdropped at three Indian airfields(Halwara, Pathankot and Adampur). The daring attempt proved to be an "unmitigated disaster". Only 22 commandos returned to Pakistan as planned, 93 were taken prisoner (including one of the Commanders of the operations, Major Khalid Butt), and 20 were killed in encounters with the army, police or civilians The reason for the failure of the commando mission is attributed to the failure to provide maps, proper briefings and adequate planning or preparation.

Despite failing to sabotage the airfields, Pakistan sources claim that the commando mission affected some planned Indian operations. As the Indian 14th Division was diverted to hunt for paratroopers, the Pakistan Air Force found the road filled with transport, and destroyed many vehicles.

India responded to the covert activity by announcing rewards for captured Pakistani spies or paratroopers. Meanwhile, in Pakistan, rumors spread that India had retaliated with its own covert operations, sending commandos deep into Pakistan territory, but these rumors were later determined to be unfounded.

## Losses

India and Pakistan make widely divergent claims about the damage they inflicted on each other and the amount of damage suffered by them. The following summarizes each nation's claims.

- According to the United States Library of Congress Country Studies: The war was militarily inconclusive; each side held prisoners and some territory belonging to the other. Losses were relatively heavy—on the Pakistani side, twenty aircraft, 200 tanks, and 3,800 troops. Pakistan's army had been able to withstand Indian pressure, but a continuation of the fighting would only have led to further losses and ultimate defeat for Pakistan. Most Pakistanis, schooled in the belief of their own martial prowess, refused to accept the possibility of their country's military defeat by "Hindu India" and were, instead, quick to blame their failure to attain their military aims on what they considered to be the ineptitude of Ayub Khan and his government.
- TIME magazine analyzing the conflict, reported that India held 690 $Mi^2$ of Pakistan territory while Pakistan held 250 $Mi^2$ of Indian territory in Kashmir and Rajasthan, Pakistan had lost almost half its armour temporarily. The same article stated that 'severely mauled by the larger Indian armed forces, Pakistan could continue the fight only by teaming up with Red China and turning its back on the U.N'.
- An excerpt from Stanley Wolpert's *India* summarizing the Indo-Pakistani War of 1965, is as follows: In three weeks the second IndoPak War ended in what appeared to be a draw when the embargo placed by Washington on U.S. ammunition and replacements for both armies forced cessation of conflict before either side won a clear victory. India, however, was in a position to inflict grave damage to, if not capture, Pakistan's capital of the Punjab when the cease-fire was called, and controlled Kashmir's strategic Uri-Poonch bulge, much to Ayub's chagrin.

- Dennis Kux's *"India and the United States estranged democracies"* also provides a summary of the war. Although both sides lost heavily in men and materiel, and neither gained a decisive military advantage, India had the better of the war. New Delhi achieved its basic goal of thwarting Pakistan's attempt to seize Kashmir by force. Pakistan gained nothing from a conflict which it had instigated.
- Newsweek magazine, however, praised the Pakistani military's ablility to hold of the much larger Indian Army. "By just the end of the week, in fact, it was clear that the Pakistanis were more than holding their own."

## Ceasefire

On September 22, the United Nations Security Council unanimously passed a resolution that called for an unconditional ceasefire from both nations. The war ended the following day.

The Soviet Union, led by Premier Alexey Kosygin, hosted ceasefire negotiations in Tashkent (now in Uzbekistan), where Indian Prime Minister Lal Bahadur Shastri and Pakistani President Ayub Khan signed the Tashkent Agreement, agreeing to withdraw to pre-August lines no later than February 25, 1966. The ceasefire was criticized by many Pakistanis who, relying on official reports and the controlled Pakistani press, believed that the leadership had surrendered military gains. The protests led to student riots. Pakistan State's reports had suggested that their military was performing admirably in the war - which they incorrectly blamed as being initiated by India - and thus the Tashkent Declaration was seen as having forfeited the gains. Some recent books written by Pakistani authors, including one by ex-ISI chief titled "The Myth of 1965 Victory", allegedly exposed Pakistani fabrications about the war, but all copies of the book were bought by Pakistan Army to prevent publication because the topic was "too sensitive".

India and Pakistan accused each other of ceasefire violations; India charged Pakistan with 585 violations in 34 days, while Pakistan countered with accusations of 450 incidents by India. In addition to the expected exchange of small arms and artillery fire, India reported that Pakistan utilized the ceasefire to capture the Indian village of Chananwalla in the Fazilka sector. This village was recaptured by Indian troops on 25 December. On October 10, a B-57 Canberra on loan to the PAF was damaged by 3 SA-2 missiles fired from the IAF base at Ambala A Pakistani Army Auster was shot down on 16 December, killing one Pakistani army captain and on 2 February 1967, an AOP was shot down by IAF Hunters. The ceasefire remained in effect until the start of the Indo-Pakistani War of 1971.

## Intelligence Failures

Strategic miscalculations by both India and Pakistan ensured that the war ended in a stalemate.

## Indian Miscalculations

Indian military intelligence gave no warning of the impending Pakistan invasion. The Indian Army failed to recognize the presence of heavy Pakistani artillery and armaments in Chumb and suffered significant losses as a result.

The "Official History of the 1965 War", drafted by the Ministry of Defence of India in 1992, was a long suppressed document that revealed other miscalculations. According to the document, on September 22 when the Security Council was pressing for a ceasefire, the Indian Prime Minister asked commanding Gen. Chaudhuri if India could possibly win the war, were he to delay accepting the ceasefire. The general replied that most of India's frontline ammunition had been used up and the Indian Army had suffered considerable tank losses. It was determined later that only 14% of India's frontline ammunition had been fired and India held twice the number of tanks as Pakistan. By this time, the Pakistani Army had used close to 80% of its ammunition.

Air Chief Marshal (retd) P.C. Lal, who was the Vice Chief of Air Staff during the conflict, points to the lack of coordination between the IAF and the Indian army. Neither side revealed its battle plans to the other. The battle plans drafted by the Ministry of Defence and General Chaudhari, did not specify a role for the Indian Air Force in the order of battle. This attitude of Gen. Chaudhari was referred to by ACM Lal as the "Supremo Syndrome", a patronizing attitude sometimes held by the Indian army towards the other branches of the Indian Military.

## Pakistani Miscalculations

The Pakistani Army's failures started with the supposition that a generally discontented Kashmiri people, given the opportunity provided by the Pakistani advance, would revolt against their Indian rulers, bringing about a swift and decisive surrender of Kashmir. The Kashmiri people, however, did not revolt. Instead, the Indian Army was provided with enough information to learn of Operation Gibraltar and the fact that the Army was battling not insurgents, as they had initially supposed, but Pakistani Army regulars.

The Pakistani Army also failed to recognize that the Indian policy makers would order an attack on the southern sector in order to open a second theater of conflict. Pakistan was forced to dedicate troops to the southern sector to protect Sialkot and Lahore instead using them to support penetrating into Kashmir.

"Operation Grand Slam", which was launched by Pakistan to capture Akhnoor, a town north-east of Jammu and a key region for communications between Kashmir and the rest of India, was also a failure. Many Pakistani commentators criticized the Ayub Khan administration for being indecisive during Operation Grand Slam. These critics claim that the operation failed because Ayub Khan knew the importance of Akhnur to India (having called it India's "jugular vein") and did not want to capture it and drive the two nations into an all-out war. Despite progress being made in Akhnur, General Ayub Khan relieved the commanding Major General Akhtar Hussain Malik and replaced him with Gen. Yahya Khan. A 24-hour lull ensued the replacement, which allowed the Indian army to regroup in Akhnur and successfully oppose a lackluster attack headed by General Yahya Khan. "The enemy came to our rescue", asserted the Indian Chief of Staff of the Western Command. Later, Akhtar Hussain Malik criticized Ayub Khan for planning Operation Gibraltar, which was doomed to fail, and for relieving him of his command at a crucial moment in the war. Malik threatened to expose the truth about the war and the army's failure, but later dropped the idea for fear of being banned.

Some authors have noted that Pakistan might have been emboldened by a war game - conducted in March 1965, at the Institute of Defence Analysis, USA. The exercise concluded that, in the event of a war with India, Pakistan would win. Other authors like Stephen Philip Cohen, have consistently commented that the Pakistan Army had "acquired an exaggerated view of the weakness of both India and the Indian military... the 1965 war was a shock".

Pakistani Air Marshal and Commander-in-Chief of PAF during the war, Nur Khan, later said that the Pakistan Army, and not India, should be blamed for starting the war. However propaganda in Pakistan about the war continued; the war was not rationally analyzed in Pakistan, with most of the blame being heaped on the leadership and little importance given to intelligence failures that persisted until the debacle of the 1971 war, when Pakistan suffered a decisive defeat at the hands of India, leading to the creation of Bangladesh.

## Involvement of other Nations

The United States of America, which had previously supplied military equipment to India and Pakistan, imposed an embargo against further supplies to both countries once the war had started. The US was apprehensive that military equipment that it had provided to be used in a battle against communism, would instead be used by the countries to fight one another. The American embargo especially affected Pakistan since the majority of its equipment was provided by America. This would cause Pakistan to believe that it could not continue the war beyond September. Following imposition of the American embargo, other NATO allies (including the UK) discontinued providing military equipment to the nations.

Both before and during the war, China had been a major military associate of Pakistan and had invariably admonished India, with whom it had fought a war in 1962. There were also reports of Chinese troop movements on the Indian border to support Pakistan. As such, India agreed to the UN mandate in order to avoid a war on both borders. India's participation in the Non-Aligned Movement yielded little support from its members. Pakistan, however, gained assistance from countries of Asia with large Islamic populations, including Turkey, Iran and Indonesia. The USSR was more neutral than most other nations during the war and even invited both nations to talks that it would host in Tashkent.

## THIRD INDO-PAK WAR WAS FOUGHT IN 1971

The peace, however, was short-lived. The third Indo-Pak war was fought in 1971 over the issue of former East-Pakistan and the creation of Bangladesh. The political division of Pakistan as East Pakistan became the sovereign and independent Bangladesh was another humiliating defeat that affected Indo-Pak relations as recalcitrance over Kashmir grew and became a prime contest for national pride and prestige. 1971 saw the signing of the Simla Treaty which cemented the border between PoK and Indian Kashmir as an international border that would be respected by both sides as any other international territorial confine (Varshney 1013). This border has come to be known as the Line of Contol (LoC) which frequently experiences border skirmishes and cross-fires.

In the midst of this growing Indo-Pak political animosity, there has also been a progressively intensifying discontent and disillusionment of the Kashmiri people against the Indian government. There has been an increasingly popular insurgency movement since December 1989 in Kashmir as various ideological groups claim the right to an independent state and oppose Indian rule in Kashmir (Ganguly, 1996, 76). These include the Jammu and Kashmir Liberation Front (JKLF), Hizb-ul-Mujahideen, and Lashkar-e-Toiba (LET) among others. During the rise and high points of the insurgency in the 1990s, Islamic insurgency groups were actively supported by Pakistan. "Almost every shop in the main bazaar of every town, large or small, in Pakistan had a Lashkar collection box to raise funds for the struggle in Kashmir" ("Profile..." 2006). If I may jump ahead in my historical analysis for a brief moment, it would be pertinent to point out that the 11th July 2006 co-ordinated attacks on the Mumbai metro system were carried out by LET ("Asia..." 2006). Many of these insurgent groups aim not only for the freedom of Kashmir from Indian rule but also to extend Islamic rule to India. They also benefit immensely from the chaotic political situation in Kashmir because it provides them with a huge bulk of a vulnerable population with enough grievances to recruit to fight for their ideologies.

The insurgency has only soured Indo-Pak relations further and in most cases delayed bilateral talks between the two countries. Further, since the September 11th attacks on the US and the global war on terror, Pakistan has been pressured to clamp down on these terrorist groups. President Musharraf has banned LET and three other terrorist groups although "after the ban [his] government did not try to break up Lashkar but it restricted the movements of its leaders and the group members were told to keep a low profile" ("Profile...").

Ganguly (1996) argues that there are two main reasons for the rise and steady presence of the insurgency in Kashmir which extends its violent nature into the rest of India. As the Indian government promoted development of its states through education, a new generation of young Kashmiris were made more cognizant of their rights and called for political mobilisation and the freedom of Kashmir (80). This was also accompanied by a "deinstitutionalisation of politics in the state, which drove the expression of political discontent into extra-institutional contexts" – mainly insurgent groups (80). The insurgency has undoubtedly embittered Indo-Pak relations and led to an intensification of the security threat that both feel. The insecurity of the region was heightened in 1998 when India announced its nuclear capability with Pakistan following soon after. Both have also not signed the Nuclear Non-Proliferation Treaty (NPT). Since then both countries have increased their defence budgets despite a number of sanctions in light of the nuclear tests (Ganguly & Biringer, 908).

With the Indian subcontinent now nuclear, the threat of the Kashmir conflict began to attract increasing international concern. Both India and Pakistan trudged along the path of uncompromised ideals. However, 1999 began with the Indian prime minister Atal Bihari Vajpayee taking an historic bus trip to Lahore on the invitation of then Pakistani premier Nawaz Sharif (Kapur, 195). There was much celebration as the Indian and Pakistani PMs exchanged garlands of flowers and the local people cheered. Hopes for a real peace building effort were rekindled. Countless Indians and Pakistanis forced to move at the time of partition dreamed of going back to their ancestral homes. Five decades after the conflict began, there seemed to be a real chance that the political process would move forward and there would a real attempt at a cessation of hostilities. However, deeply-rooted historical conflicts with identities, political interests, and national pride at stake are rarely forgotten with an unusual bus ride into enemy territory.

While political niceties between the Indian and Pakistani leaderships were going on, Parvez Musharraf, then chief of the Pakistani army, was planning an incursion into Indian territory by Pakistani troops and Kashmiri militants in an effort that was reminiscent of the 1965 war.

The LoC passes through extremely rugged territory among the craggy slopes of the Himalayan range with impassable weather for most of the year. There had been a tacit agreement between India and Pakistan that certain areas of the LoC would be unmanned during the peak of winter with the expectation that neither side would take advantage of this vulnerability and respect the international border ("War..."). The hope was that the Indian army would not detect the infiltrators until May which they didn't. This gave the Pakistani army and militants considerable time to occupy strategic positions along the LoC. The main Srinagar-Leh national highway was in clear range which gave them tactical advantage as it was the only route the army had to the higher reaches of the border between India and Pakistan. Had the incursion been successful, the LoC would have inevitably been redefined because India would not have been able to fight back with its only highway connecting them to the infiltrators being manned by the infiltrators themselves.

The Indian offensive was launched on 26th May 1999 and called Operation Vijay (victory). Patriotism was flying high as India was deeply offended by the under-handed infiltration with a clear goal of redefining the international border and claiming Indian territory. The war ended with India successfully pushing back the infiltrators across the original LoC and Pakistan condemned by the international community for what was a clear act of unprovoked aggression and infiltration into Indian territory. Soon after, Musharraf led a military coup against Prime Minister Sharif and declared himself President. With mistrust high between the two countries and the demise of democracy in Pakistan, any diplomatic progress that had been made toward peace was stalled.

September 11th brought the Indo-Pak conflict over Kashmir back into the limelight as the US pressured Pakistan into banning terrorist organisations and providing refuge for the Taliban. The Indian and Pakistani people share a common history and a hard struggle against colonialism. Yet they were separated along religion which can be a deeply contentious identity issue. I would argue that the Kashmir conflict between India and Pakistan is deeply rooted in identity and emotion. The pride of the Indian and Pakistani people relies on the future of Kashmir. The insurgency has shown that what the Kashmiris themselves want is independence and autonomy. Thus, you have the three main stakeholders in the conflict at cross-purposes, each fighting for a non-negotiable national identity. It is no wonder that this is a classically defined intractable conflict.

But to define the stakeholders as simply the Pakistanis, the Indians, and the Kashmiris would naturally be too simplistic and belie the complexity of the conflict. The promised plebiscite to the Kashmiris is long overdue; there isn't even a permanent provision for the state in the Indian constitution. However, the state of Jammu and Kashmir consists of three distinct territories with three diverse religious populations. The Kashmir conflict makes them all important stakeholders especially as most of the people living there have lived their lives under constant threat of violence. The future of Kashmir will determine not only the future of the Kashmiris, but also the people of Ladakh, Jammu, and other parts of J&K. An important question that needs to be asked is what an independent Kashmir would mean for the rest of the state.

The Kashmir conflict has also inflamed religious animosity between Hindus and Muslims in India which threatens the secularity that the country proudly claims. The 1992 Mumbai and 2002 Gujarat Hindu-Muslim riots horrified not only the international community but also the Indian population. India was reminded of the deep cleavages in its population. The Hindu nationalist party (BJP) in government at the time was undoubtedly threatening to a significant size of the population. Though the majority of Indians are Hindus, on account of sheer size of the population, India has a fair number of Muslims, Christians, and Buddhists among other religions. The Kashmir conflict threatens the delicate balance that the diversely secular Indian population lives in. Military insurgency groups such as the LET are increasingly attempting to ruin this balance in hopes for a resolution to Kashmir. The 2005 bombings in a public market in New Delhi during the festive celebrations of the Hindu festival of Diwali and the Muslim festival of Eid-ul-Fitr and the 2006 Mumbai metro bombings by the LET were strategically implemented to fracture religious communities and tolerance in India and weaken the Indian government.

## THE 1971 INDIA-PAKISTAN WAR

On the 3rd of December 1971, the Pakistani Air Force (PAF) struck a number of Indian airfields in northern India. By midnight, India was officially at war with Pakistan. Two weeks later, the war was over. The Indian Army had overrun erstwhile East Pakistan (Bangladesh) and taken 93,000 POWs. It was one of the swiftest military campaigns in recent history.

### The Setting

The partition of the Indian Subcontinent in 1947 created two independent countries: India and Pakistan. India, which became independent on 15 August 1947, stood for a secular, equitable polity based on the universally accepted idea that all men are created equal and should be treated as such. Pakistan, which officially came into existence a day earlier, was based on the premise that Hindus and Muslims of the Subcontinent constitute two different nationalities and cannot co-exist. The Partition created two different countries with most Muslim majority areas of undivided India going to the newly created nation, Pakistan (Land of the Pure). Pakistan was originally made up of two distinct and geographically unconnected parts termed West and East Pakistan. West Pakistan was made up of a number of races including the Punjabis (the most numerous), Sindhis, Pathans, Balochis, Mohajirs (Muslim refugees from India) and others. East Pakistan, on the other hand, was much more homogeneous and had an overwhelming Bengali-speaking population.

## The Roots of Discord

Although the Eastern wing of Pakistan was more populous than than the Western one, political power since independence rested with the Western elite. This caused considerable resentment in East Pakistan and a charismatic Bengali leader called, Sheikh Mujibur Rehman, most forcefully articulated that resentment by forming an opposition political party called the Awami League and demanding more autonomy for East Pakistan within the Pakistani Federation. In the Pakistani general elections held in 1970, the Sheikh's party won the majority of seats, securing a complete majority in East Pakistan. In all fairness, the Sheikh should have been Prime Minister of Pakistan, or at least the ruler of his province. But West Pakistan's ruling elite were so dismayed by the turn of events and by the Sheikh's demands for autonomy that instead of allowing him to rule East Pakistan, they put him in jail.

## Origins of the Crisis

The dawn of 1971 saw a great human tragedy unfolding in erstwhile East Pakistan. Entire East Pakistan was in revolt. In the West, General Yahya Khan, who had appointed himself President in 1969, had given the job of pacifying East Pakistan to his junior, General Tikka Khan. The crackdown of 25 March

1971 ordered by Tikka Khan, left thousands of Bengalis dead and Sheikh Mujibur Rehman was arrested the next day. The same day, the Pakistani Army began airlifting two of its divisions plus a brigade strength formation to its Eastern Wing. Attempts to dis-arm Bengali troops were not entirely successful and within weeks of the 25 March massacres, many former Bengali officers and troops of the Pakistani Army had joined Bengali resistance fighters in different parts of East Pakistan.

The Pakistani Army conducted several crackdowns in different parts of Bangladesh, leading to massive loss of civilian life. The details of those horrific massacres, in which defenceless people were trapped and machine-gunned, is part of Bangladeshi history. Survivors compare it to the Nazi extermination of Jews. At the same time, the Pakistani Administration in Dhaka thought it could pacify the Bengali peasantry by appropriating the land of the Hindu population and gifting it to Muslims. While this did not impress the peasantry, it led to the exodus of more than 8 million refugees (more than half of them Hindus) to neighbouring India. West Bengal was the worst affected by the refugee problem and the Indian government was left holding the enormous burden. Repeated appeals by the Indian government failed to elicit any response from the international community and by April 1971, the then Indian Prime Minister, Mrs. Indira Gandhi, decided that the only solution lay in helping Bengali freedom fighters, especially the Mukti Bahini, to liberate East Pakistan, which had already been re-christened Bangladesh by its people.

Pakistan felt it could dissuade India from helping the Mukti Bahini by being provocative. The Pakistan Air Force (PAF) in East Pakistan took to attacking suspected Mukti Bahini camps located inside Indian territory in the state of West Bengal. In the Western and Northern sectors too occasional clashes, some of them quite bloody, took place.

Pakistan was suggesting that should India continue with its plans it should expect total war as in 1965. Only this time, the Pakistanis would concentrate their forces in the West and thereby aim at capturing as much as Indian territory as possible. The Indians, on the other hand, would be fighting a war on two fronts (while at the same time keeping a fearful eye on the Chinese borders). Given this scenario, the Pakistanis felt that India at best would be able to capture some territory in East Pakistan and lose quite a bit in the West. In the end, the Pakistanis knew that the Western powers would intervene to stop the war and what would matter is who had the most of the other's territory.

Confident that another war would be as much of a stalemate as the 1965 Conflict, the Pakistanis got increasingly bold and finally on 3 December 1971 reacted with a massive co-ordinated air strike on several Indian Air Force stations in the West. At midnight, the Indian Prime Minister Mrs. Indira Gandhi in a broadcast to the nation declared that India was at war with Pakistan. As her words came on in million of Indian homes across the Subcontinent, the men at the front were already engaged in bitter combat...

## PAF Strikes

For all practical purposes, the war started at about 5:40 pm on 3 December when Pakistan Air Force (PAF) combat aircraft struck nine Indian airfields along the Western borders. The air strikes were followed by a massive attack on the strategic Chhamb sector in the north. In the East, it was the Indian Army which went on the offensive. By late that night, artillery shells were raining down all along the Western and Eastern borders. India and Pakistan were locked in a two-front war.

In the West, the Indian Army had very limited offensive aims and was relegated more to a holding role. The initiative lay with Pakistan. In this theatre, Pakistan had near parity with India in armour and artillery while India had more infantry divisions. Pakistan's most successful thrust was in Chhamb where the 23rd Pakistani Division (along with two additional infantry brigades, one extra armoured brigade and Corps artillery units) under the able leadership of Major General Iftikhar Khan completely overwhelmed the forward defensive positions of the Indian 10 Division commanded by Major General Jaswant Singh.

Chhamb village was taken and the Pakistanis threatened to advance towards Jammu, the summer capital of the state of Jammu & Kashmir. Heavy fighting continued in this sector for a week until the indecisiveness of the Indian Divisional commander forced the Indian Corps Commander to intervene personally and launch heavy attacks to push the Pakistanis back to a non-threatening position. The Pakistanis surprisingly failed to take advantage of their initial successes in this sector and actually depleted the forces available to their commander, who was killed on 10 December in a helicopter crash.

Acting in accordance with its strategy to grab as much territory in the West as possible, Pakistan also launched a major attack on Punch in the state of Jammu & Kashmir. This attack, unlike the one on Chhamb, was completely repulsed, although here the Indian Army was at a locational disadvantage since the Pakistanis controlled the heights around the town. Smaller attacks were launched by Pakistan in Punjab at Fazilka and Hussainiwala. Here the forward Indian defences were breached but the Pakistani Army could not sustain its attacks. A more ambitious armoured thrust in the deserts of Rajasthan was similarly stopped in the famous Battle of Longewal. In all, it appeared that the Pakistani military high command could not make up its mind as to where it should deliver its main punch and kept pulling back until it was too late.

The Indian Army chief, General Sam Maneckshaw, had a completely different set of problems. His strategy had to take into account the Chinese, with whom the Indian Army had fought a full blown war only nine years earlier. The Chinese were now firm Pakistani allies and had been making threatening noises ever since India resolved to intervene in the East Pakistan issue. General Maneckshaw, despite the disappointment of his Corps and divisional commanders, had to hold back his Army in the West, keep a watchful eye on the long and difficult Chinese borders and, at the same time, ensure that his Eastern Army secured its objective of grabbing a good chunk of East Pakistani territory within 2 to 3 weeks. The Indian aim was to install a Bangladeshi interim government in East Pakistani territory before the cessation of hostilities. It was not all clear in the beginning whether things would work out quite the way as planned.

## MODEST AIMS, AMBITIOUS ACTION

One of the less remarked upon aspects of the 1971 war was the varied character of the key men who planned and executed the operations. Best known was of course the flamboyant Indian Army Chief, General Sam Maneckshaw, a Parsee who had won the Military Cross in WW II.

To the Indian public, it was General Maneckshaw with his twirled moustache, Gorkha cap and baton, who was the symbolic hero. Yet, there were below him, an equally varied and extraordinary set of men, who planned and executed their own battles.

The Western Army was commanded by an Anglo-Indian Lt. Gen. K.P.Candeth and the Eastern Army, headquartered at Calcutta, by a Sikh, Lt. Gen. J.S.Aurora. General Aurora's a brilliant Chief of Staff was Major. Gen. J.F.R.Jacob, the scion of an old Jewish family of Calcutta. Together these men planned and executed the lightning operations of December 1971.

The 4th morning saw Indian forces and Mukti Bahini guerrillas ready for battle with the Pakistanis, who were by now well dug in and waiting for the Indian assault. The Indian forces easily outnumbered the Pakistanis by a ratio of about 2:1. However, according to conventional infantry wisdom, an attacking Army requires a three-is-to-one superiority in numbers to attack. India did not have that. Besides, the Pakistani Army commander in the East, General A.A.K.Niazi, was determined merely to delay the Indian advance. For, in this war, the real battle was against time. The longer it took the Indian to secure their limited objectives, the greater the probability of the United Nations intervening to stop the war and effect a stalemate. Pakistan was confident that a stalemate was all that the Indians could get. Towards this strategy, General Niazi, had fortified the towns and approaches to the East Pakistani heartland and had boasted before the war began that should hostilities begin, he would take the battle inside India.

The brief given by the Indian Army chief, General Maneckshaw, to the Eastern Command was very limited. The aim was to occupy only two areas of East Pakistan - Chittagong and Khulna - so that an interim Bangladeshi government could be established. The capture of the whole of East Pakistan was not even conceived. A major problem was the geography and terrain of East Pakistan. Three major rivers - the Brahmaputra, the Ganga and the Meghna - divided East Pakistan into four natural regions. Each of the rivers were major ones - all of them wider than any European river. Each sub-region was further divided into several pockets cut by smaller rivers and their tributaries. The idea that an attacking army could bridge these, fight the enemy and then take territory, all within a couple of weeks, was ludicrous.

Lt. General Aurora's Chief of Staff, Major General Jacob, however, did not entirely agree with the Indian Army top brass. "I think the aim of the government was to take as much territory as possible in East Pakistan so as to establish an Bangladeshi government in their own territory," he recalled in an interview with SAPRA INDIA. "Army Headquarters issued an operations instruction according to which our main objectives were to take Chittagong and Khulna ports, which were termed the entry ports. But we at Eastern Command felt differently. We felt that Dhaka was the geo-political centre of Bangladesh and therefore any campaign to be successful had to capture Dhaka."

The Eastern Command went ahead with its own plans, although Army Headquarters felt it was too ambitious and could not be achieved. Jacob's commander, Lt. Gen. Aurora, provided full support for his Army's own plans and allowed Jacob to pull down troops kept in reserve for a possible attack by the Chinese. Some of these troops had to be brought into battle so hurriedly that the only way was to paradrop them. This was accomplished with the help of the IAF and soon soldiers geared to fight the Chinese in the high mountains found themselves in the tropical riverine areas of Tangail in East Pakistan.

"We realised that any campaign to be successful had to be swift. The United Nations was putting great pressure on us and also the Russians had indicated that they did not want to exercise their veto any more," Jacob explained.

"Therefore any campaign had to be quick. We realised that Niazi (the Pakistani Army commander in East Pakistan) was going to fortify the towns and defend them in strength. We therefore decided not attack any towns but bypass them using subsidiary tracks to get to our objective: Dhaka."

The immense practical problem of moving thousands of troops and tonnes of equipment across rivers and marshes was accomplished largely due to the efforts of the Army Corps of Engineers, and with a lot of local help.

The IAF chipped in by using helicopters to lift entire battalions across larger rivers that could not be quickly bridged by the Engineers. In most places, the swiftly moving contingents quickly overcame enemy resistance and moved forward. The Pakistanis for the most part, were completely taken by surprise.

Within 6 days of the war, Indian troops were deep inside East Pakistani territory and moving fast. The Mukti Bahini section of the advancing forces played a crucial role in guiding the Indian Army through the treacherous riverine areas and providing critical intelligence. It is doubtful whether the Indian Army could have moved so fast and decisively without the help of the Bangladeshis. At any rate, by the seventh day of the war, the Pakistani Army High Command, headquartered in Rawalpindi, was in a complete panic.

## Using Sea Power

The 1971 war was the first, and only, occasion when the Indian political leadership exhibited a proper understanding of the use of military power for achieving a clear national aim. In past conflicts, Indian leaders either had no clear aim in mind and were merely reacting to events or they were confused about how best to use the military power available to them. During the 1962 India-China war, for instance, the Indian government ordered the Indian Air Force to withdraw its fighter bomber squadrons from the north east and not to hit the invading Chinese.

IAF bombers could have changed the course of the 1962 war had it been allowed to hit the thin and tenuous Chinese logistics lines. Similarly, in the 1965 India-Pakistan conflict, the Navy was ordered to keep its ships in port and not engage in any offensive action against Pakistan. The Pakistani Navy was given a free hand and it managed to lob a few shells at one point in the Western Coast. The Indian Navy's chance to see some action came only in 1971 December.

Since East and West Pakistan were two separate geographical entities more than 1,600 miles apart, the only way Pakistani forces in East Pakistan could be sustained was through the sea. The Indian Prime Minister, Mrs. Indira Gandhi, decided that the Navy would be given the strategic task of denying both East and West Pakistan access to war supplies. The aim in short was a complete naval blockade of both parts of Pakistan. The bigger aim was of course to ensure that the conflict was not perpetuated beyond the time required to capture a chunk of East Pakistani territory.

The Indian Navy's best and biggest warship at that time was its sole aircraft carrier, INS Vikrant, a carefully preserved World War II vintage carrier built in Britain. Ideally, a task force centred around the Vikrant should have been used to block Karachi, which at that time was West Pakistan's sole deep water port. However, one of Vikrant's main boilers was out of operation and the ship could not maintain the kind of speed required for manoeuvring in a situation where the air threat would be considerable. It was decided that the Vikrant would be used to blockade the ports in East Pakistan, and destroy the riverine craft used by the Pakistanis there.

## Vikrant in Action

The day war was declared, the Vikrant, which had been anchored off the northern-most tip of the Andaman & Nicobar chain of islands, moved towards the principal East Pakistani port, Chittagong. The Pakistanis, having learnt that Vikrant was positioned in the Bay of Bengal, despatched one of their submarines, PNS Ghazi, to the east. The Pakistani submarine thought it could sneak into Vizag harbour, the principal naval port in the Indian east coast. It was, however, detected and sunk before it could cause any damage. The Vikrant continued unhindered. Rear Admiral (retired) P.D.Sharma, who was then an aviator aboard the Vikrant, recalls what it was like:

"Fighter pilots practice for years and when they finally get an opportunity to see real action, it is thrilling - it is the moment one has been waiting for all one's life. And it was so for us aboard the Vikrant on 4th December 1971...

"The first sortie was mounted against Cox's Bazaar. Eight Sea Hawks went in led by the squadron commander. I was in the second sortie which attacked Chittagong. This was in the afternoon of the 4th because it took some time for the Vikrant to close in the range to Chittagong.

"We went in low level, pulled up and carried out repeated attacks on the airfield. In the first attack itself we inflicted considerable damage. We withdrew for the night and sailed towards the Mangla-Khulna area. Our next attacks were on those harbours. Then we came back to Chittagong. And by the time we were through with that area, especially Chittagong harbour, Chittagong airfield and the approaches to Chittagong, the scene was something to be seen. The place had been devastated. There were ships that had turned turtle, there were half-sunk ships by the quay side, the airfield was pockmarked with craters and no ship could even think of approaching the place."

## THE ATTACK ON KARACHI

The most dramatic naval plan was drawn up by the Western Naval Command. It was decided that the main attack on Karachi harbour would be launched by tiny PT-15 missile boats instead of regular warships. There were several reasons for this decision. Regular ships without air cover would be vulnerable whereas the tiny missile boats would present difficult, fast-moving targets. Moreover, the Navy wanted to try out the missiles to see how effective they could be in real action, although this kind of use of missile boats, which were designed for coastal defence and not for long range offensive action of any kind, was highly unorthodox. At any rate, three missile boats were chosen for the mission and despatched in the dead of night from Bombay harbour.

Leading the missile boat squadron was Commodore (Retired) Babru Bahan Yadav:"The task given to us was not easy. Our ships were little more than boats and did not have the range to go all the way to Karachi on their own steam. So an oiler was placed about half-way to the target and we were able to refuel and carry on.

"As we neared their coast, we found some of their ships patrolling the area. The boat on my left was detailed to engage the contact. That boat was the first Indian warship to fire a missile in anger. Two missiles were fired and both were direct hits. It is interesting to recall that the radar contact which was on our screen slowly diminished and then suddenly disappeared. We were very jubilant at that time. Later, we found that this has been a Pakistani destroyer.

Very soon another ship was located right in front of my boat. We fired a couple of missiles as well but did not sink it. The boat on our right was ordered to attack the ship. It did so and managed to cripple it completely. We thought we had sunk it but later the Pakistanis claimed that the ship had been badly crippled and put out of action but not sunk. Anyway, as we continued, both the other boats could not keep up and had to turn back. Only Nipat, the boat I was on, could proceed towards Karachi harbour. We pressed on and fired missiles on Karachi which hit the oil installations there. The attack took place just 1 minute before midnight and we could see the flames from the oil installations lighting up the sea. It looked like Diwali (Indian festival of lights and firecrackers)."

It took a few more days for Commodore Yadav's boat to return to harbour as they had to take evasive action and ran out of fuel. In the meanwhile, the Pakistanis who were hunting for the boat put out a message that an Indian vessel had been sunk. Nipat, the only boat not accounted for at that time, was presumed sunk. But Nipat returned, thanks to the ingenuity of its engineers who managed to take out pump oil and use it to run the engines.

The Indian Navy accomplished the task assigned to it within the first few days of the war. No enemy shipping could move in or out of its harbours. Merchant ships did not dare approach Karachi. Control of the seas around both wings of Pakistan was with the Indian Navy.

## KARGIL WAR

Before the Partition of India in 1947, Kargil was part of the Baltistan district of Ladakh, a sparsely populated region with diverse linguistic, ethnic and religious groups, living in isolated valleys separated by some of the world's highest mountains. The First Kashmir War (1947–48) concluded with the Line of Control (LOC) bisecting the Baltistan district, with the town and district of Kargil lying on the Indian side in the Ladakh subdivision of the Indian state of Jammu and Kashmir. After Pakistan's defeat in the Indo-Pakistani War of 1971, the two nations signed the Simla Agreement promising not to engage in armed conflict with respect to that boundary.

The town of Kargil is located 205 km (120 miles) from Srinagar, facing the Northern Areas across the LOC. Like other areas in the Himalayas, Kargil has a temperate climate. Summers are cool with frigid nights, while winters are long and chilly with temperatures often dropping to "48 °C ("54 °F).

An Indian national highway (NH 1) connecting Srinagar to Leh cuts through Kargil. The area that witnessed the infiltration and fighting is a 160 km long stretch of ridges overlooking this highway. The military outposts on the ridges above the highway were generally around 5,000 metres (16,000 ft) high, with a few as high as 5,485 metres (18,000 ft). Apart from the district capital, Kargil, the populated areas near the front line in the conflict included the Mushko Valley and the tiny town of Drass, southwest of Kargil, as well as the Batalik sector and other areas, northeast of Kargil.

One of the reasons why Kargil was targeted was that the terrain surrounding it, lent itself to pre-emptive seizure of unoccupied military positions. With tactically vital features and well-prepared defensive posts atop the peaks, a defender of the high ground would enjoy advantages akin to a fortress.

Any attack to dislodge a defender from high ground in mountain warfare requires a far higher ratio of attackers to defenders, and the difficulties would be exacerbated by the high altitude and freezing temperatures.

Kargil was also just 173 km (108 mi) from the Pakistani-controlled town of Skardu, which was capable of providing logistical and artillery support to Pakistani combatants. In addition to these tactical advantages, the Kargil district had a Muslim majority, which may have led Pakistani forces to expect local support for the infiltration as it had been expected in Operation Gibraltar.

## BACKGROUND

After the Indo-Pakistani War of 1971, there had been a long period with relatively few direct armed conflicts involving the military forces of the two neighbors - notwithstanding the efforts of both nations to control the Siachen Glacier by establishing military outposts on the surrounding mountains ridges and the resulting military skirmishes in the 1980s.

During the 1990s, however, escalating tensions and conflict due to separatist activities in Kashmir, some of which were supported by Pakistan, as well as the conducting of nuclear tests by both countries in 1998, led to an increasingly belligerent atmosphere. In an attempt to defuse the situation, both countries signed the Lahore Declaration in February 1999, promising to provide a peaceful and bilateral solution to the Kashmir conflict.

During the winter of 1998 -1999, some elements of the Military of Pakistan were covertly training and sending Pakistani troops and paramilitary forces, some allegedly in the guise of mujahideen, into territory on the Indian side of the LOC. The infiltration was code named "Operation Badr"; its aim was to sever the link between Kashmir and Ladakh, and cause Indian forces to withdraw from the Siachen Glacier, thus forcing India to negotiate a settlement of the broader Kashmir dispute.

Pakistan also believed that any tension in the region would internationalise the Kashmir issue, helping it to secure a speedy resolution. Yet another goal may have been to boost the morale of the decade-long rebellion in Indian Administered Kashmir by taking a proactive role. Some writers have speculated that the operation's objective may also have been as a retaliation for India's Operation Meghdoot in 1984 that seized much of Siachen Glacier.

According to India's then army chief Ved Prakash Malik, and many other scholars, much of the background planning, including construction of logistical supply routes, had been undertaken much earlier. On several occasions during the 1980s and 1990s, the army had given Pakistani leaders (namely Zia ul Haq and Benazir Bhutto) similar proposals for infiltration into the Kargil region, but the plans had been shelved for fear of drawing the nations into all-out war.

Some analysts believe that the blueprint of attack was reactivated soon after Pervez Musharraf was appointed chief of army staff in October 1998. After the war, Nawaz Sharif, Prime Minister of Pakistan during the Kargil conflict, claimed that he was unaware of the plans, and that he first learned about the situation when he received an urgent phone call from Atal Bihari Vajpayee, his counterpart in India. Sharif attributed the plan to Musharraf and "just two or three of his cronies", a view shared by some Pakistani writers who have stated that only four generals, including Musharraf, knew of the plan. Musharraf, however, asserted that Sharif had been briefed on the Kargil operation 15 days ahead of Vajpayee's journey to Lahore on February 20.

## War Progress

There were three major phases to the Kargil War. First, Pakistan infiltrated forces into the Indian-controlled section of Kashmir and occupied strategic locations enabling it to control NH1. The next stage consisted of India discovering the infiltration and mobilizing forces to respond to it. The final stage involved major battles by Indian and Pakistani forces resulting in India capturing positions held by Pakistani forces and the withdrawal of Pakistani forces back across the Line of Control.

## OCCUPATION BY PAKISTAN

During the winter season, due to extreme cold in the mountainous areas of Kashmir, it was a common practice for both the Indian and Pakistan Armies to abandon some forward posts on their respective sides of the LOC and to reduce patrolling of areas that may be avenues of infiltration. When weather conditions became less severe, forward posts would be reoccupied and patrolling resumed. During February 1999, the Pakistan Army began to re-occupy the posts it had abandoned on its side of the LOC in the Kargil region, but also sent forces to occupy some posts on the Indian side of the LOC.

Troops from the elite Special Services Group as well as four to seven battalions of the Northern Light Infantry (a paramilitary regiment not part of the regular Pakistani army at that time) covertly and overtly set up bases on the vantage points of the Indian-controlled region. According to some reports, these Pakistani forces were backed by Kashmiri guerrillas and Afghan mercenaries. Pakistani intrusions took place in the heights of the lower Mushkoh valley, along the Marpo La ridgeline in Dras, in Kaksar near Kargil, in the Batalik sector east of the Indus river, the heights above of the Chorbatla sector where the LC turns North as well in the Turtok sector south of the Siachen area.

## INDIA DISCOVERS INFILTRATION AND MOBILIZES

Initially, these incursions were not detected for a number of reasons: Indian patrols were not sent into some of the areas infiltrated by the Pakistani forces and heavy artillery fire by Pakistan in some areas provided cover for the infiltrators. But by the second week of May, the ambushing of an Indian patrol team, acting on a tip-off by a local shepherd in the Batalik sector, led to the exposure of the infiltration. Initially with little knowledge of the nature or extent of the encroachment, the Indian troops in the area assumed that the infiltrators were jihadis and claimed that they would evict them within a few days.

Subsequent discovery of infiltration elsewhere along the LoC, and the difference in tactics employed by the infiltrators, caused the Indian army to realize that the entire plan of attack was on a much bigger scale. The total area seized by the ingress is generally accepted to between 130 km$^2$ - 200 km$^2$; Musharraf however, stated that 500 square miles (1,300 km$^2$) of Indian territory was occupied.

The Government of India responded with Operation Vijay, a mobilisation of 200,000 Indian troops. However, because of the nature of the terrain, division and corps operations could not be mounted; the scale of the subsequent fighting was mostly at the regimental or battalion level. In effect, two divisions of the Indian Army, numbering 20,000, plus several thousand from the Paramilitary forces of India and the air force were deployed in the conflict zone.

The total number of Indian soldiers that were involved in the military operation on the Kargil-Drass sector was thus close to 30,000. The number of infiltrators, including those providing logistical backup, has been put at approximately 5,000 at the height of the conflict. This figure includes troops from Pakistan-administered Kashmir that were involved in the war providing additional artillery support. The Indian Air Force launched Operation Safed Sagar in support of the mobilization of Indian land forces, but its effectiveness during the war was limited by the high altitude, which in turn limited bomb loads and the number of airstrips that could be used.

The Indian Navy also readied itself for an attempted blockade of Pakistani ports (primarily Karachi port) to cut off supply routes. Later, the then-Prime Minister of Pakistan Nawaz Sharif disclosed that Pakistan was left with just six days of fuel to sustain itself if a full-fledged war had broken out.

## INDIA ATTACKS PAKISTANI POSITIONS

The terrain of Kashmir is mountainous and at high altitudes; even the best roads, such as National Highway No. 1 (NH 1) from Leh to Srinagar, are only two lanes. The rough terrain and narrow roads slowed traffic, and the high altitude, which affected the ability of aircraft to carry loads, made control of NH 1A (the actual stretch of the highway which was under Pakistani fire) a priority for India. From their observation posts, the Pakistani forces had a clear line-of-sight to lay down indirect artillery fire on NH 1A, inflicting heavy casualties on the Indians. This was a serious problem for the Indian Army as the highway was its main logistical and supply route. The Pakistani shelling of the arterial road posed the threat of Leh being cut off, though an alternative (and longer) road to Leh existed via Himachal Pradesh.

The infiltrators, apart from being equipped with small arms and grenade launchers, were also armed with mortars, artillery and anti-aircraft guns. Many posts were also heavily mined, with India later stating to having recovered more than 8,000 anti-personnel mines according to an ICBL report. Pakistan's reconnaissance was done through unmanned aerial vehicles and AN/TPQ-36 Firefinder radars supplied by the US. The initial Indian attacks were aimed at controlling the hills overlooking NH 1A, with high priority being given to the stretches of the highway near the town of Kargil. The majority of posts along the Line of Control were adjacent to the highway, and therefore the recapture of nearly every infiltrated post increased both the territorial gains and the security of the highway. The protection of this route and the recapture of the forward posts were thus *ongoing objectives* throughout the war.

The Indian Army's first priority was to recapture peaks that were in the immediate vicinity of NH1a. This resulted in Indian troops first targeting the Tiger Hill and Tololing complex in Dras, which dominated the Srinagar-Leh route. This was soon followed by the Batalik-Turtok sub-sector which provided access to Siachen Glacier. Some of the peaks that was of vital strategic importance to the Pakistani defensive troops were

Point 4590 and Point 5353. While 4590 was the nearest point that had a view of NH1a, point 5353 was the highest feature in the Dras sector, allowing the Pakistani troops to observe NH1A. The recapture of Point 4590 by Indian troops on June 14 was significant, notwithstanding the fact that Point 4590 resulting in the Indian Army suffering the most casualties in a single battle during the conflict. Though most of the posts in the vicinity of the highway were cleared by mid-June, some parts of the highway near Drass witnessed sporadic shelling until the end of the war.

Once India regained control of the hills overlooking NH 1A, the Indian Army turned to driving the invading force back across the Line of Control. The Battle of Tololing, among other assaults, slowly tilted the combat in India's favor. Nevertheless, some of the posts put up a stiff resistance, including Tiger Hill (Point 5140) that fell only later in the war. A few of the assaults occurred atop hitherto unheard of peaks – most of them unnamed with only Point numbers to differentiate them – which witnessed fierce hand to hand combat.

As the operation was fully underway, about 250 artillery guns were brought in to clear the infiltrators in the posts that were in the line-of-sight. The Bofors field howitzer (infamous in India due to the Bofors scandal) played a vital role, with Indian gunners making maximum use of the terrain that assisted such an attack. However, its success was limited elsewhere due to the lack of space and depth to deploy the Bofors gun. It was in this type of terrain that aerial attacks were used with limited effectiveness. The IAF lost a MiG-27 strike aircraft which it attributed to an engine failure as well as a MiG-21 fighter which was shot down by Pakistan; Pakistan said it shot down both jets after they crossed into its territory and one Mi-8 helicopter to Stinger SAMs. During attacks the IAF used laser-guided bombs to destroy well-entrenched positions of the Pakistani forces.

In many vital points, neither artillery nor air power could dislodge the outposts manned by the Pakistan soldiers, who were out of visible range. The Indian Army mounted some direct frontal ground assaults which were slow and took a heavy toll given the steep ascent that had to be made on peaks as high as 18,000 feet (5,500 m). Since any daylight attack would be suicidal, all the advances had to be made under the cover of darkness, escalating the risk of freezing.

Accounting for the wind chill factor, the temperatures were often as low as “11 °C to “15 °C (12 °F to 5 °F) near the mountain tops. Based on military tactics, much of the costly frontal assaults by the Indians could have been avoided if the Indian Military had chosen to blockade the supply route of the opposing force, virtually creating a siege. Such a move would have involved the Indian troops crossing the LoC as well as initiating aerial attacks on Pakistan soil, a manoeuvre India was not willing to exercise fearing an expansion of the theatre of war and reducing international support for its cause.

Two months into the conflict, Indian troops had slowly retaken most of the ridges they had lost; according to official count, an estimated 75%–80% of the intruded area and nearly all high ground was back under Indian control.

## AFTERMATH

### India

From the end of the war until February 2000, the Indian stock market rose by over 30%. The next Indian national budget included major increases in military spending.

There was a surge in patriotism, with many celebrities expressing their support for the Kargil cause. Indians were angered by media reports of the death of pilot Ajay Ahuja, especially after Indian authorities reported that Ahuja had been murdered and his body mutilated by Pakistani troops. The war had produced higher than expected fatalities for the Indian military, with a sizeable percentage of them including newly commissioned officers. One month after conclusion of the Kargil war, the Atlantique Incident - where a Pakistan Navy plane was shot down by India - briefly reignited fears of a conflict between the two countries.

After the war, the Indian government severed ties with Pakistan and increased defence preparedness. India increased its defence budget as it sought to acquire more state of the art equipment. Media reported about military procurement irregularities and criticism of intelligence agencies like RAW, which failed to predict the intrusions or the identity/number of infiltrators during the war.

An internal assessment report by the armed forces, published in an Indian magazine, showed several other failings, including "a sense of complacency" and being "unprepared for a conventional war" on the presumption that nuclearism would sustain peace. It also highlighted the lapses in command and control, the insufficient troop levels and the dearth of large-calibre guns like the Bofors. In 2006, retired Air Chief Marshal, A.Y. Tipnis, alleged that the Indian Army did not fully inform the government about the intrusions, adding that the army chief Ved Prakash Malik, was initially reluctant to use the full strike capability of the Indian Air Force, instead requesting only helicopter gunship support. Soon after the conflict, India also decided to complete the project- previously stalled by Pakistan - to fence the entire LOC.

The end of the Kargil conflict was followed by the 13th Indian General Elections to the Lok Sabha, which gave a decisive mandate to the NDA government. It was re-elected to power in September–October 1999 with a majority of 303 seats out of 545 in the Lok Sabha. On the diplomatic front, Indo-U.S. relations improved, as the United States appreciated Indian attempts to restrict the conflict to a limited geographic area. Relations with Israel – which had discreetly aided India with ordnance supply and matériel such as unmanned aerial vehicles and laser-guided bombs, as well as satellite imagery – also were bolstered.

## Pakistan

Faced with the possibility of international isolation, the already fragile Pakistani economy was weakened further. The morale of Pakistani forces after the withdrawal declined as many units of the Northern Light Infantry suffered heavy casualties, and the government refused to acknowledge the dead bodies of its soldiers, an issue that provoked outrage and protests in the Northern Areas. Pakistan initially did not acknowledge many of its casualties, but Sharif later said that over 4,000 Pakistani troops were killed in the operation and that Pakistan had lost the conflict. Responding to this, Pakistan President Pervez Musharraf said, "It hurts me when an ex-premier undermines his own forces," and claimed that Indian casualties were more than that of Pakistan.

Many in Pakistan had expected a victory over the Indian military based on Pakistani official reports on the war, but were dismayed by the turn of events and questioned the eventual retreat. The military leadership is believed to have felt let down by the prime minister's decision to withdraw the remaining fighters. However, some authors, including ex-CENTCOM Commander Anthony Zinni, and ex-PM Nawaz Sharif, state that it was General Musharraf who requested Sharif to withdraw the Pakistani troops.

With Sharif placing the onus of the Kargil attacks squarely on the army chief Pervez Musharraf, there was an atmosphere of uneasiness between the two. On October 12, 1999, General Musharraf staged a bloodless *coup d'état*, ousting Nawaz Sharif. Benazir Bhutto, an opposition leader and former prime minister, called the Kargil War "Pakistan's greatest blunder". Many ex-officials of the military and the ISI (Pakistan's principal intelligence agency) also believed that "Kargil was a waste of time" and "could not have resulted in any advantage" on the larger issue of Kashmir.

A retired Pakistani Army General, Lt Gen Ali Kuli Khan, lambasted the war as "a disaster bigger than the East Pakistan tragedy", adding that the plan was "flawed in terms of its conception, tactical planning and execution" that ended in "sacrificing so many soldiers." The Pakistani media criticized the whole plan and the eventual climbdown from the Kargil heights since there were no gains to show for the loss of lives and it only resulted in international condemnation.

Despite calls by many, no public commission of inquiry was set up in Pakistan to investigate the people responsible for initiating the conflict. The PML(N) published a white paper in 2006, which stated that Nawaz Sharif constituted an inquiry committee that recommended a court martial for General Pervez Musharraf, but Musharraf "stole the report" after toppling the government, to save himself. The report also claims that India knew about the plan 11 months before its launch, enabling a complete victory for India on military, diplomatic and economic fronts. A statement in June, 2008 by a former army corps commander of Pakistan that Sharif "was never briefed by the army" on the Kargil attack, reignited the demand for a probe of the episode by legal and political groups.

Though the Kargil conflict had brought the Kashmir dispute into international focus – which was one of the aims of Pakistan– it had done so in negative circumstances that eroded its credibility, since the infiltration came just after a peace process between the two countries was underway. The sanctity of the LOC too received international recognition. President Clinton's move to ask Islamabad to withdraw hundreds of armed militants from Indian-administered Kashmir was viewed by many in Pakistan as indicative of a clear shift in US policy against Pakistan.

After the war, a few changes were made to the Pakistan army. In recognition of the Northern Light Infantry's performance in the war - which even drew praise from a retired Indian Lt. General - the regiment was incorporated into the regular army. The war showed that despite a tactically sound plan that had the element of surprise, little groundwork had been done to gauge the politico-diplomatic ramifications.

And like previous unsuccessful infiltrations attempts, such as *Operation Gibraltar*, which sparked the 1965 war, there was little coordination or information sharing among the branches of the Pakistan military. One U.S. Intelligence study is reported to have stated that Kargil was yet another example of Pakistan's (lack of) grand strategy, repeating the follies of the previous wars.

# 6

# China's Relationship with Pakistan and Conflict Sino-indian Relations

China's relationship with Pakistan touches on three sensitive issues that are of great importance to India's national security, namely territory and borders, nuclear issues, and access to the Indian Ocean. When the United States imposed sanctions on Pakistan following the country's nuclear test in 1998, China stepped in to become the country's largest arms supplier and helped Pakistan develop an indigenous weapons industry. Even more importantly, China played a crucial role in Pakistan's acquisition of nuclear weapons.

More recently China's strategic and commercial objectives have come to the fore in its decision to develop a port at Gwadar in Pakistan (which is located about 180 nautical miles from the Strait of Hormuz), adding credibility to claims that China is attempting to encircle India. Similarly, China's ambiguous position on the Kashmir conflict—and the fact China's acquired territory in Pakistani-administered Kashmir—makes it party to the conflict and adds to India's lingering suspicions about Chinese intentions. It has been argued in the past that China, through its relationship with Pakistan, seeks to contain India and maintain its status as a regional, sub-continental power, and no more. But as Pakistan's relations with the United States worsen while India's relations with the United States improve, the rules of the game may be changing. In the Sino-Pakistan relations it has been the strong military ties and the issue of Kashmir that disturb India most. In this context China needs to manage the relationship with Pakistan in a proper manner so as not to arouse too many misgivings in New Delhi. At the same time, China's own stakes in Pakistan also need understanding from India. Pakistan is China's door to the Islamic world and an important partner in the battle against Islamic extremism. Pakistan's location is also significant for China in securing energy routes for its economic development, and, at the strategic level, Pakistan is an important balancing card to play in India-China-U.S. equations.

From the Indian point of view, China's relations with Pakistan have contributed to a deterioration in regional stability by enabling Pakistan to counter-balance India by developing nuclear weapons and missiles. More recently, the access that China has gained through Gwadar to the Indian Ocean is likely to accelerate the emerging rivalry. While China may have had the leverage in the past to restrain or discourage Pakistan from engaging in or perpetuating hostile relations with India, it has either not been able to or has chosen not to encourage Pakistan to engage constructively in resolving major regional security issues, choosing instead to maintain a low profile, as seen for example in Afghanistan.

In South Asia, some believe, China has implemented a more balanced policy since the 1990s. It has taken into account the perception of India to develop relations with other South Asian countries. Some observers note that China has taken a relatively neutral position on the sensitive issues between India and Pakistan since then.

Over the years, the Sino-Indian relationship has also acquired an independent dynamism and cannot be easily hamstrung by the strong alliance between China and Pakistan. The drive of India-China ties comes from within each country—the need to further economic development and to forge better understanding. The two, despite their differences, are destined for deeper economic interdependence.

Relations in the Sino-Pakistan-India triangle can be best described as contained volatility. With each of these countries armed with nuclear weapons and beset with fragile inter-community relations that spill over into terrorism, the imperative for institutionalizing dialogue and mutual understanding has never been stronger.

## CHINA-PAKISTAN RELATIONSHIP

For China, Pakistan is essentially a surrogate army. Owing to traditional military rivalry, India has for decades maintained a Pakistan centric strategic policy which keeps its military tied up and limits its options against China. According to Husain Haqqani, of Carnegie Endowment for International Peace, "For China, Pakistan is a low-cost secondary deterrent to India". "For Pakistan, China is a high-value guarantor of security against India." In this mutually beneficial friendship however, owing to Pakistan's limited strategic capability against India, China is essentially a needed ally, while China does not necessarily rely on Pakistan. China-Pakistan relations are diverse, and the Chinese have a strong investment presence in Pakistan. According to Jing Huang, senior fellow in Asia Studies at the Brookings Institution, "Pakistan would welcome investments from China more than anywhere else because Chinese are our brothers and time-tested friends". The two countries have cooperated on a variety of large-scale infrastructure projects in Pakistan, including highways, gold and copper mines, major electricity complexes and power plants, and numerous nuclear power projects. Pakistan helps China on a range of issues, including "providing intelligence, fighting terrorism, and repairing relations with the Muslim world".

However, this strategic relationship has adopted a sinister dimension of proliferation of sensitive nuclear and missile technology to Pakistan. Commercially, as China began its economic reform and opening up in the early 1980s, defence industries and arms exporting companies were under tremendous pressure to tap into the lucrative international arms market. Pakistan became a valued customer for Chinese arms. Finally, given US concern about and emphasis on missile proliferation issues, Beijing has also found it useful to exploit them as bargaining leverage in dealing with Washington on issues important to China: US arms sales to Taiwan, TMD deployment in East Asia, among others. American intelligence reports have alleged that China has transferred complete M-11 missiles, missile related technology, and manufacturing assistance to Pakistan.

The M-11 is a single stage, solid fuelled missile with a reported range of 290 km and a payload of 800 kg. While technically the M-11 missile does not fall within the MTCR parameter, they have the inherent capability of being able to deliver a 500 kg payload over 300 km. The fact that China has resisted joining the MTCR as a formal member, coupled with its ambiguous interpretation and implementation of its bilateral commitments with the United States, raises questions as to the seriousness of Chinese commitment to arms control and nonproliferation.

Significantly, some news reports suggest Chinese security agencies knew about Pakistani transfers of nuclear technology to Iran, North Korea, and Libya. China also had longstanding ties with Abdul Qadeer Khan, known as the father of the Pakistani nuclear program, and head of an international black market nuclear network. "The Pakistani nuclear program is largely the result of Sino-Pakistani relations" says Huang.

China-Pakistan nuclear cooperation began in the early 1980s. The United States government and many Western analysts believe that China assisted Pakistan in developing nuclear explosives prior to its accession to the NPT in 1992. In 1983, US intelligence agencies reported that China had transferred a complete nuclear weapon design to Pakistan, along with enough weapons-grade uranium for two nuclear weapons. China also reportedly helped Pakistan operate its Kahuta uranium-enrichment plant. According to media reports the amount transferred was enough for making 10 nuclear weapons

China also provided assistance and transferred dual-use materials that could be applied in the development of nuclear weapons. Beijing insists that China's assistance involved the provisions of peaceful technical information rather than weapons-related technologies or materials. According to Chinese Foreign Ministry spokesman Qin Gang, nuclear energy cooperation between China and Pakistan is "absolutely for peaceful purpose."

China allegedly involved Pakistani scientists in a nuclear test at its Lop Nur test site in 1989. On December 31, 1991, China signed a contract to build the Chashma 300-MW nuclear power reactor for Pakistan, and has agreed to build an additional three more reactors Chasma II (which is already under construction) and Chasma III and Chasma IV (III and IV are to be contractually agreed upon).

Beijing has adopted a number of measures to improve its proliferation image including publicly adopting responsible nuclear export policies after joining the International Atomic Energy Agency (IAEA) in 1984 and furthered its commitment by acceding to the Nonproliferation Treaty (NPT) in 1992. In addition, Beijing has formally enunciated three principles governing its nuclear exports: (1) acceptance of IAEA safeguards; (2) peaceful use only; and (3) no re-transfers to a third country without China's prior consent.

In 1993 China and the International Atomic Energy Agency (IAEA) signed an agreement to apply IAEA safeguards to a Chinese nuclear power station sold to Pakistan (INFCIRC/418). In 1994, China reportedly turned down a Pakistani request to "correct" Pakistan's nuclear weapons and to use the Chinese Lop Nur testing range. In recent years, China has also promulgated domestic laws regulating nuclear and dual-use exports. It has also played a highly constructive role in the six party talks in restricting the North Korean nuclear weapons program and also international efforts in curbing the Iranian nuclear program. Beijing, while advocating a nuclear deal for Pakistan, has indicated that a more detailed study of the Pakistani request would be needed by the Chinese leadership.

However, significant concerns continue to emanate out of Chinese exports, particularly to Pakistan. In 1995, a major controversy erupted over suspected sales of 5,000 specially designed ring magnets from the China Nuclear Energy Industry Corporation (CNEIC) to a non-safeguarded Pakistani nuclear laboratory, which was allegedly involved in nuclear weapons work. China initially denied that the sale had taken place; a Chinese Foreign Ministry spokesman called the reports "groundless" and warned the United States not to impose sanctions based on "rumours." Pakistan also denied that any transfer of sensitive nuclear technology had taken place. However, in talks with US officials, China eventually privately admitted that the sale had taken place, but argued that China should not be penalized for two reasons. First, China insisted that CNEIC had arranged the sale without the knowledge or consent of the central government. Second, China argued that the ring magnets were not magnetized, and the Nuclear Suppliers Group (NSG) Trigger List only covers ring magnets magnetized at a specific tolerance. Suspicions of sensitive technological transfers resurfaced in August-September 1996, when reports indicated that China had agreed to sell a special industrial furnace and high-technology diagnostic equipment to a Pakistani nuclear facility, equipment which reportedly can be used in the construction of nuclear bombs. The reports were dismissed by the Chinese and investigators could not find sufficient evidence against China.

The May 1998 tests by Pakistan in response to similar tests by India, further fuelled suspicions over Pakistan's nuclear program. While scientists claimed it to be an indigenous test, many commentators allege that the tests could not have been possible without the explicit help of China. In response to Pakistan testing its nuclear weapons, China practically laid all blame on India. According to a statement from the foreign office "The present situation in South Asia has been caused solely by India. India conducted nuclear tests in disregard of strong opposition by the international community." In February 2001, the press reported that China's Seventh Research and Design Institute, which is overseen by the China National Nuclear Corporation, supplied 50 ceramic capacitors to Pakistan's New Labs plutonium reprocessing plant. The

Institute was reportedly paid through a bank account maintained by an official at the Pakistani embassy in Beijing. The Chinese-supplied Khushab reactor can generate enough plutonium for at least one nuclear weapon per year, and probably more. According to US think tank Institute for Science and International Security (ISIS), Pakistan is close to increasing several-fold its ability to make weapon-grade plutonium through developments at Khushab. The Khushab nuclear site in Punjab province originally consisted of one heavy-water reactor with a power of about 50 MW and a heavy water production facility. Details about the construction of the second and third reactors emerged in 2006 and 2007. "No electricity production equipment is seen in the (satellite) images. This is consistent with the purpose of the reactors being to produce plutonium for nuclear weapons," the report said. Chinese proliferation activities during the eight years of the Clinton administration resulted in Chinese entities subject to sanctions 17 times. In four years of the Bush administration, Chinese entities have been sanctioned a total of 50 times. In 2004 alone, 14 Chinese entities were sanctioned a total of 23 times.

Five companies—China Great Wall Industry Corporation, China Precision Machinery Import/Export Corporation, China North Industries Corporation (NORINCO), Wha Cheong Tai Company, Ltd., and Zibo Chemical Equipment Plant—and one Chinese national, Q.C. Chen, have all been sanctioned at least four times by the United States and are often referred to as "serial proliferators" by U.S. officials

For some entities, such as the China Great Wall Industry Corporation and China Precision Machinery Import/Export Corporation, the sanctions have been spread out over more than a decade. But for NORINCO and Zibo Chemical Equipment Plant, the sanctions have all occurred since 2003 and 2002, respectively.

## Wider Proliferation Circle

Chinese proliferation to Pakistan has indirectly fuelled weapons activities across the world, especially owing to the role of disgraced Pakistan nuclear scientist Abdul Qadeer Khan. In

2004, as a result of on-site investigations into Libya's nuclear weapons program new details of the Pakistan-China collaboration were studied. As part of disarmament inspections, early Chinese nuclear weapons designs were handed over to IAEA inspectors by Libyan scientists, wrapped in plastic bags bearing an address in Islamabad.

Several recent developments have once again highlighted not only the central role that Beijing in developing Pakistan's nuclear arsenal, but also Dr. Khan's intimate links with China's nuclear establishment. According to Professor Mohan Malik of Security Studies at the Asia-Pacific Centre for Security Studies, Honolulu, "the Chinese seem to have been thoroughly beaten in the proliferation game by their own clients and allies-Pakistan and North Korea".

Reacting to reports about the Khan nuclear network, the Chinese Foreign Ministry spokesperson urged Islamabad to undertake the investigations "properly" and bring them to a conclusion "quickly." Professor Malik, draws attention to the Chinese preference for conducting investigations "properly" and ending them "quickly". This, he argues, reveals Beijing's apprehensions over exposing the Chinese nuclear establishment's long standing ties with Khan. Mallik argues that Khan's numerous visits to China's nuclear installations over the last three decades and gains accrued to China's weapons program from the Dutch centrifuge technology stolen by him in the mid-1970s are particularly sensitive issues for Beijing. A senior member of the Pakistan Muslim League (Quaid-e-Azam) told a Pakistani journalist that "Chinese officials had expressed a desire for the proliferation inquiry to end quickly as they feared that Dr. Khan would publicly detail his network's 'China connection,' thereby embarrassing a crucial ally that Pakistan considers a strategic counterweight to India."

Although the bomb designs sold to Libya were of a 1960s Chinese vintage, an analysis of Pakistan's May 1998 nuclear tests reveals that China may have supplied more advanced nuclear weapons designs of the late 1980s and early 1990s to Pakistan, which may have been shared with other countries. The close cooperation between Chinese and Pakistani military agencies also leaves little doubt that the Chinese had greater knowledge about Khan's proliferation activities than is publicly reported.

## PAKISTAN: NUCLEAR FEARS

There has been a growing fear among western nations over the security of Pakistan's nuclear arsenal, particularly over fears that the volatile country would possibly lead to weapons falling into the hands of terrorists. Earlier this year, IAEA director El Baradei, expressed his fear that "nuclear weapons could fall into the hands of an extremist group in Pakistan or in Afghanistan." Pakistan's poor proliferation record with its top nuclear scientist indicated for proliferation to regimes in Libya, North Korea and Iran have further fuelled western fears.

Consistent reports indict Pakistan's military intelligence of close ties with terrorist organizations. There have also been linkages of top Pakistan nuclear scientists with extremist groups and this has led to strong suspicions that the arsenal is in unsafe hands, and therefore should be safeguarded or destroyed at the earliest. It is in this regard, that the United States has been strongly skeptical in pushing forward for a nuclear deal with the country.

Significantly, the one nation, which would have the greatest fears over the safety of the Pakistan nuclear facilities, is unperturbed. Indian National Security Advisor, K Narayanan has said that Pakistan's nuclear weapons are largely in safe hands. According to him, "I would say it (Pakistani nuclear arsenal) is relatively safe or I would say it is largely safe." He said that apprehensions about Pakistan's nuclear weapons falling in the hands of radicals has led to the US paying "very close attention" to the concerns, and added that India already has a contingency plan in place to deal with a situation of nuclear weapons falling into wrong hands and getting used by elements in Pakistan.

This was reiterated by States Assistant Secretary of State for South and Central Asian Affairs Richard Boucher, when he said "Pakistan's nuclear arsenal is in safe hands" and that the United States would help Pakistan. According to Gurmeet Kanwal, director for the Centre for Land Warfare Studies, India, "The Pakistani military authorities are extremely concerned about such eventualities and have made elaborate arrangements to ensure that all their nuclear warheads are stored safely. They claim that carefully formulated personnel, reliability policies and electronic safety mechanisms have been developed and incorporated by Pakistan's Nuclear Command Authority."

Articulating the difficulties a rogue organization would have in getting control of nuclear weapons, he adds "The Musharraf regime has ensured that hard-line radical elements are ruthlessly weeded out from the nuclear security detail. Hence, it can be concluded that if some rogue elements were to try to gain control over the nuclear warheads, they would have to be prepared to fight their way through several layers of highly motivated personnel who are armed to the teeth."

Could these measures satisfy China into accepting a nuclear deal for Pakistan and dismissing global concerns surrounding any nuclear transfer to Pakistan?

## Chinese View

Beijing's national security strategy is a principle of "containment through surrogates", that requires proliferation to countries that can countervail its perceived rivals and enemies. The Chinese military has long practiced what John Mearsheimer calls "managed proliferation"-it calls for providing nuclear or missile technology to China's friends and allies (Pakistan, Iran, North Korea) so as to contain its rivals through proxies (India in South Asia, the United States in the Middle East and Japan in East Asia). Toshi Yoshihara and Richard Sokolsky elaborate, "Beijing has relied on the threat of proliferation as a counterweight to U.S. policies that threaten China's interests."

According to Professor Richard Russell of the National Defence University, "China works against American counter-proliferation policy until they get caught, and then deny charges, only to subsequently, and much belatedly, recant to say that it will not happen again."

China views with great concern the Indo-US strategic partnership, and actively continues to balance its opposing goals of counter weighting India and yet developing friendly relations with it. In order to do so, it finds it expedient to engage in a double speaks. For example, Chinese leaders were supportive of the Indo-US deal, yet engaged in nearly fatal delaying tactics during the NSG vote. On realizing that its opposition would be futile, it engaged in hopes that the NSG would address "the aspirations of all parties", an obvious reference to Pakistan. Privately, Chinese officials admitted that Pakistan was on their back in opposing the India specific waiver, and pointed out to angry Indian officials that it did not come in the way of blocking the vote.

However, China has far more significant leverage over Pakistan and cannot be bullied into adopting a pro-Pakistan stance. An example of this was witnessed during the recent red mosque crises in Pakistan. In response to violence against Chinese workers in Pakistan, Musharraf made the following statement: *"The Chinese, who are such great friends of ours- they took the Chinese hostage and tortured them. Because of this, I was personally embarrassed. I had to go apologize to the Chinese leaders, "I am ashamed that you are such great friends and this happened to you".*

## PAKISTAN-CHINA RELATIONS AND ITS PHASE

Pakistan's relations with China have always been the most important of its relationships with other countries. It is based on trust, respect, and mutual benefit. Over the past 55 years, since the two countries established their diplomatic relations, this relationship has evolved in a manner to serve the interests of both countries. To understand the evolution of this relationship from a correct perspective, it is important to have a brief overview of the relationship between the two countries.

Pakistan was the first Islamic country and third noncommunist state to accord recognition to the People's

Republic of China. Although Pakistan established diplomatic relations with China in 1951, the actual consolidation of relations started in the early 1960s, when Pakistan changed its previous stance and supported China's seating in the UN in 1961. In the 1962 Sino-Indian border war, the US rushed military assistance to India, which Pakistan, being an allay of the West, considered detrimental to its security concerns and moved out of the Western orbit (SEATO and CENTO). At that point in time, a commonality of interests seemed to be emerging between Pakistan and China. It was the shared sense of an evolving geostrategic environment in which the two countries amicably negotiated and signed an agreement on the demarcation of their common border in March 1963. In the following years, Pakistan on its part sincerely helped China to end the isolation that both the superpowers wished to impose on China, by signing an air-transport agreement and trade agreement and helping China maintain contact with a number of countries, especially the Islamic world. Similarly, China played a commendable role in its support of Pakistan in achieving a ceasefire in the 1965 Indo-Pakistan war by issuing stern warnings to India. Following the war, China, also in an attempt to compensate for war losses, supported Pakistan with military equipment including tanks and aircraft. In the 1960s, Pakistan-China relations evolved on firm foundations of mutual trust and confidence.

In the early 1970s, Pakistan played an important role in facilitating secret communications between the US and China that resulted in Henry Kissinger's secret visit to China followed by President Richard Nixon's historic visit. Sino-US normalization of relations was perceived in Indian strategic thinking as the emergence of a US-Pakistan-China strategic triangle, which prompted India to sign a treaty of peace, friendship and cooperation with the Soviet Union. It could be termed as a kind of a security treaty because Article IX of the treaty stipulated that in "the event of either party being subject to an attack or threat thereof, the high contracting parties shall immediately enter into mutual consultations in order to remove such threat and to take appropriate effective measures to ensure peace and security of their countries." 1 This development introduced a new dimension to the region, especially if seen in the context of the Cold War, and also created more space for further consolidation of Pak-China relations.

The other development, which had profoundly influenced Sino-Pak relations, was the Indo-Pakistan war in 1971, followed by the Chinese military and economic assistance to Pakistan. Later, on the issue of Bangladesh's application for membership to the UN, China, on Pakistan's request, exercised its veto power for the first time to stall the move, which helped Pakistan to secure in a bargain the release of its POWs and the return of troops to their prewar positions.

The Indian nuclear explosion of 1974 introduced a new dimension to the strategic balance in the region and gave fresh impetus to expanding Pak-China defence cooperation. Between 1971 and 1978, China assisted Pakistan in building two defence-related mega projects, first, the Heavy Rebuild Factory for T–59 tanks, and second, the F–6 Aircraft Rebuild Factory. Chinese intent to make Pakistan self-reliant in the production of a conventional weapons system, without attaching any political strings to its assistance, cultivated deep-rooted respect and goodwill for China in Pakistan.

The end of the 1970s witnessed international developments of immense consequences that continued to impact on the entire region throughout the following decades and even today. These were the Iranian Islamic Revolution in February 1979, the declared hostility of the new Iranian leadership towards the US, and in the later part of the year, the invasion of Afghanistan by the Soviet Union. Invasion of Afghanistan created a situation of two hostile fronts for Pakistan—India and Afghanistan—threatening peace and stability in the region. At this crucial juncture, China stood firmly by Pakistan and condemned the invasion of Afghanistan as a "hegemonic action" that posed a threat to peace and stability not only for the region but for the entire world. Pakistan and China had a shared perspective and developed coordinated strategies to deal with the Afghan situation. China provided covertly, in the following years, military supplies worth $200 million annually to the Afghan resistance groups, and extended political support to Pakistan at all international fora.

Throughout the 1980s, Pakistan-China relations continued to develop into a comprehensive relationship. While China improved its relations with India towards the end of the 1980s, Pakistan did not feel that China's improving relations with India were at the cost of China's relations with Pakistan. Although there was a visible shift in the Chinese stance on Kashmir, Pakistani policy makers believed that China's improved relations with India would act as a restraining factor on Indian belligerency towards Pakistan. Pakistan always supported China on all issues important to Chinese national interests such as sovereignty over Hong Kong, Taiwan, and Tibet and issues relating to human rights and democracy. China always appreciated and counted on Pakistan's strong support as a trusted friend over all these issues at international fora. Following the withdrawal of Soviet forces from Afghanistan in 1988– 1989, the regional strategic dynamics changed once again. The US, after having achieved its strategic interest of rolling back communist aggression, claimed victory over the former Soviet Union and abandoned Afghanistan. Pakistan's support was no longer required by the US, so it came under US sanctions for secretly developing nuclear weapons; an issue to which the US turned a blind eye for a decade during the Afghan War. Throughout the 1990s, Pakistan remained under US sanctions and China was the primary source of Pakistan's military hardware procurements. During this period, Pakistan-China defence-related cooperation also substantially increased. China's support for Pakistan's nuclear and missile programs became a constant irritant in Sino-US and Sino-Indian relations, especially the issue of supply of M-11 missiles and 500 ring magnets to an "unsafeguarded" nuclear facility. China, on its part, despite tremendous US pressure to cut off high-technology links with Pakistan, remained steadfast in its commitment to strengthen Pakistan's defence capability.

In May 1998, Indian nuclear tests destabilized the strategic balance in South Asia. As a prelude to these tests, the Indian defence minister and prime minister described China as a long-term security threat. While commenting on the Indian assertion, the official Chinese media reported that "India's explosions have sabotaged the fragile trust built up with Beijing over the past decade." Following the Indian nuclear tests, Sino-Indian relations suffered a severe setback. Deterioration in Sino-Indian relations reinforced Pakistan's importance in China's South Asia policy. Pakistan and China held high-level consultations on the situation in South Asia. China expressed its understanding of Pakistan's compulsion to go nuclear. It gave Pakistan the confidence to reestablish the strategic balance in South Asia by conducting its own nuclear tests. The depth of Pakistan-China relations was reflected from the fact that it was after Pakistan had acquired demonstrable nuclear weapons capability that the Chinese leadership gave assurance to the visiting US president Bill Clinton in June 1998 of cooperating with the US on the issue of nuclear proliferation. In 1999, during the Kargil conflict between the two nuclear states, India and Pakistan, China adhered to a strict neutral position. China was concerned over the possibility of escalation of the conflict, and asked both countries to defuse tensions. The Chinese position of neutrality was duly acknowledged by India, and provided both countries with an opportunity to mend their fences and once again improve their bilateral relations. Pakistan also had a complete understanding of China's interest to improve bilateral relations with India, especially in the context of evolving Indo-US strategic partnership.

After the events of 9/11, Pakistan and China consulted each other on the unfolding situation in the region. On September 18, 2001, a special envoy of the then Chinese president, Jiang Zemin, arrived in Islamabad to meet General Pervez Musharraf and other officials and discussed the situation emerging as a consequence of the 9/11 attacks. Pakistan's decision to side with the US and to provide use of its airspace and base facilities had initially raised some concerns in Chinese policy-making circles. However, the exchange of high-level visits clarified the Pakistani position that under no circumstances would Pakistan allow its cooperation with the US to undermine

Chinese strategic interests. During the India-Pakistan military standoff in 2001–2002, China continued with its position of neutrality and played an important role in defusing tensions between India and Pakistan through telephone diplomacy. Since India escalated the tensions, despite Pakistan's repeated requests for negotiation, China's role to pacify the situation was considered more favorably by the Pakistani authorities and people.

The Chinese leadership stated that "it is in the interests of both countries and the expectation of the international community for both Pakistan and India to maintain the utmost restraint and safeguard the peace and stability of South Asia." China's proactive diplomacy to engage the US and India in the volatile South Asian situation was received well in Pakistan and indeed helped to ease tensions. There was complete understanding between Pakistan and China, and the Chinese leadership appreciated Musharraf government's policies on antiterrorism and peaceful resolution of contentious issues with India.

President Musharraf, in his December 2001 visit to China, explicitly expressed support of the Chinese campaign against Muslim separatists in Xinjiang. He urged the Chinese Muslims to be very patriotic and to work for the betterment of their country. He declared that Pakistan would extend full support to China to fight against East Turkestan terrorist forces. This was the first time that a Pakistani leader went public in support of Chinese policies to curtail Muslim separatists in Xinjiang. In view of Chinese concerns that there is a link between the separatist forces in Xinjiang and the jihad organizations in Pakistan and Afghanistan, Pakistan has also institutionalized antiterrorism dialogue with China and the two sides have agreed to share intelligence on terrorism. In December 2003, the Pakistan Army in a military operation near the Pak-Afghan border killed Hahsan Mahsum, the leader of the East Turkestan Islamic Movement, while extraditing a number of alleged terrorists to China. In recent years, antiterrorism-related cooperation between the two countries has constantly been expanding. On August 6, 2004, China and Pakistan conducted their first joint antiterrorism military exercise named "Friendship 2004," in Xinjiang.

In April 2005, during Premier Wen Jiabao's visit to Islamabad, the two sides signed a treaty of friendship, cooperation and good neighborly relations as well as an agreement on combating terrorism, separatism and extremism. The comprehensive antiterrorism cooperation from Pakistan has effectively removed the apprehensions of the Chinese side, holding in regard the support of the Uighur Muslim separatists from some of Pakistan's religious groups. Pakistan-China defence-related cooperation has always been the most important component of their overall bilateral relations.

The tradition of high-level exchange of visits for consultations between the armed forces of the two countries has provided sustenance to the bilateral relations, as the institution of the armed forces plays a special role in political decision making in both countries. In recent years, a mechanism of defence and security consultation has been institutionalized between the two countries. Since March 2002, three rounds of consultations have taken place. In order to enhance military-to-military cooperation, China and Pakistan, in October 2003, conducted a joint maritime search-and-rescue exercise near Shanghai. That was the first time for the navy of the People's Liberation Army (PLA) to conduct an exercise with a foreign country. Similarly, in November 2005, during their visit to Pakistan, Chinese naval ships conducted a second joint maritime search-and-rescue exercise with the Pakistan Navy. That was again the first time for the PLA Navy to conduct a joint exercise in waters abroad. Pakistan and China share a common interest in the security of the sea lanes of communication, and both support a multilateral framework for guarding energy and trade sea routes. Defence production-related cooperation has also expanded in recent years between the two countries. Pakistan and China have jointly developed JF–17 Thunder—a multi-role fighter aircraft. Pakistan and China finalized a deal in April 2005, under which China Dockyard in Shanghai will build four F–22P frigates for the Pakistan Navy and transfer the technology as well. Cooperation on other ongoing defence projects is continuing to the satisfaction of both. At the political level, Pakistan and China have unanimity of views on issues like the war on terrorism, Iraq, Afghanistan, and the Iranian nuclear program. Both countries wish to strengthen the authority of the UN and oppose unilateralism and concepts such as "coalition of the willing" or "concert of democracies" outside the UN ambit to deal with international security issues.

## PAKISTAN-CHINA STRATEGIC RELATIONS

On January 1, 2011, in a heartwarming ceremony held in the Pakistan-China Friendship Centre at Islamabad, yet another gift from the People s Republic of China, the Pakistan-China Friendship Year was launched. The Friendship Year, which coincides with the 60th Anniversary of the establishment of diplomatic relations between the two countries, provides a timely occasion to take stock of their bilateral ties which have been described by the most adulatory metaphors possible. There could have been no better backdrop for this exercise than the recently concluded visit by Chinese Premier Wen Jiabao to Pakistan on 17-19 December, 2010. In glaring contrast to the summit level visits from USA, UK, France and Russia in quick succession confined to India alone, the Chinese Premier paid back- to-back official visits to India as well as Pakistan. In his arrival statement in Islamabad on 17 December, 2010 Premier Wen Jiabao declared that it was a firm policy of the Chinese Government to further cement and deepen the strategic partnership of cooperation with Pakistan, which his visit will push to a new high. Addressing the Pakistani Parliament on 19 December, 2010, Premier Wen Jiabao lyrically waxed that "the friendship between China and Pakistan is deeply rooted in the hearts of the two peoples. It is in our blood, and has become our noble and firm.conviction." These sentiments were reciprocated in equal measure by the rhapsodic Pakistani leadership and people. They stressed that pursuing friendship with China was the bedrock of Pakistan s foreign policy, enjoying national consensus. The Joint Statement issued at the conclusion of the visit on 19 December, 2010 expressed the shared view that "the China-Pakistan all-weather strategic partnership of cooperation ... has gone beyond bilateral dimensions and acquired broader regional and international ramifications."

This assessment represents the culmination of a process which spans the last 60 years. The Pak-China relationship has been marked by deep mutual trust, confidence and understanding, rooted as it is in their strict adherence to the universally acknowledged Five Principles of Peaceful Coexistence and Charter of the United Nations as well as strong opposition to hegemony of all kinds and hues. Their friendship has been

tested in the crucible of time. The two countries have always stood by each other through thick and thin. This relationship emerged in a given set of circumstances when the world was in the grip of Cold War between the capitalist and the Socialist world, the ideological rift between the two leading socialist states, USSR and China, had started developing. China was then relatively an isolated and less developed country and both Pakistan and China perceived India as a common threat.

However, the context in which this unique relationship took root and prospered has been undergoing a change. Pakistan became instrumental in facilitating contact between two erstwhile enemies, China and USA, leading to the recognition of People s Republic of China by USA and the establishment of diplomatic ties between the two states. Following the disintegration of the Soviet Union, the United States has emerged as the sole super power, adding to the complexity of its relations with a rising China. The ideological and territorial conflicting relations between China and the former Soviet Union have given way to cooperative ties between them. China and India who went to war with each other in 1962 have since normalized their relations, the casus belli, i.e., the unresolved border dispute notwithstanding. Their bilateral trade and economic cooperation is racing fast ahead. Lately, the growing bonhomie between USA and India has introduced a new destabilizing element in the region, directly impacting Pakistan and China.

And China itself too has been undergoing a monumental change. Following Deng's policy of internal reforms and opening to the outside world, China has transformed from a puritanical socialist economy to a system of socialism with Chinese characteristics. Or is it now Capitalism with Chinese characteristics? Resultantly, China has become (after USA) the second largest economy in the world, whose responsible policies are indispensable for international financial and monetary stability and to cope with the challenges of global warming as well as energy and food security. And as a permanent member of the UN Security Council with increased military and political clout it has been playing a valuable stabilizing role in the maintenance of international peace and security and to counter the menaces of terrorism, extremism, fundamentalism, separatism and nuclear proliferation. At the same time, contemporaneously India has been incrementally acquiring the sinews of a major economic and military power with resultant enhanced influence in world affairs. The end of Cold War era saw the crystallization of Chinese foreign policy propelled by its domestic agenda. Henceforth, the Chinese were primarily concerned with fostering an international climate of peace and stability which they deemed essential for wholeheartedly pursuing the goal of development and modernization at home. They in particular endeavoured to have friendly ties with all neighbours, including India.

## People's Republic of China – Pakistan Relations

People's Republic of China–Pakistan relations began in 1950 when Pakistan was among the first countries to break relations with the Republic of China on Taiwan and recognise the PRC. Following the 1962 Sino-Indian War, Pakistan's relations with the PRC became stronger; since then, the two countries have regularly exchanged high-level visits resulting in a variety of agreements. The PRC has provided economic, military and technical assistance to Pakistan. Bilateral relations have evolved from an initial Chinese policy of sympathy and support for the creation of a independent homeland for the Muslims of South Asia in 1947 to an unusual partnership that links a small but militarily powerful Pakistan, dependent on China for its economic and military strength, with China trying to balance competing interests in the region. Diplomatic relations were established in 1950, military assistance began in 1966, a strategic alliance was formed in 1972 and economic co-operation began in 1979. The relationship has been described by Hu Jintao as "higher than the mountains and deeper than oceans". Favourable relations with China have been a pillar of Pakistan's foreign policy. China strongly supported Pakistan's opposition to Soviet Union involvement in Afghanistan and was perceived by Pakistan as a regional counterweight to India. China and Pakistan also share a close military relation, with China supplying a range of modern armaments to the Pakistani defence forces. China supports Pakistan's stance on Kashmir while Pakistan supports China on the issues of Xinjiang, Tibet, and Taiwan. Lately, military cooperation has deepened with joint projects producing armaments ranging from fighter jets to guided missile frigates. Chinese cooperation with Pakistan has reached high economic points with substantial investment from China in Pakistani infrastructural expansion, including the noted project in the Pakistani deep water port in Gwadar. Both countries have an ongoing free trade agreement. Pakistan has served as China's main bridge between Muslim countries. Pakistan had earlier played a leading role in bridging the communication gap between China and the West, through Henry Kissinger's secret visit before the 1972 Nixon visit to China.

Pakistan has an enduring, multi-dimensional and deep-rooted relationship with China. The long-standing ties of friendship between the two countries are underpinned by mutual trust and confidence. A close identity of views and mutuality of interest remain the hallmark of bilateral ties. Pakistan has always supported China on all issues of importance to the latter, especially those related to the question of China's sovereignty e.g. Taiwan, Xinjiang, and Tibet and other sensitive issues such as human rights. The Chinese leadership has always appreciated Pakistan's steadfast support on issues of their concern. They are also generous in acknowledging the significant role of Pakistan in the early 1970s, which enabled China to break its isolation from the West and the US, when Henry Kissinger secretly visited Beijing. Pakistan also helped China become a member for the United Nations and has also been instrumental in providing excellent relations of China with the Muslim world. China has also supported Pakistan through thick and thin. The Kashmir issue has always been supported, while in 2008 during Pakistan-Indian tensions, it promised unlimited financial and military aid. Pakistan and China have also been involved in technology exchanged. Although earlier, it would be mostly sharing, it now remains in the favour of Chinese.

## Diplomatic Relations

Diplomatic relations between Pakistan and China were established on 21 May 1951. The 50th Anniversary of the establishment of the diplomatic relations was an occasion of great significance both in historic terms as well as for a strong public manifestation of the durability and the strength of their relations. A series of high level exchanges, hallmark of which was Premier Zhu Rongji's visit to Pakistan on 11–14 May 2001 and President of Pakistan's visit to China later in 2001 as part of the commemorative events for the golden jubilee celebrations. In addition, high profile cultural and business activities were undertaken, including Pakistan's participation in the Beijing International Trade Fair in April 2001, civil awards for Chinese nationals in recognition of their contribution to international relations between Pakistan and China and cooperation in various fields and the issuing of first day covers/commemorative stamps to mark the occasion. To mark the 50th Anniversary of relations between China and Pakistan, the Pakistan Post issued a set of 3 commemorative postage stamps on 12 May 2001. Pakistan and China further celebrated the 50th Anniversary by releasing First Day of Issue Covers simultaneously in Beijing and Islamabad on 21 May. Special ceremonies were held in the respective capitals to mark the release of First Day of Issue Covers containing postage stamps of the respective countries on both the First Day Covers duly covered with special postmarks on 21 May 2001. With the government of President Asif Ali Zardari under intense pressure from the United States, there are calls from notable politicians and defence analysts for Pakistan to adopt a foreign policy which considers China and not the US to be Pakistan's strongest ally and most significant stakeholder. China's emergence as the leading global economic power coupled with recent rumours of an Indo-Western policy that could promote a destabilisation followed by a potential disintegration of Pakistan has helped this suggestion gain further credibility.

Washington has historically been accused of using Pakistan in time of need and then deserting it for a policy that favours stronger relations with India to take advantage of the large consumer market there. China, on the other hand has been a time-tested friend of Pakistan's. The recent Mumbai attacks serve as an ideal example of this where the US joined hands with India in accusing Pakistan whereas China warned all other powers to restrain an invasion of Pakistan. It is in this respect that the focus in the coming years would be on the speed and scale of development at Gawadar port. Some circles in Pakistan believe that the process of this development should be expedited as a matter of urgency because it would deepen Chinese interest in Pakistan substantially.

## Pakistan-China Military Relations

The People's Republic of China's military relationship with Pakistan's military has often been regarded by the leaders of both countries as all weather and time tested. This relationship between two Asian countries, who are joined with a common border, is important in the world's geo-strategic alliances. The policy of having good relations between the armed forces was taken by the leaders to counter the balance of power in the Asia. On the one hand Indian and Soviet Union, and on the other hand Pakistan and China's policies to counter it. In recent years this relationship has deepened even further by having defence agreements between Pakistan and China.

China has been a steady source of military equipment to the Pakistani Army and also has helped Pakistan to set-up mass weapons production factories and also have given technology assistance and modernized facilities. In the last 20 years, the countries are involved in the joint venture of several projects to enhance military and weaponry systems, which includes JF-17 Thunder fighter aircraft, K-8 Karakorum advance training aircraft, space technology, AWACS, Al-Khalid tank, Babur cruise missile. The armies have a schedule for organising joint military exercises. China is the largest investor in the Gwadar Deep Sea Port, which is strategically located at the mouth of the Strait of Hormuz. However Gwadar port is currently embazzled in multilateral diplomatic standoff.

China has offered to Pakistan military aid in order to fight against the terrorist activities on their (Pakistan's) soil. Beijing will further cooperate with Islamabad in dealing firmly with terrorists. After the aid the Islamic Republic of Pakistan will also purchase military equipment from China to fight terror to which China have agreed. This will strengthen cooperation between two Armed Forces.

In the past, China played a major role in the development of Pakistan's nuclear infrastructure, especially when increasingly stringent export controls in Western Countries made it difficult for Pakistan to acquire materials and uranium enriching equipment from elsewhere. China has supplied Pakistan with equipment to enrich its indigenous uranium to weapons grade.

In the 1990s, China designed and supplied the heavy water Khushab reactor, which plays a key role in Pakistan's production of plutonium. A subsidiary of the China National Nuclear Corporation also contributed in Pakistan's efforts to expand its uranium enrichment capabilities by providing 5,000 custom made ring magnets, which are a key component of the bearings that facilitate the high-speed rotation of centrifuges. China also provided technical and material support in the completion of the Chashma Nuclear Power Complex and plutonium reprocessing facility, which was built in the mid 1990s. China has also launched Pakistan's first satellite to orbit in 1990 due to Pakistan's lack of a spaceport. The Relations of China and Pakistan were disturbed during the government of President

Pervez Musharraf because he was more inclined towards the United States of America than China.

## Economic Relations

In October 2009, Pakistan and China agreed to 'propel' trade between the two countries. Both sides opposed to all forms of terrorism, extremism and separatism, resolved to cooperation with each other to fight the above-mentioned three forces, said the Statement adding, China conveyed its complete support to Pakistan's commitment and efforts to fight terrorism and appreciated the sacrifices made by the government and people of Pakistan in this regard. Five Year Development programe on Economic trades and free trade agreement in goods and investments was also signed. China also agreed to further develop and boost Pakistan's Mineral and Energy sector as well as broaden financial and banking sector cooperation.

Both sides inked almost twelve agreements/MOUs during the visit in the fields of economic and technical cooperation, free trade, minerals, petroleum and natural resources, environmental protection, radio and television, space technology, agriculture sector, properties exchange between foreign ministries of the two countries, museum of natural history, cricket field and project of X-Ray container/vehicle inspection system.

## Cultural Relations

The prime minister congratulated the government and the people of China on behalf of the people of Pakistan on the cultural week. Chinese Ambassador Lou Zhaohui said that China greatly values its deep rooted friendship with Pakistan, stressing that the friendship is all weather and in all dimensions of life. Chinese artists staged performances including Chinese acrobats, folk songs and a magic show. A large audience watched and showed great interest in the Chinese culture.

## Public Opinion

The relationship between China and Pakistan's is considered to be their equivalent to the Israel – United States relations.

When a US delegate once confronted a Chinese diplomat about Beijing's uncompromising and unconditioned support for Pakistan, the Chinese reportedly responded with a heavily-loaded sarcastic remark by saying "Pakistan is our Israel".

According to a Pew survey of Pakistan public opinion last year, 84 percent of respondents said they had a favorable view of China and 16 percent had a favorable view of the United States. These results showed that Pakistan is the most pro-China country in the world.

### Issues

The ETIM is a Waziri based mujihadeen organization that is said to be allied with the Taliban, which received funding from rouge elements in the ISI. This could to a potential diplomatic confrontation between Pakistan and China.

## SINO-PAKISTAN TIES: AN "ALL-WEATHER" FRIENDSHIP?

In 1950, based in part on their convergent interests toward India, Pakistan was among the first countries to recognize the People's Republic of China and break diplomatic ties with the Republic of China. Sino-Pakistan ties gained particular momentum after the 1962 Sino-Indian war, when China and Pakistan signed a boundary agreement recognizing Chinese control over portions of the disputed Kashmir territory. Since then, maintaining close ties with China has been a priority for Islamabad, and Beijing has provided extensive economic, military, and technical assistance to Pakistan over the years. And it was Pakistan that in the early 1970s enabled China to cultivate its ties with the West with the United States in particular, becoming the conduit for Henry Kissinger's landmark secret visit to China in 1971 and has been instrumental in bringing China closer to the larger Muslim world. Pakistan has supported China on all issues of importance to the latter, especially those related to the question of China's sovereignty, such as Taiwan, Xinjiang, and Tibet, as well as other sensitive issues such as human rights. China has reciprocated by supporting Pakistan's stance on Kashmir.

China has emerged as Pakistan's largest defence supplier, with joint projects that produce armaments ranging from fighter jets to guided missile frigates. Pakistan's military modernization is dependent on Chinese largesse, with China supplying Pakistan with short-range M-11 missiles and helping Pakistan develop the Shaheen-1 ballistic missile.8 In the last two decades, the two states have been actively involved in a range of joint ventures, including the JF-17 fighter aircraft used for delivering nuclear weapons, an Airborne Warning and Control System, and the Babur cruise missile (the dimensions of which exactly replicate those of the Hong Niao Chinese cruise missile).

In a major move for its indigenous defence industry, China is supplying its most advanced homemade combat aircraft, the third-generation J-10 fighter jet, to Pakistan in a deal worth around $6 billion. Negotiations are also underway between the two for the purchase of six new submarines by Islamabad. Beijing is helping Pakistan to build and launch satellites for remote sensing and communication, even as Pakistan is reportedly already hosting a Chinese space communication facility at Karachi.

China also played a major role in the development of Pakistan's nuclear infrastructure and emerged as Pakistan's benefactor at a time when increasingly stringent export controls in Western countries made it difficult for Pakistan to acquire materials and technology. The Pakistani nuclear weapons program is essentially an extension of the Chinese one. Arms-control advocate Gary Milhollin aptly noted, "If you subtract China's help from Pakistan's nuclear program, there is no nuclear program." In the 1990s, China designed and supplied the heavy water Khusab reactor, which plays a key role in Pakistan's production of plutonium.

China also provided technical and material support for the completion of the Chashma Nuclear Power Reactor and plutonium reprocessing facility, which was built in the mid-1990s. Although China has long denied helping any nation attain a nuclear capability, the father of Pakistan's nuclear weapons program, Abdul Qadeer Khan, acknowledged the crucial role China played in his nation's nuclear weaponization when China gave 50 kilograms of weapon grade enriched uranium, drawings of nuclear weapons, and tons of uranium hexafluoride for Pakistan's centrifuges. This is perhaps the only case where a nuclear weapon state has actually passed on weapons-grade fissile material as well as a bomb design to a non-nuclear weapon state.

On the economic front, China and Pakistan have a free trade agreement, with China accounting for around 11 percent of Pakistan's imports. The two sides are committed to achieving a trade target of $15 billion by 2015.13 China's "no-strings attached" economic aid to Pakistan is more appreciated than the aid it receives from the United States (which often comes with riders attached), even as Chinese assistance is nowhere near what the United States has given to Pakistan; the United States provided $349 million in military and economic assistance to Pakistan in 2010 alone. Though Beijing did provide a soft loan of about $500 million to Islamabad to tide over Pakistan during the economic crisis in 2008, it did not end up giving a large-scale bailout package as was expected, thereby forcing Pakistan to go to the International Monetary Fund. China's economic cooperation with Pakistan is growing, with substantial Chinese investment in Pakistani infrastructural expansion, including the noted project in the port in Gwadar, which is strategically located at the mouth of the Strait of Hormuz. The railroad from Gwadar through the Karakoram Mountains leading into Xinjiang in western China would provide China with an alternative energy supply route (China is building this strategic transport corridor despite Indian objections to its activities in Pakistan Occupied Kashmir).

China's presence in the Bay of Bengal via roads and ports in Burma, as well as in the Arabian Sea via the Gwadar port, has been a cause of concern for India. It has been suggested that Gwadar could provide China with a "listening post" from where it could "monitor U.S. naval activity in the Persian Gulf, Indian activity in the Arabian Sea, and future U.S.—Indian maritime cooperation in the Indian Ocean." Though Pakistan's naval capabilities do not, on their own, pose any challenge to India, the combination of Chinese and Pakistani naval forces could indeed be formidable for India to counter. With access to crucial port facilities in Egypt, Iran, and Pakistan, China is well-positioned to secure its interests in the region.

## CHINA'S CONTINUING SALIENCE IN PAKISTANI FOREIGN POLICY

With India's recent rise as an economic and political power of global significance, Sino-Indian ties are now at a critical juncture as India tries to find the right policy mix to deal with its most important neighbour. Meanwhile, Chinese strategists remain concerned about U.S. attempts to encircle China and the profound effect on Chinese security of an eventual integration of India into a U.S. alliance.

China, according to this view, needs to remain vigilant against the growing network running "from Japan to India" that would suffocate China. As India struggles to emerge as a global power with an ambitious foreign policy agenda, China can effectively scuttle Indian ambitions by continuing with its diplomatic and military support to Pakistan. Much to India's chagrin, China has given ample indications in the recent past that it wants to follow that path. With the civilian government of President Asif Ali Zardari under intense pressure from the United States to do more to fight terrorism emanating from Pakistani soil, there are calls in Pakistan to adopt a foreign policy that considers China and not the United States to be Pakistan's strongest ally and most significant stakeholder. China's emergence as the leading global economic power coupled with recent attempts by India and the United States to forge a closer relationship has helped this suggestion gain further credibility.

Washington has historically been accused of using Pakistan in times of need and then deserting it for a policy that favours stronger relations with India to serve the larger U.S. strategic agenda. Pakistan remains angry about U.S. indifference after the United States used it to funnel aid to Afghan mujahideen and then turned its back on Pakistan after the Soviet withdrawal. Whereas only around nine percent of Pakistanis view the United States as a partner, around 80 percent of the Pakistani population considers China a friend.

The Obama administration's July 2011 decision to suspend a portion of U.S. aid to the Pakistani military has led many in Islamabad to become even more forceful in underlining Beijing's importance for Pakistan. Reacting to the U.S. move, Islamabad's ambassador to Beijing, Masood Khan, was quick to suggest that "China will stand by us in difficult times as it has been doing for the past years." Though Beijing cannot replace Washington as an aid-provider to Pakistan, the tension in U.S.—Pakistan ties provides an opportunity for Beijing to deepen its relationship with Islamabad. As it is, China is considered a more reliable ally that has always come to Pakistan's aid when India has been on the rise, even to an extent that China has conveniently turned a blind eye to Pakistan's strategy of using terror as an instrument of policy against India. Not surprisingly, Pakistan has given China a "blank cheque" to intervene in India—Pakistan peace talks. Pakistan also seems to have allowed Chinese engineers to examine the remains of the stealth helicopter destroyed during the raid that killed Osama bin Laden despite a direct request from the United States that China not be allowed to do so.

## Forecast for the "All-Weather" Relationship

With India's ascent in the global hierarchy and U.S. attempts to carve out a strong partnership with India, China's need for Pakistan is only likely to grow. As tensions rose between India and Pakistan after the November 2008 terror attacks in Mumbai, Pakistan's Chairman of the Joint Chiefs of Staff Committee went to China to seek that country's support, which was readily given. The visit resulted in the signing of a new agreement on military cooperation between the two nations, with Beijing agreeing to expedite the delivery of F-22 frigates to Pakistan's Navy.

Beijing has justified its arms sales to Pakistan on the grounds that India was buying similar weapon systems from the United States (it also is buying military hardware from the Russians). China has consistently defended Pakistan's desire for high capacity weapons systems as normal for an independent nation seeking to bolster its security. In the years preceding the attacks in Mumbai, China blocked UN sanctions against the dreaded Lashkar-e-Taiba (LeT) and Jamaat-ud-Dawa (JuD), the organizations that planned and executed the attacks, despite a broad global consensus favouring such a move. Only when tensions surfaced between Beijing and Islamabad on the issue of Chinese Uighur separatists receiving sanctuaries and training on Pakistani territory did China agree to a ban on JuD. More recently, China has refused to reconsider its objection in the United Nations to proscribing the Jaish-e-Mohammed's Maulana Masood Azhar and some prominent LeT operatives based in Pakistan, despite New Delhi's presenting detailed information on them to Beijing. With the exception of China, other major global powers such as Britain, France, Germany, and Russia supported the U.S.—India nuclear deal as they were eager to sell nuclear fuel, reactors, and equipment to India. China, on its part, made its displeasure clear by asking India to sign the NPT and dismantle its nuclear weapons. The official Xinhua news agency of China commented that the U.S.—India nuclear agreement "will set a bad example for other countries." Since the U.S.—India deal is in many ways a recognition of India's rising global profile, China was not very happy with the outcome and indicated that it would be willing to sell nuclear reactors to Pakistan. It was a not so subtle message to the United States that if Washington decides to play favourites, China retains the same right.

Not surprisingly, China's plans to supply two nuclear reactors to Pakistan in defiance of international rules have gathered momentum. Chinese authorities have confirmed that the China National Nuclear Cooperation has signed an agreement with Pakistan for two new nuclear reactors at the Chashma site Chashma III and Chashma IV in addition to the two that it is already working on in Pakistan. This will be in clear violation of the Nuclear Suppliers Group (NSG) guidelines that forbid nuclear transfers to countries that are not signatories to the NPT or do not adhere to comprehensive international safeguards on their nuclear program. China has suggested that "there are compelling political reasons concerning the stability of South Asia to justify the exports," echoing Pakistan's oft-repeated compliant that the U.S.—India nuclear pact has upset stability in the region. The decision to supply reactors to Pakistan which has a record of dealing with North Korea, Iran, and Libya reflects China's growing diplomatic confidence and underscores its view of Pakistan as a prized South Asian strategic power. Recent suggestions emanating from Beijing that China is likely to set up military bases overseas to counter U.S. influence and exert pressure on India have been interpreted in certain sections in New Delhi as a veiled reference to China's interest in having a permanent military presence in Pakistan. Even though it might not be politically possible for the Pakistani government to follow through on such threats and openly allow China to set up a military base, New Delhi fears that Islamabad might allow Beijing use of Pakistani military facilities without any public announcement. Indian concerns have also risen that China and Pakistan are coordinating their efforts in regard to border issues with India. The presence of the Chinese military in the Gilgit—Baltistan area of Pakistan Occupied Kashmir, purportedly to repair and upgrade the Karakoram Highway, has enormous implications for Indian security.

Overall, it has been rightly observed that China's policy toward Pakistan is "an object lesson in how to attain long-term national goals by calm calculation, forbearance, and diplomatic skill." Nevertheless, there are indeed limits to China—Pakistan ties. The relationship remains fundamentally asymmetrical: Pakistan wants more out of its ties with China than China is willing to offer. Today, while Pakistan's domestic problems are gargantuan, China will be very cautious in involving itself even more. In September 2011, China Kingho Group, one of China's largest private coal mining companies, pulled out of what was to be Pakistan's largest foreign-investment pact, citing concerns for the security of its personnel. Moreover, the closer China gets to Pakistan, the faster India would move into the U.S. orbit.

Amid worries about the potential destabilizing influence of Pakistani militants on China's Muslim minority in Xinjiang, Beijing has also taken a harder line against Pakistan. The flow of arms and terrorists from across the border in Pakistan remains a major headache for Chinese authorities, and Islamabad's inability and/or failure to curb extremism makes it difficult for the Chinese to trust Pakistan completely. If Pakistan wants to keep receiving support from China, then it needs to demonstrate progress on this issue.

As tensions rose between China and Pakistan in the aftermath of violence in the border town of Kashgar in Xinjiang in August 2011, President Zardari went to talk directly with local leaders and businessmen in Xinjiang, recognizing that if he was not able to mend fences with local leadership, Sino-Pakistani ties might be in real jeopardy.

China, at least publicly, has continued to emphasize that its relationship with Pakistan is far more important than isolated incidents of violence. To be clear, Chinese involvement in Pakistan is unlikely to match the U.S. profile in the country in the short to medium term, and it is not readily evident if China even wants to match the United States.

But flirtation with Pakistan gives China crucial space for diplomatic maneuvering vis-a'-vis India and the United States, and it will continue to utilize the relationship in pursuit of its larger strategic objectives. Pakistan is not going to be a common interest that binds China with either India or the United States any time soon. China was the only major power that openly voiced support for Pakistan after bin Laden's assassination, defending Islamabad and emphasizing that the Pakistani government may not have known about bin Laden's presence on its territory. During Prime Minister Gilani's visit, Chinese Premier Wen Jiabao affirmed that "Pakistan has made huge sacrifices and an important contribution to the international fight against terrorism, that its independence, sovereignty, and territorial integrity must be respected, and that the international community should understand and support Pakistan's efforts to maintain domestic stability and to realize economic and social development." Wen went on to state that China would like to be an "all-weather strategic partner," and would do its best to help the Pakistani government and people get through their difficulties. To underscore its commitment, China agreed to immediately provide Pakistan with 50 new JF-17 Thunder multi-role jets under a co-production agreement, even as negotiations continued for more fighter aircrafts including those with stealth technology. Despite this generosity, Pakistan wanted even more from China underscored by its expressed desire to have China take over the operation of Gwadar port in the Arabian Sea west of Karachi, in which Beijing has invested heavily in recent years and which serves an important role in the projection of China's naval prowess in the region. Pakistan has suggested that the port could be upgraded to a naval base for Chinese use. China, however, immediately rejected this offer, not wanting to antagonize the United States and India with the formal establishment of a base in Pakistan.

Ever since Chinese and Pakistani leaders underscored their nations' commitments to each other's core security interests at the Bandung Conference in 1955, Pakistan has occupied a unique position in China's foreign policy calculus. Their relations have been described as "arguably the most stable and durable element of China's foreign relations." India has been the main factor that has influenced China's and Pakistan's policies vis-a'-vis each other. China, viewing India as a potential challenger in the strategic landscape of Asia, has tended to use Pakistan to counter Indian power in the region, while Islamabad has gained access to civilian and military resources to balance Indian might in the sub-continent. The China—Pakistan partnership serves the interests of both by presenting India with a potential two-front theatre in the event of war with either country. Each is using the other to balance India as India's disputes with Pakistan keep India preoccupied, distracting New Delhi from the task of reaching its potential as a major regional and global player.

Although some U.S. and Indian voices are asking the Obama and Singh administrations, respectively, to partner with China to restore stability in Pakistan, Pakistan's utility for China is only likely to increase, particularly as India continues its ascent in the global inter-state hierarchy and pursues a more ambitious foreign policy posture primarily to counter China, resulting in a further tightening of the Sino-Pakistan entente cordiale.

## PAKISTAN-CHINA NUCLEAR DEAL AND NON-PROLIFERATION

Pakistan-China nuclear cooperation has always been under the certain obligations to non-proliferation concerns. It has been ensured from the very first day of cooperation between the two countries that mutual cooperation shall be only for peaceful purposes and will be subject to IAEA safeguards, which is evident by the *Article V(1&2)* of the Nuclear Cooperation agreement 1986 that *"The cooperation pursuant to this Agreement shall be solely for peaceful purposes and the two Governments agree that the recipient country shall request the International Atomic Energy Agency to apply its safeguards."* Moreover, all reactors provided by international community to Pakistan are safeguarded by IAEA. China has been a time-tested friend of Pakistan who has always been the sole supporter of Pakistan in any event of trouble. In spite of a huge criticism by international community, China has extended its cooperation with Pakistan, which is in line with the international obligations; therefore Pakistan would never create an awkward position for China before the international community by misusing any technology or equipment provided by China. Pakistan has also faced a lot of loss due to the so-called AQ Khan story and would not be able to face another incident like the earlier if happens; therefore, it has strengthened the security of its nuclear program according to international standards. Now, there is no chance of nuclear embezzlement in Pakistan.

The non-proliferation concerns of international community on Pakistan-China nuclear deal can be mitigated through the credible domestic legislation in both countries. According to NTI website, Chinese nuclear exports are governed by some certain principles, i.e. "(1) acceptance of IAEA safeguards; (2) peaceful use only; and (3) no re-transfers to a third country without China's prior consent. China has also promulgated domestic laws regulating nuclear and dual-use exports." (China's Nuclear Exports and Assistance to Pakistan 2003)

Pakistan has also adopted credible measures in this regard. Pakistan is member of multiple non-proliferation conventions at international level and it has sufficient controls on its nuclear related entities.

Recently Pakistan has given its stance about the efforts to promote non-proliferation at Nuclear Security Summit in Washington DC held on 12-13 April 2010, and assured the world community about the establishment of effective Command & Control system, Strict Regulatory Regimes, Extensive Export Control Regime and International Cooperation consistent with its National Policies.

Pakistan government has also taken credible legislative measures domestically against proliferation including nuclear, chemical, and biological transactions, which can provide an assurance to international community about Pakistan's commitment to non-proliferation. Pakistan has taken multiple measures which are supported with rules regarding licensing, diversion and 'catch all clause' providing heavy penalties of imprisonment up to 14 years or Rs. 5 million fines, or both, or confiscating the property of the convict inside Pakistan or outside Pakistan, depending upon the nature of the crime. (IAEA 2004) A brief view of these measures is given below

- Pakistan Nuclear Safety and Radiation Protection (PNSRP) Ordinance, 1984 and PNSRP Regulation, 1990. Controls the transaction of radioactive materials and nuclear substances.
- Statutory Notification No. SRO-782 (1), 1998 provides controls over the export of fissionable material.
- Chemical Weapons Convention Implementation Ordinance, 2000 (Ordinance No.LIV of 2000). Regulates the transaction of chemicals under chemical weapons convention obligations.
- Pakistan Nuclear Regulatory Authority Ordinance, 2001. Ordinance. PNRA is established to regulate all kinds of

imports and exports of radioactive materials and sources of radiation.

Berkeley Journal of Social Sciences Vol. 1, Issue 3, March 2011

- Export Control Act 2004, "The materials, equipment and services which could contribute to the designing, development, production, stockpiling, maintenance or use of nuclear and biological weapons and their delivery systems shall be subject to the provisions of this law." (Hussain 2006)
- Biological Weapon Bill 2010 (Proposed), It is proposed by the ministry of foreign affairs Pakistan to enact a law against the Biological weapon offenders, and suggests a death penalty for those who use or attempt to use Biological weapons, and suggests life imprisonment for those who develop, manufacture, import, export, or possess them. (News 2010)

An evaluation of the elements of effective export control system and its presence in Pakistan has been evaluated by Nazir Hussain, According to an analysis of Pakistan India laws about prevention of proliferation at Stimson centre, "India's and Pakistan's export control legislation nearly mirror one another in substance and structure. Both pieces of legislation explicitly define relevant terms, and there is near symmetry in the layout and organization of the various provisions."

Pakistan's nuclear posture also shows that it has adopted a strategy of 'minimum credible deterrence' with lower nuclear threshold. Following its MCD strategy, Pakistan does not need to have a huge number of nuclear weapons, therefore, Pakistan need not to clandestinely divert peaceful civilian nuclear technology to the military purposes. Moreover, Pakistan's nuclear program is Uranium based, which was developed purely through indigenous means. Pakistan has its own Uranium enrichment plants and sufficient natural Uranium reserves at its own soil; therefore, it does not need international resources for the development of its nuclear weapon program that may invite huge undue international concerns. The Khaleej Times editorial suggests that "the US needs to realize that it cannot control or dictate developments between third states no matter how distasteful they may be. It must not forget that China would not have done this if it was not comfortable with controls and security measures implemented by Pakistan. It is also a good opportunity for Pakistan to alleviate previous concerns about proliferation and prove it is a responsible nuclear state, one that deserves due respect."

The so called allegations of nuclear terrorism regarding Pakistan's nuclear weapon, is also a part of international propaganda against Pakistan's nuclear arsenal. One should be aware that stealing, manufacturing, and launching a nuclear weapon is not a task that can be fulfilled by some terrorists. Nuclear weapons are high-tech weapons which involve a complex mechanism for explosion. Such kind of knowledge cannot be obtained or used without having an organized institutional support. Moreover, Nuclear weapons are useless in the absence of credible delivery system, which is also very complicated and impossible to be designed, manufactured, and launched. Nuclear weapons cannot be launched through simple rocket launchers. Without having the involved technical equipments and the knowledge about their complicated operations, it is impossible for any group to use those weapons. It takes a lot of time and efforts to become capable of acquiring and launching nuclear weapons, which is even more difficult for sovereign states to obtain despite having huge resources and capabilities. In this scenario, how it is possible that Pakistan's nuclear weapons can fall into the hands of terrorist. The whole debate in this regard is baseless and just meant for the purpose of creating fuss against Pakistan.

## The Problem of Pakistan

India's geographically closest and most frequently problematic relationship is with its neighbour and prodigal twin, Pakistan. India's rise as a great power will have its most immediate impact on the extremely dangerous stalemate which exists between the two states. Many security concerns converge in Pakistan, as: the state has been a key supporter of the

Taliban in Afghanistan, factions of which the Pakistani Army is now fighting in a de facto civil war; elements within the state support Islamic terrorist organisations that periodically attack India, provoking regional crises; and, the Pakistani Army has a growing nuclear arsenal, which could be vulnerable to misuse by malicious elements within the state. India and Pakistan engaged in wars in 1965 and 1971, with crises about continuing Pakistani support for insurgents in the disputed Indian state of Jammu and Kashmir erupting periodically, and threatening war in 1990. Following Indian and Pakistani nuclear tests in May 1998, Pakistani incursions across the Line of Control in the Kargil region of Kashmir led to another limited war, and the veiled nuclear threat by Pakistani Foreign Secretary Shamshad Ahmed that, 'We will not hesitate to use any weapon in our arsenal to defend our territorial integrity.'1 Major terrorist attacks in Jammu and Kashmir on 1 October 2001 and in the Indian capital Delhi on 13 December 2001 again threatened war, though merely resulted in major military manoeuvres by India, code-named *Operation Parakram*. The lack of military retaliation by India despite grave provocation seems to suggest that India is successfully deterred by Pakistan's nuclear capability, and this in turn only fuels the eagerness of some elements within Pakistan to provoke India. Pakistan has adopted an "asymmetric nuclear escalation posture", which has deterred Indian conventional military power and thus enabled Pakistan's 'aggressive strategy of bleeding India by a "thousand cuts" with little fear of significant retaliation.'

India is four times larger and seven times more populated than Pakistan. As Pakistan averages only 300 miles in width, it is susceptible to a central assault that would split the country in two. A number of important Pakistani cities also lie close to the international border in the Indus River basin. As Pakistan is thus extremely vulnerable to conventional attack by India's larger military, it defines such an attack as an existential threat to the Pakistani state. Pakistani Lt. Gen. Khalid Kidwai thus outlined that Pakistan would use its nuclear weapons if: India attacks Pakistan and conquers a large part of its territory; India destroys a large part of Pakistan's land or air forces;

India blockades Pakistan in an effort to strangle it economically; or, India pushes Pakistan into a state of political destabilisation.3 This asymmetric escalation posture is designed for a rapid first use of nuclear weapons against conventional attacks, thus leaving India without the ability to punish terrorist attacks through conventional retaliation. As elements within Pakistan continue to provoke India, this creates an extremely dangerous imbalance reliant on India's restraint to maintain peace.

Vipin Narang notes that, 'Scholars who study the South Asian nuclear balance have argued that if a limited clash between India and Pakistan were to expand into a full-scale conventional war, escalation to the nuclear level would likely result.'4 Most of the "war-game" scenarios played out by the US military also foresee any conventional conflict between India and Pakistan escalating to the use of nuclear weapons within the first 12 days.5 New analyses of this eventuality reveal that a conflict between India and Pakistan, in which 100 nuclear bombs were dropped on cities and industrial areas within the two countries, would kill more than 20 million people from the blasts, fires and radioactivity. In addition, the explosions could produce enough smoke to cripple global agriculture. Smoke generated by burning cities could create a climatic response that immediately reduces sunlight, cools the planet, and reduces precipitation worldwide. This "nuclear winter" would reduce or eliminate agricultural production over vast areas, simultaneously decreasing crop yields nearly everywhere. Approximately one billion people worldwide today live on marginal food supplies and would be directly threatened with starvation.6 While some analysts maintain that nuclear weapons would be used in only a measured way, the chaos, fear and interruption of communications that would follow nuclear war's commencement leads some to doubt that attacks would be limited in any rational manner. Additionally, Pakistan could face a decision to use its entire nuclear arsenal quickly or lose it to Indian forces which seize its military bases. Thus, unrestrained nuclear war in South Asia potentially has cataclysmic regional and global consequences.

Following the terrorist attack by Kashmiri militants in December 2001 and the subsequent military standoff with Pakistan in *Operation Parakram*, the Indian Army announced a new limited war doctrine in April 2004 called the Cold Start doctrine, which aims to allow conventional retaliation without posing an existential threat to Pakistan. Under Cold Start, the Indian army would avoid delivering a catastrophic blow to Pakistan, and instead make shallow territorial gains, 50-80 kilometres deep, that could be used in post-conflict negotiations. This doctrine aims to deny Pakistan the justification of "regime survival" for employing nuclear weapons in response to a conventional Indian attack. However, Walter C. Ladwig III foresees that, 'An operational Cold Start capability could lead Pakistan to lower its nuclear red line, put its nuclear weapons on a higher state of readiness, develop tactical nuclear weapons, or undertake some equally destabilising course of action.'7 The danger of escalation is further compounded by the relatively immature "command and control" and early warning systems of both the Indian and Pakistani nuclear arsenals. There also remains the danger of nuclear accident as, if one nation accidentally detonates a nuclear warhead on one of its own military bases, it probably will not have adequate surveillance intelligence to know that it has not been attacked by its enemy, and thus may falsely "retaliate" against the other country.

Meanwhile, in the context of the continuing conflict in Afghanistan, Pakistan believes that the United States would intervene to prevent war, as it relies on Pakistani troops along the Afghan border and supplies for American forces are transported through Pakistan. Thus, Pakistan believes the only potential military action available to India is air-strikes against Islamist training camps, which itself is not a serious problem, and may actually help Islamabad by killing destabilising jihadists while generating massive support among

Pakistanis for their government. The dual problems of nuclear escalation and American reliance on Pakistan for counter-insurgency meant that following terrorist attacks in Mumbai by Pakistani group Lashkar-e-Taiba on 26 November

2008, which killed 163 people, India was unable to respond with conventional military strikes. Any attack by India might either destabilise the Pakistani Government, or escalate the conflict to nuclear exchange. In the event of state disintegration, Pakistani nuclear weapons could fall into the hands of militant elements who would attempt to use those weapons against India or the West.

Unfortunately, there is no easy path to stabilising reform within Pakistan. Pakistan essentially has a feudal political establishment, run by a civilian aristocracy of wealthy agricultural landowners and industrialists, and the Army.8 The civilian political parties primarily function as patronage networks, without deep-seated ideological differences, and merely struggle to control state resources.

As a key aim of the agricultural and industrial élites is to avoiding paying income taxes, the Pakistani Government is also chronically in debt. The Army is seen by most Pakistanis as the primary defender of the nation and the ultimate guarantor of domestic stability. The ever-present threat of India is used to justify the Army's disproportionate share of national resources, and the Army itself also owns and manages a large agricultural and industrial empire. Domestically, the Army is the ultimate power-broker between the political parties, and has acted on several occasions to remove the party in power. As successive governments have received bailouts from international financial institutions, neither the civilian political élites nor the Army have felt any real incentive to institute fundamental change.

For the time-being, the Army is objectively the most stable and responsible force to control the country. The Pakistani military is the only state institution that works effectively, and without it Pakistan would probably have disintegrated long ago. The dire alternatives are representatives of the rising wave of radical Islam who arose from the madrassas under the patronage of General Zia ul-Haq, and gained their training in the US-backed *mujahedeen* struggle against the Soviet occupation of Afghanistan. These elements, and more recent jihadist recruits, are currently involved in Kashmiri terrorist organisations like Jaysh-e-Mohammad, and Lashkar-e-Taiba, as well as in the Afghani and Pakistani Taliban which occupy Pakistan's border provinces. While the Pakistani Army and intelligence services are often unwilling to directly challenge these forces (and, indeed, currently cultivate relations with the Kashmiri groups and the Afghani Taliban), and external (and, particularly, American) attempts to move forces into Pakistani territory would almost certainly make things worse, this unstable situation is likely to continue.

As India's power increases, so will its ability to strategically encircle Pakistan, through relations with Iran and Afghanistan, and via naval power. At the same time, India's patience for Pakistan's continuing terrorist provocations will probably lessen. Nevertheless, Pakistan's deterrent capabilities remain, as attacks on the Pakistani state – either unsuccessful or successful – are likely to result in either nuclear exchange or widespread chaos and bloodshed. If India continues restraint, however, and reaches out to more moderate elements within the military and civilian political parties, it could leverage its growing economic strength to gradually help a more moderate Pakistani state develop.

## The Challenge of China

On a grander strategic level, relations between India and China will be highly significant as India emerges as a great power. There is a growing interdependence between the two Asian giants, as China is now India's number-one trading partner, with more than $52 billion in bilateral trade, and estimates are that China-India trade will surpass US-China trade by 2020. China's powerful manufacturing sector complements India's combination of a raw materials and cutting-edge technology economy. Strategically, a strong and influential India helps to create a more multipolar world, consistent with Chinese interests, although China increasingly regards India as its main Asian rival. China is thus involved in a complex game of encirclement with India. China has armed Pakistan with nuclear weapons and ballistic missile technology, and has built 'strong military-to-military ties with Burma, Pakistan, Nepal, Bangladesh, and Sri Lanka as part of what Indians see as a strategy to tie India down, Gulliver-like, in its region.'9 China is also developing deep-water ports throughout the Indian Ocean to support its projected blue-water naval capacity.

Meanwhile, on the border, China continues to press its claims to vast tracts of Indian territory. Over the past years, increased friction in the border area between India and China has led to incursions by Chinese troops, the wounding of several Indian border police, and a build-up of military forces on both sides, as Beijing has been uncharacteristically assertive in its claims to sections of India's Arunachal Pradesh state. The Indians responded by moving 30,000 troops and their latest warplanes into the area, leading some analysts to predict a China-India war within five years.

China rejects the McMahon Line that forms the border, and places the traditional Sino-Indian border at the base of the Himalayan foothills. Stratfor's George Friedman argues that, for China, control of Tibet is of vital strategic importance, providing a barrier against its populous and economically and militarily-advancing neighbour. The high mountain passes of Tibet provide virtually impenetrable terrain which is easy to protect militarily. Along the frontier directly south of this border, in India, is one of the largest population concentrations in the world. If China were to withdraw, Beijing fears that this population could migrate into Tibet, and Tibet could gradually turn into a beachhead for Indian power that would directly abut Sichuan and Yunnan provinces. The Chinese thus see control of Tibet as a matter of fundamental national security. They also see the 1959 decision by Indian Prime Minister Jawaharlal Nehru to give asylum to the Dalai Lama, and the continuing support for the Tibetan government-in-exile, as perpetuating this threat. Thus, 'Beijing's price for a border settlement and for normalisation of ties with India, appears to be that India dismantle the

Tibetan settlement in Dharamshala and request the Dalai Lama take up residence in another country.'On a broader front,

80 per cent of China's oil and gas supplies transit the Indian Ocean and South China Sea, so the Chinese navy is increasingly making its presence felt in the area in order to secure its lines of supply. For China, like India, the steady flow of imported resources is not just an issue of economic growth, but also of the longevity of the Chinese Communist Party. Chinese leaders increasingly fear that adversaries could blockade sea lanes and strategic bottlenecks such as the Strait of Malacca, and are thus moving to an offshore defence policy that will include "distant ocean defence". China's actions, however, may impinge upon India's interests and destabilise relations.

Jason Blazevic argues that, following "defensive realist" strategies, each nation will attempt to gain power for self-preservation and other nations will see this move as a strategic threat, thus decreasing collective security. As part of this competition, China has been developing a so-called "string-of-pearls" strategy, expanding influence into ports in Burma, Sri Lanka and Pakistan. According to a report by US defence contractor Booz Allen Hamilton, 'China is building strategic relationships along the sea lanes from the Middle East to the South China Sea in a way that suggests defensive and offensive positioning to protect China's energy interests.'11 China emerged as the biggest military spender in the Asia-Pacific in 2006, and now has the fourth-largest defence expenditure in the world. Its navy is also considered the third-largest in the world behind only the US and Russia, and is superior to the Indian Navy. In this context, India perceives Chinese actions as power maximisation, and fears that China's forward-basing strategy will be used to contain India and rapidly achieve hegemony in the Indian Ocean.

Meanwhile, China and India have adopted nuclear "assured retaliation" postures (what they sometimes refer to as "credible minimum deterrence"), which rely on a small but secure and survivable nuclear force that assures a retaliatory strike against a primary opponent. In many ways, this seems like the most stable aspect of the competition between India and China, though it is yet to be seen what reaction a new generation of

*Surya* missiles might provoke in China. Meanwhile, analysts like Stephen Walt expect that China will follow a consistent but non-provocative build-up of its military capabilities and diplomatic alliances over the long-term, aiming to gradually edge the United States out of a hegemonic position. India is likely to mirror this build-up and thus tension, and possible low-level confrontation, may result on the India-China border and in the Indian Ocean region.

## INDIA AND PAKISTAN: ON THE NUCLEAR THRESHOLD

This briefing book contains material from the National Security Archive's project on U.S. policy toward South Asia, which is documenting nuclear developments in India and Pakistan from the 1950s to the present. The archive is collecting U.S. government records that illustrate American policies and perspectives. Information is being collected from the National Archives and the presidential libraries, and through Freedom of Information Act (FOIA) and Mandatory Review requests, used to obtain the declassification of now-secret materials. A selective and focused collection of documents will be made available to researchers.

The project is creating a comprehensive history of nuclear developments in South Asia, including weapons programs in India and Pakistan, as well as international efforts to curtail proliferation in the region. Information about factors that influenced nuclear issues, such as the unresolved enmity between India and Pakistan, and India's perception of China as a security threat, will also be incorporated. The U.S. has generally opposed nuclear proliferation in South Asia, while seeking to preserve good relations with both India and Pakistan. At times, however, its commitment has been questioned, because it has seemed to subordinate nonproliferation policy to other concerns. During the Soviet occupation of Afghanistan, for instance, the U.S. provided massive levels of economic and military aid to its ally, Pakistan. The assistance was widely criticized, because Pakistan was demonstrably importing nuclear-related material, from China and other nations. Few doubted that it was engaged in an active nuclear weapons development program.

China's role as a leading provider of sensitive technology to Pakistan has repeatedly strained U.S.-China relations, and has complicated efforts to expand U.S.-China trade. The Archive's South Asia project is using the FOIA to seek the declassification of documents discussing this issue, and other contemporary and controversial topics. Materials collected for this project will, of course, reflect a U.S. perspective. As noted, nonproliferation policy is influenced by other concerns, including competition among the major powers. The Archive's efforts are directed toward enhancing understanding of U.S. decisions and the issues that influenced policy formulation. The analyst for the South Asia nuclear project is Joyce Battle, who prepared this briefing book. She is also the analyst for the Archive's documentation projects on the Persian Gulf and U.S. policy toward Iraq. Materials collected for the latter project were published in a document set, Iraqgate: Saddam Hussein, U.S. Policy and the Prelude to the Persian Gulf War, 1980-1994.

## Briefing Book Documents

The documents in the briefing book date from 1961 to 1983. In 1961, India had an advanced civilian nuclear program, while Pakistan's was in its early stages. In 1983, nine years had elapsed since India's explosion of a nuclear device, and Pakistan's nuclear weapons program was well under way. During the early 1960s, India under Prime Minister Jawaharlal Nehru strongly advocated global disarmament, but was apprehensive about China's nuclear weapons program. India's concern increased following its October 1962 territorial war with China. The stakes were raised by China's first nuclear weapons test in October 1964. Many observers thought it increasingly likely that India would respond to China's actions by seeking its own weapons capability. War with Pakistan in 1965 further alarmed India: it was angered by China's outspoken support for Pakistan during the conflict, and disappointed by what it viewed as insufficient Western attention to its security needs. The U.S.

considered various options that might dissuade India from developing nuclear weapons, including scientific cooperation aimed at enhancing India's national prestige. It also joined in cooperative arrangements with both India and Pakistan to monitor nuclear and missile developments in China and the Soviet Union. India, for its part, launched a campaign seeking security guarantees to shield it from Chinese nuclear attack, arguing that such assurances might make a nuclear weapons program of its own unnecessary. Various options were proposed: U.S. guarantees, joint U.S.-Soviet guarantees, guarantees from all the nuclear states, British guarantees, or guarantees in conjunction with the nuclear nonproliferation treaty, then being negotiated. U.S. policy makers seriously considered these proposals, although some doubted that they would deter India from developing a bomb.

The Embassy in New Delhi viewed India's overtures sympathetically, while the Defence Department opposed any commitment to India that would alienate Pakistan, a U.S. military ally. In 1967, both President Lyndon Johnson and Defence Secretary Robert McNamara supported the concept of guarantees during meetings with a visiting Indian representative. Later that year, U.S. and Soviet officials were still discussing security guarantees, hoping to induce India to sign the nuclear nonproliferation treaty. No agreement was ever reached, however, in part because India itself concluded that such commitments would not guarantee its security in the event of actual nuclear conflict. In May 1974, India tested a nuclear device, although it called the event a "peaceful nuclear explosion."

Its terminology did not forestall censure, both within the international community and from domestic critics. The test had serious consequences: India lost much of the foreign technical assistance that had till then sustained its civilian nuclear program. A Pakistani reaction to India's test of a nuclear explosive was predicted, and confirmed within a few years. By the mid-1970s, intelligence reports indicated that Pakistan had an active nuclear weapons program, and in 1983 the State Department noted that it had "unambiguous evidence" of this fact. Documents in this briefing book illuminate aspects of the internal debate among U.S. officials, as they attempted to formulate effective policies toward nuclear proliferation in South Asia while protecting sometimes conflicting interests and objectives.

## Nuclear Threat Reduction in India and Pakistan

The Carnegie Endowment for International Peace (CEIP) published a draft report, 'Universal Compliance: A Strategy for Nuclear Security', in June 2004. The report proposes a strategic blueprint for US leadership to rethink international nuclear nonproliferation and global nuclear security. In this report, the recommended measures for nuclear risk reduction between India and Pakistan include:

- o Establishment of national risk reduction centres in both countries to administer agreed upon confidence-building measures.
- o Acommitment not to develop, produce, and use 'tactical' nuclear weapons.
- o Agreement not to flight-test missiles in the direction of the other country.
- o Agreement to flight-test missiles only from designated test ranges.
- o Provision of advance notification of the movement of missiles for training purposes.

The Henry L. Stimson Centre's report, 'Reducing Nuclear Dangers in South Asia', argues that: "The stability-instability paradox that was formulated in the West to characterise the dangers of nuclear deterrence is alive and well in South Asia. This paradox holds that, while offsetting nuclear capabilities might indeed prevent a full-blown conventional or nuclear war, the presence of these fearsome weapons could also encourage the use of violence at lower levels in the expectation that escalation would be contained by a mutual desire to avoid the nuclear threshold." And that, "Kashmir has been inflamed since the advent of covert nuclear capabilities on the subcontinent, and tensions have grown even more pronounced with the demonstration of overt nuclear capabilities in 1998. The region is now experiencing crises with greater frequency and severity."

The report includes extensive deliberations during two workshops, November 14-18, 2002, and May 20-23, 2003, with participants from the US, India and Pakistan, convened by the Stimson Centre to discuss escalation control and scenarios that could lead to crossing of the nuclear threshold. It provides the following 'doable' steps in the near term:

- o Establishment of national risk reduction centresto serve as focal points for the administration of confidence-building measures.
- o Missile-related measures to formalise and properly implement the agreement concerning prior notification of missile launches; to formalise and extend the time-line for such notifications; to forego missile flight tests in the direction of the other country; to flight test missiles only from designated test ranges; and to provide advance notification of the movement of missiles for training purposes.
- o Clarifying terminology or developing common terminology on nuclear-related programmes, deployment, and doctrine could reduce misunderstanding and increase crisis stability.
- o Leadership declarations affirming responsible nuclear stewardshipcould help defuse nuclear dangers and facilitate an improvement in bilateral relations.
- o Increased awareness of nuclear dangers, particularly with regard to the possible acquisition of nuclear materials by terrorist groups, would be advisable.

In the Stimson Centre's report, the proposals collected in the workshops on escalation control are grouped in five categories: improving bilateral relations; nuclear risk reduction and strategic restraint; safety and security measures; and, improving intelligence through communication.

Both the reports, by CEIP and the Stimson Centre, have this presumption that 'deterrence' may not work between India and Pakistan as similar to the Cold War experience. Such assumptions are not completely invalid for the two countries did resort to nuclear rhetoric during the 1999 Kargil conflict and indulged in 'nuclear signalling' during the period of crisis in 2001-2. In addition, the absence of a doctrine without no-first-use policy and repeated calls from the Pakistani side to lower the threshold could have a certain bearing on the thinking of Western analysts. Already, the strategic debate had reached a slightly higher level than was normally prevalent in the subcontinent when the Indian Army Chief stated that a limited war with Pakistan is possible.

For any future war in the subcontinent, the two most likely scenarios discussed in the Cooperative Monitoring Centre Occasional Paper of Sandia National Laboratories, are: a breakdown along the common border in Kashmir, and failure of nuclear policy. The authors propose an alternative approach through which India and Pakistan can begin to cooperate in managing their common border to prevent a breakdown. The ultimate concern in the report about the existence of nuclear weapons is the possibility of their use in a time of conflict. The following are the enumerations in the Cooperative Monitoring Centre Occasional Paper that focuses on the monitoring of nuclear safety, security, and stability:

- o The ability to assess the current operational and deployment status of nuclear weapons is perhaps the most critical factor in near-term crisis prevention.
- o Developing measures to prevent escalation.
- o National decisions to include both technical and procedural mechanisms to restrict use of weapons and delivery systems will permit more time to attempt diplomatic solutions to conflict before initiating weapons use.
- o Another element of nuclear stability is determining the readiness of launch systems. There may be a number of indicators associated with launcher alert status. These include: Flight parameters loaded, other software updates (if appropriate); Vehicle fuelled (missile or

aircraft); Crews readied; Delivery vehicle in launch location (moved to launch point); Transporter system in ready position (e.g., transporter erector launcher [TEL] in raised launch position); Weapon armed. While most of these indicators of launch preparation are difficult to monitor, some, such as missile fuelling and launcher movements, might be monitored through electronic sensors.

- There is the possibility of use through miscalculation or misinterpretation.
- Sharing information on any of the concerns for safety, security or accident will require an infrastructure of capabilities and procedures. These include methods for providing timely, reliable, secure, accurate, and authenticated communications.
- Ensuring safety of nuclear weapons and materials will primarily be a state responsibility because of the highly classified nature of most safety issues. These issues involve detailed design, as well as material and handling details. An expanded mission for hotlines between the Directors-General of Military Operations and between the Heads of State might be established to address this critical issue.

Acknowledging the fact that only the Indian and Pakistani governments can decide whether and on what basis, to establish new risk reduction measures, the 'Working Group Report of the Centre for Strategic and International Studies (CSIS)' recommends the following steps for nuclear risk reduction:

- A new communications mechanism-nuclear risk reduction centres (NRRCs) in India and Pakistan-should be established to complement existing bilateral channels.
- The main functions of the NRRCs would be to provide each party a dedicated, secure means of: (a) notifying the other side about activities or events on its territory that might be wrongly perceived or misinterpreted that could lead to conflict, (b) sharing information that the two countries are obliged to exchange under existing

security agreements, and (c) seeking and receiving clarifications about àmbiguous events on the other' sterritory. Other functions could include the conduct of joint exercises of certain NRRC notification procedures, technical back-up during crises, and support for consultations on the implementation of existing confidence-building measures (CBMs).

o Adequate infrastructure already exists in South Asia to support a wide range of secure communication options, including data, voice, video, or a combination of these. The approximate cost for a dedicated cable permitting teletype and voice communication would be US$10,000-50,000 annually. For a dedicated satellite channel permitting teletype, voice, and video, the annual cost would be roughly US$560,000.

o The centres would operate on a continuous, round-the-clock basis. Written messages using agreed formats would be the norm, although voice and video capability would also be desirable. It would be the prerogative of each government to decide where it would institutionally house its NRRC and to determine how its NRRC would relate to other government organisations. The Indian and Pakistani solutions to these questions need not be symmetrical.

The Working Group Report concluded, that "the circumstances in South Asia today are very different from the circumstances surrounding the current US-Russian relationship and the relationship that existed when the US-Soviet Centres were brought into being. To tailor a new communications mechanism to the needs of South Asia, the mechanism could appropriately take on a wider range of functions than the US and Russian Centres."

Rodney W.Jones assumes that there lies intense political conflict over Kashmir and that the escalation in South Asia has the potential of becoming a nuclear war. In one of the papers presented during the fourth nuclear stability roundtable during March 12-13, 2002, in Washington on 'Military Asymmetry and

Instability in Emerging Nuclear States: India and Pakistan,' he suggests the following conditions of nuclear stability in the region:

- o High nuclear threshold (strong conventional defence)
- o Secure second strike capabilities (robust C4I)
- o Rough parity in size and defence space
- o Neither falling behind the other's first strike edge (good early warning?) Supposing that "nuclear deterrence might provide the security that allows a general improvement in security relations" in South Asia, the UNIDR (United Nations Institute for Disarmament Research) research paper depicts various aspects of nuclear confidence-building measures between India and Pakistan. Commenting on the current conflict situation between the two countries, the authors of the paper subscribe to developing CBMs in connection with the 'central issue-Kashmir'. An interim suggestion is made to work on the possibilities of addressing the 'central sore-cross-border terror raids' from Pakistan.

With regard to nuclear CBMs, according to the UNIDR paper, India and Pakistan should share the development of respective nuclear doctrines and security concepts to have clarity over 'red lines'; develop mechanisms on notification of ballistic and cruise missile tests; create nuclear risk reduction centres with robust safety systems to deal with the issues of accidental or unauthorised use; and install a secure and dedicated line of communication including safe command and control systems between the national authorities (the nature or constitution of national authority remains undefined). The paper categorically puts the 'Kashmir issue' to be discussed as in the final stages of CBMs between the two countries.

The UNIDR study concludes that the two countries should seize the ripe moment (that has begun since the two countries agreed to peace talks during the sidelines of the SAARC summit in January 2004) in the context of possibility of conflict. "Any future terrorist incident might provoke India into punitive action, which in the worst case might lead to uncontrolled or accidental responses, all the way to a nuclear exchange. This suggests that, although the nuclear aspects will have to be part of the general discussions on security, it might also be worth considering whether they can be made separable, in case the moment passes too quickly."

The aspect of geographical proximity of the two countries is also discussed in one of the reports dealing with nuclear threat reduction measures. Based on some hypothetical South Asian launch point-target combinations, the missile travel time between India and Pakistan is estimated between 8 to 13 minutes.

Taking account of the danger of false alarms and miscalculations, the Pugwash Discussion Paper of 2002 suggests that a posture of De-alert (most basic measures would be to keep the weapons de-mated from delivery systems; use of locking devices), and installation of best available safety measures into the weapons, like use of Insensitive High Explosive (IHE) and fire-resistant pits would significantly reduce the risk of inadvertent or unauthorised use of weapons.

From the above discussed strategic policy recommendations, there emerge two sets of proposals that could draw attention of the diplomats and strategic planners of India and Pakistan. In the first set, one can identify mechanisms for escalation control and nuclear force management within each state. The second set includes possible measures of nuclear CBMs by the two countries to work towards long lasting stability in the region.

## HOW CAN THEY BE IMPROVED? INDIA-CHINA RELATIONS

### Economic Constraints

Despite the development that has occurred so far, however, there are still many constraints in bilateral relations between China and India, affecting political, economic and security co-operation. In economic relations, the current status of India-China co-operation does not match the economic scales of the two countries. There is a huge opportunity for them to expand the size of their markets and deepen their economic interdependence. In 2011, the trade volume between China and India was only equal to one-sixth of that between China and the United States and one-third of that between China and South Korea. Given the large populations in each of these countries, it is obvious thatneither country has fully explored the market opportunities available in the other. Moreover, India has been worried about a trade deficit with China; for instance, India had a US$27 billion deficit with China in 2011. Such a trade imbalance could lead to nervousness in the bilateral relationship. According to the *Wall Street Journal*, India has been putting pressure on the Chinese Government to import more Indian products and has set high tariffs to protect Indian industries. Further, the relative backwardness of the domestic infrastructure in India is another constraint on co-operation that restricts deeper economic collaboration and personnel exchanges.

## Border Issues

The India-China border and other territorial disputes, along with the issue of Tibet, restrict the establishment of political trust. Such a bilateral security dilemma is difficult to solve and is not conducive to co-operation. India has been concerned with China's infrastructure building in Tibet, which it views as a strengthening of China's strategic advantage in the region. According to the Indian media, Prime Minister Singh agreed to station an additional 90,000 troops along India's border with China in 2012. Although India has officially recognised that Tibet is part of China, it still hosts the Tibetan independence force. Moreover, given that China and Pakistan maintain a quasi-alliance, while India and Pakistan are still hostile to each other, the power-balance game is still being played in the region. China is also very sensitive about India's recent involvement in oil exploration in the South China Sea and its actions to strengthen maritime co-operation with Japan, which has disputes with China over islands in the region. The so-called "String of Pearls" strategy, which suggests that China is constraining India by constructing ports and bases in the Indian Ocean region, has been heavily covered by the Indian media.

## Perception Problems

Finally, the peoples of China and India lack a comprehensive and rational understanding of each other. In India, China is often viewed as a dangerous competitor; the media particularly portrays China this way. In China, a few nationalists tend to express a strong dislike of India and do not recognise that the country should be viewed as a regional and global power. A recent poll showed that two-thirds of Chinese respondents had negative views of India and only 23 per cent of Indian interviewees believed that the relationship between China and India was co-operative. The mutual distrust between the two peoples has undoubtedly affected the development of the relationship between their countries and may continue to do so.

## Multi-Sector Co-operation

The development of economic co-operation is the main pillar of India-China relations. The volume of India-China trade increased from US$100 million in 1988, to US$73.9 billion in 2011. China has become India's biggest trading partner and India is China's seventh largest trading partner. The two governments have set the goal of increasing their trade volume to US$100 billion by 2015. With increasingly closer trade relations, mutual investment has developed quickly as well. By December 2011, China's accumulated investment in India had reached US$57.6 million and India's investment in China had reached US$44.2 million. Their mutual investment is still booming.

In their political interaction, a multi-channel and multi-level political dialogue platform has been set up, with frequent bilateral visits for in-depth discussions to resolve difficult issues and problems. On 26 September 2011, the first Sino-Indian Strategic and Economic Dialogue was launched, in which Chinese and Indian economic and foreign affairs policymakers began frank and direct discussions. National leaders of the two countries have frequent meetings in bilateral, regional and global forums. Taking 2012 as an example, in March President Hu Jintao travelled to India to take part in a joint Brazil, Russia, India and China meeting and spoke with Prime Minister Manmohan Singh of India. Then, in June, Premier Wen Jiabao met with Prime Minister Singh at the "Rio+20" United Nations Conference on Sustainable Development in Brazil. In November, Premier Wen again met with Prime Minister Singh in Cambodia, during the East Asia Summit. The leaders' diplomacy strongly promotes the development of the relationship between their countries.

China and India have also begun co-operating on security issues, particularly on border and non-traditional security issues. In January 2012, State Councillor Dai Bingguo and Indian National Security Advisor Shivshankar Menon met to discuss border issues; this was the fifteenth meeting of its kind. The two parties agreed to build a mechanism for consultation and co-ordination on border affairs. The first meeting of the mechanism was held in March 2012. China and India have also reached a basic consensus on strengthening maritime security co-operation and a maritime affairs dialogue is currently being planned. Cultural exchanges and co-operation between China and India continue to expand. This has become an important driving force for promoting the development and deepening of relations between the two countries. For example, in 2011 and 2012, 500 Indian and 500 Chinese young people were invited to visit the other country and to participate in cultural activities. That same year, 606,000 people travelled from India to China and 118,000 travelled from China to India, illustrating how frequently the people of the two countries interact.

## True Strategic Partners

We believe that China and India should become strategic partners in the true sense, rather than viewing each other as hostile competitors. Currently, it seems that a certain degree of asymmetry exists in China's and India's perceptions of each other. In particular, India does not trust China politically and views it as a competitor. In contrast, to the extent that India features in Chinese strategic thinking, it is viewed more as a development partner, rather than a competitor. These different views affect the efficiency of co-operation, which has already led to misunderstandings between the two and some estrangement. Therefore, to achieve fully the goal of co-operation based on common interests, China and India should first adjust their view of each other's role in their foreign policy, by viewing each other as real strategic partners, beyond mere rhetoric. On the regional level, China and India are stakeholders in maintaining regional peace, stability and prosperity. They should go beyond zero-sum thinking and employ a co-operative attitude to resolve their differences and address common regional challenges. Globally, they should play a greater role in the process of reforming global governance.

## Prerequisites for Success

The key to achieving this partnership is to abolish both the Cold War mentality and the concept of "sphere of influence". India and China should not see South Asia or East Asia as being solely under their respective spheres of influence. For its part, India should understand that China respects the special role that India plays in South Asia and work with Beijing to promote the development and stability of the region. China's active approach in South Asia and the South Asian Association for Regional Co-operation does not aim at eliminating the influence of India; its involvement concerns the fact that it shares borders with South Asian countries. If we judge a country geographically, China could also be seen as a South Asian country, in the sense that the South Asian-influenced Tibetan Plateau comprises a quarter of China's overall territory. Historically, culturally and geographically, China has had close ties with South Asian countries and India does not need to be nervous about China's engagement with the region. Taking economic development as an example, China's south-western provinces, such as Sichuan and Yunnan, have strong interests in promoting business connections with South Asia, as they see this region as a major market and investment destination.

China's investment in the ports of the region ispurely for commercial purposes. This investment is important because China needs commercial ports on the Indian Ocean for transportation across the region, which is very important for China's trade and its energy supplies.

In turn, China should also accept the reality that India is an important player in East Asia. India, as an emerging power, has been seen as an economic opportunity by many regional countries. For example, the prime minister of Singapore, Lee Hsien Loong, once commented that the historical origin of Singapore was due to trade between China and India. It now seems that history is repeating itself, as an opportunity exists for Singapore in linking the two countries. It is natural for India to pursue its interests in the region, as East Asia is the most robust economy in the world, particularly since the Global Financial Crisis.

Some Chinese intellectuals have expressed concern that India could ally with the US to constrain China. Judging from developments since 2010, however, there is no evidence that India has formed a strong alliance with the US to compete with China. For example, India refused to join in the proposed quadrilateral security mechanism comprising the US, Japan, India and Australia. Regardless of the effort the US has put into trying to draw India closer by emphasising shared values and democratic institutions, Indian policymakers have remained as neutral as possible and developed foreign policy based on India's own national interests. India has its own goal of great power status and understands that a good relationship with China is the key to achieving it. Both countries are latecomers to the international system and passive receivers of the existing international norms and rules. Hostility between these two countries will only weaken the alliance between the emerging countries in attempting to reform the global order. Based on the above, the authors recommend following measures to improve India-China relations:

- Upgrading the current Sino-Indian Strategic and Economic Dialogue meetings to a higher level – for example, by having future dialogues led by the Chinese State Councillor and Indian National Security Advisor, with the full participation of diplomatic, economic and military policymakers;

- Strengthening co-ordination and communication in regional and global institutions;
- Nurturing a more positive image of each other, both in government and society;
- Working on non-traditional security issues, such as the maritime security co-operation, and making it a basis for better mutual understanding;
- Careful handling of sensitive issues – particularly such issues as the Tibetan independence movement, the South China Sea and the so-called "String of Pearls"; and,
- Promoting open regionalism and rejecting the idea that East Asia and South Asia should be viewed as separate blocs and defined regions.

## Future Prospects

Although these constraints exist, we still believe there is a positive future for the bilateral relationship, because the two countries share many common interests in a wide variety of areas. For example, their economic structures are complementary. Further, China is a manufacturing power and India is a major worldwide player in the service industry. Both countries face similar problems in domestic economic and social development and can share their experiences and support each other in approaching these. Regarding security, from China's point of view, if China cannot handle its relationship with India effectively, it will not be able to shape an ideal security environment, which is crucial for its domestic development. For India, a good relationship with China will not only benefit India's development but also be an important way to enhance its international influence.

On the regional level, China and India actively participate in multilateral co-operation processes, such as the free-trade schemes in South-East Asia. Both countries have concluded a free-trade agreement with the Association of South-East Asian Nations.

The recently launched negotiations for the Regional Comprehensive Economic Partnership also include them. If concluded by 2015, as intended, this partnership will become one of the world's largest free-trade areas. Moreover, both countries recognise that non-traditional security issues in the region, such as terrorism, transnational crime, piracy, natural disasters and other challenges, can only be tackled through joint efforts and regional co-operation. One example is the sub-regional co-operation between China, India, Burma and Bangladesh, which focuses on economic co-operation, as well as non-traditional security issues, such as narcotics. On a global level, broad common interests exist between China and India, such as reform of international financial institutions, maintenance of an open international trade system and tackling the challenge of climate change. As developing countries, China and India can strengthen coordination in global institutions to protect their national interests. China and India's strategic partnership has already had a great impact, especially in dealing with North-South relations. This is why, worldwide, an increasing number of people are beginning to talk about a possible future for "Chindia".

## INDIA-CHINA RELATIONS: AN INDIAN PERSPECTIVE

There is a growing perception now that the global economic gravity has shifted to Asia and that India and China, the emerging economic powerhouses in the region, will shape the Twenty-first century. In making such feelings a reality however, the nature of the future dynamics of domestic conditions as well as external relations of the two nations appears a crucial factor; this article attempts to focus in particular on the future prospects for India-China ties on the premise that this, along with the roles of other Asian powers like Japan, is going to be important in the matter of guaranteeing the stability and prosperity of the region as well as rest of the world. The article tries to present the Chinese side with Indian perspectives of key developments. Chinese perspectives are already being made available in India in a similar manner. The writer feels that put together, such exchanges will facilitate creation of a better mutual understanding between the two sides, impacting favourably on the overall India-China relationship.

## Growing Optimism

Broadly speaking, India-China ties at government levels remain stable at this juncture; New Delhi and Beijing have established a 'strategic and cooperative partnership for peace and prosperity' and signed a document on 'shared vision for the 21st century', signifying that the Sino-Indian ties have gone beyond the bilateral context and acquired a global character. Accordingly, India and China are cooperating on international issues related to the diversification of global energy mix, climate change, arms control and disarmament, non-traditional security threats, counter-terrorism, WTO, WMD, human rights and South-South Co-operation. Bilaterally, the two sides now aim at building 'a relationship of friendship and trust, based on equality, in which each is sensitive to the concerns and aspirations of the other'.

They are not viewing each other as a security threat and are by and large satisfactorily implementing confidence building measures in the disputed border, besides carrying out joint military exercises. Special Representatives of India and China have so far held thirteen rounds of border talks, though with no tangible results. Most important is that with an attitude of promoting ties looking beyond the unsolved and 'complex' border dispute, India and China are speeding up their trade and economic contacts. Bilateral trade is fast gathering momentum, with the volume to the tune of US$ 40 billion now and projections for US$ 60 billion by 2010.

China has emerged as India's largest trading partner, replacing the US, in April 2008- February 2009 period. Also significant is the ongoing momentum in their exchanges of high level visits reflecting the desire of each party to forge stronger ties, of which the recently concluded state visit of Indian

President Ms Patil to China is a prominent example. Notwithstanding the encouraging picture brought out above, there are issues deeply dividing India and China; resolving them once for all is of utmost necessity, to further strengthen their relations. There are some talks in India about the past civilisational contacts helping resolution of the issues; they however lack substance. As modern nation states, the India and China have developed geo-political interests, which often tend to clash. What follows is a discussion on the conditions contributing to India-China frictions and the likely scenario in bilateral ties in future.

## Problem Areas—Boundary Issue

As this writer sees, the boundary issue comes foremost in the list of problem areas. It is most sensitive one for both India and China as it relates closely to territorial integrity and sovereignty in respect of each side. It therefore needs to be handled carefully by the two nations. China's understanding of Indian perspectives on the boundary issue will remain incomplete if it does not take into account the traditional doubts prevailing in India on China having been territorially ambitious. Examples being quoted in India in this regard include Mao's description of China's 'palm' (Tibet) and 'five fingers' (Nepal, Sikkim, Bhutan, NEFA and Ladakh); references are also being made in India to the PRC's sense of 'historical loss' of territories expressed through their maps and atlas series, published in eighties. Such maps had even been seen claiming that India's Assam, even Andamans, were 'historically' parts of China.

Proceeding from 'doubts' to substantive points, it is being seen in India that the border positions of India and China are in conflict with each other and hence are difficult to solve. China's claims are based on its historical stand – all its borders, including with India, are as defined during the Qing dynasty period which ended in 1912.The root of the border problem with India lies in Beijing's position that a large chunk of its territory, especially the 90,000 Sq km area in the Eastern sector, were illegally taken away by the British India, after the 1914 Simla Convention and that India inherited the British legacy. This has provided the rationale for Beijing in rejecting the McMahon line, a product of the Convention and in claiming the entire Arunachal Pradesh state of India as part of Chinese territory, called by it as 'Southern Tibet' Authoritative scholars in China have categorically stated that Beijing cannot recognize the McMahon line; if it did so, it would amount to Chinese admission of the 1962 conflict as a 'war of aggression' as well as an implicit acknowledgement that Tibet was once independent of China. On the other hand, for India, McMahon line remains the 'de facto' border with China.

The Sino-Indian border problem remains complicated with the Chinese claiming recently the 2.1 Sq km 'finger area' of Sikkim, the status of which as an Indian state has already been recognized by Beijing 'de facto'. On the current scenario, meriting attention are India's concerns arising from various factors – the reported Chinese intrusions, said to number 270 in 2008, into the Indian border, the adverse reaction of Beijing to the visit of the Indian Prime Minister Dr. Manmohan Singh to Arunachal Pradesh, China's bid to stop the loans for Arunachal Pradesh from the Asian Development Bank and strong Chinese state-controlled media criticisms of India's dispatch of additional troops to and positioning of advanced fighter aircraft in its Eastern border. Adding to India's discomfort has also been the rise in the level of Chinese media rhetoric against India, noticed in 2009; this has however subsided now.

Sino-Indian border talks, despite thirteen rounds of talks so far between two Special representatives, have not led to any tangible result in finalising a 'frame work' for a boundary settlement in accordance with the Agreement on Political Parameters, reached in 2005. While Beijing's stand is to approach the border issue in the spirit of 'mutual understanding and mutual accommodation', India wants 'ground realities' to be taken into account. About the reported Chinese claim over Tawang, an interesting argument is that besides strategic factors, the same has been due to the China's fears that Buddhist monasteries in the border including the one in Tawang have been centres of Tibetan resistance to the Chinese authority and as such, they should be taken over by it. Interestingly, the

Chinese have introduced some new elements to the border question by questioning the already agreed position of keeping areas with settled populations out of the dispute. Is China ready for accommodation on the border issue? The statement made by the PRC Ambassador to India in November 2006 that both sides should make compromises on the 'disputed' Arunachal may be meaningful in this regard.

China's general stand is to 'shelve' the difficult border issues like the one with India and instead work for 'common development'. For e.g the PRC wants to 'shelve' the South China Sea territorial dispute, leave the Senkaku issue with Japan for 'future generations' to solve and 'put aside the Sino-Indian border dispute waiting for a suitable climate for solution' (Deng Xiaoping to the then Indian leader Vajpayee, Beijing, 1979). What is being noticed in India is that China never gives up its claims on sovereignty over disputed areas. An example is Japan-China settlement on exploring the disputed Chunxiao gas field in the East China Sea.

Though Beijing has agreed for joint development of the field, it has declared that China's sovereignty over the field is indisputable. The Chinese 'shelving' formula needs close scrutiny of India in particular. As this writer views, this formula has inherent flaws – for some at least, the projected completion of China's military modernization in 2050 may create new pressures on the leaders in Beijing at that time to become aggressive on all border issues. What are therefore needed are serious efforts from India and China at their border talks, leading to a 'compromise' based solution to the issue, much sooner than later.

## Other Bilateral Issues —Tibet Issue

Tibet issue is prominent among other problems. It can be said that with India accepting the Tibet Autonomous Region as an integral part of China and standing firmly against any anti-China activity of the Dalai Lama from India's soil, this issue does not figure in Sino-Indian state to state relations. However, Beijing appears to be having reservations on India's motives with respect to the Dalai Lama. The State-controlled media allegation, made on the eve of Manmohan Singh – Wen Jiabao meeting in Thailand, that the Dalai Lama is colluding with India whenever Sino-Indian border talks are held, along with the Chinese official view that the proposed visit to Arunachal Pradesh by the Dalai Lama in November 2009, 'further exposes the anti-China and separatist nature of the Dalai clique' and a subsequent authoritative comment that such visits cast a new shadow on Sino-Indian relations, firmly point to Beijing's approach linking the Dalai Lama factor with the Sino-Indian border question.

China's fears need to be understood in the context of March 2008 unrest in Tibet, posing a challenge to China's sovereignty over that territory, even weakening Beijing's position in its border negotiations with India. Also, the question as to why India is tolerating the Tibetan Government in Exile in its soil, seems to be bothering China. Premier Wen Jiabao's description of the Tibet issue as a 'sensitive' one in relations with India, assumes significance in the context of what has been said above. The writer feels that Chinese suspicions on India-Dalai Lama relations are not going to disappear soon; the picture may change if talks between Beijing and the exiled spiritual leader succeed, but chances in this regard appear to be bleak at least for the moment.

## China-Pakistan Nexus

China-Pakistan nexus is the next major bilateral issue. A better understanding is required in China about India's sensitivities on this account. The Chinese military, missiles and nuclear help to Pakistan continues, but Beijing is not in a position to give a guarantee to India that Pakistan will not leverage such support from China, to fight against India. Not surprisingly, New Delhi perceives that China's military assistance to Pakistan has direct implications for India.

## China's Defence Modernisation

On the third issue of China's military modernization programme, India's concerns are being expressed through its important government documents, for e.g. the Defence Ministry's

Annual Report (2008-2009) has said that the programme has implications for India's defence and security. Asking Beijing to show greater transparency in its defence policy and postures, particularly on the double-digit growth in defence spending in last two decades, it has observed that China's stated aim in its Defence White Paper for 2008 to develop missiles, space based assets and blue water naval capabilities will have an effect on the overall military environment in the neighbourhood of India. The Chinese side should properly address such concerns of India.

## China's policy towards India's Neighbourhood

India's concerns also relate to China's attempts to establish a strategic presence in India's neighbourhood, for e.g port projects like Gwadar (Pakistan), Hambantota(Sri Lanka), Chittagong (Bangladesh). They are giving rise to fears in India of a Chinese encirclement of the country, under what has come to be known as a 'string of pearls strategy'. The PRC has taken care to officially repudiate such concerns, by asserting that it has no plans to try for domination of the shipping lanes in the Indian Ocean and has no intentions to establish a chain to encircle India. An India-China understanding on the issue is a must for further improving bilateral relations.

## India-US Relations

Chinese critical positions on the India-US relations are also a matter of India's concern. The Chinese have welcomed the India-US Strategic Dialogue and are themselves promoting ties with the US. Still, China seems to nurture fears about US-India collusion against it. Its official media description of India's policy as one 'befriending the far and attacking the near' is unmistakably an indirect, but strong criticism of the developing strategic relations between India and the US.

## East Asia Integration

It would be necessary for China to pay attention to the Indian perception that it hesitates to accept India's leading role in the East Asian regional integration process on the plea that the process should only be based on ASEAN+3 (China, Japan and South Korea) cooperation, and that ' outsiders' like India, Australia and New Zealand have no place in it.

## India's Defence Strategy

Reports in India about the country's defence strategy visualizing war on two fronts- Pakistan and China, have been commented upon in China. A Chinese comment (China Youth Daily) has said that India's real target is China, not Pakistan. Indian strategic planners have only done a scenario building; war is not an option for India, which wants to settle its historic problems with its two neighbours peacefully. Under the strategy, both land and sea power are getting emphasis in India, which reflects a logical consideration of the country's geopolitical position.

## How to Read Chinese Media?

The Indian public does not understand the reasons for appearance of hawkish views on India in some of China's strategic journals/websites. Global Times and writer, like Colonel Dai Xu, have often given controversial views on India. How far such views reflect official thinking remains a question in India. Is the People's Liberation army (PLA) influencing China's foreign policy making? Even the US Defence Secretary Robert Gates has hinted to such possibilities (Shangrila Dialogue, Singapore, 2010).The answer to such misgivings may lie in the need for reporting transparency in China.

## Economy

Questions are being asked in China on how India will use its economic power. They are similar to doubts in India and abroad about China's intentions once its modernization programme gets completed, say in 2050. China has announced peaceful development as its goal. India's objectives are on the same lines – enriching the entrepreneurial and economic potential of the country through a suitable reform strategy as well as integrating the country with the world's economic system under a new order. India's increasing role in G-20 mechanism speaks for the latter in particular. Another basic point relates to attempts to compare the development models of India and China. Which one is the better? A debate may be unending in this regard- generally, the Indian model based on democracy is being viewed favourably from a long term point of view than that of China which rests on a one-party system. The main difference is that while China has been following a model based on investment flow from abroad and exports. India has been giving a boost to entrepreneurship and free enterprise. In the opinion of the writer, the Indian superiority in the service sector notwithstanding, it will not be easy for India to catch up fast with China, which has already emerged as a manufacturing giant.

What will be India's global interests as an emerging power is another topic getting focus in China. As Dr Manmohan Singh, the Indian Prime Minister puts it, India's goal is to gain its rightful place in the comity of nations, making full use of the opportunities offered by a globalised world, operating on the frontiers of modern science and technology and using modern science and technology as important instruments of national economic and social development. The emerging India's partnerships with the US, China and other powers, India's role in the G-20 mechanism etc stand to explain its interests in the 21st century. Realising its responsibilities as a growing power, India is cooperating with other nations on addressing issues of global concern like terrorism, climate change, disarmament, world trade etc. In conclusion, it can be said that there are mixed views on China in India; Indians are noticing the prevailing good atmosphere in bilateral relations at state levels, but their concerns are continuing on China's strategic intentions vis-à-vis India. More and more people to people contacts between the two sides can bring a beneficial change to such conditions.

## PAKISTAN, CHINA UNDERPIN INDIA'S SECURITY DOCTRINE

Any national security doctrine of India has to cater to the possibility of threats from two sources-China and Pakistan.

The threat from China was rated high until 1988 because of the unresolved border dispute between the two countries, the clandestine military and nuclear assistance given by the Chinese government to the Pakistani armed forces in order to keep the Indian security forces preoccupied on two fronts, and the support extended by the Chinese intelligence agencies to the tribal insurgent groups of India's Northeast. The border dispute led to a war between the two countries in 1962. Between 1967 and 1979, many of these insurgent groups went to Yunnan in China via north Myanmar and were trained and armed by the Chinese intelligence.

The visit of Rajiv Gandhi, the then Indian prime minister, to China in 1988 and his meeting with Deng Xiaoping set in motion the process of improving bilateral relations. In 1988 and thereafter, the two countries agreed on a number of confidence-building measures, set up a joint working group to discuss the border problem on a sustained basis and decided not to let the pending border dispute come in the way of an improvement in relations in the economic, cultural and other fields. The Chinese intelligence, which had already started reducing its clandestine assistance to the tribal insurgent groups from 1979, totally stopped it after 1988. Despite this, China continues to pre-occupy the attention of India's national security managers due to the following reasons:

The very slow progress of the talks on the border issue, giving rise to misgivings that Beijing probably wants to keep this issue alive till it has totally pacified Tibet to its satisfaction. Though there is no more unrest in Tibet, which has been developing economically, the Dalai Lama still enjoys a large following there. The Chinese are determined that when the present Dalai Lama dies, his successor will be a man of their choice. They appreciate that this could give rise to serious unrest, which could be exploited by the Tibetan Diaspora in India and elsewhere. By keeping the border issue alive, China wants to retain a pressure point which it can exploit should India show reluctance to keep the Tibetan refugees under control.

In national security matters, the Chinese, unlike the Indians, work on a long-term basis and try to develop today options that they may need years hence should circumstances so warrant. For example, China's continued clandestine assistance to Pakistan in the military nuclear field and in the acquisition of a missile-based delivery capability.

Even as Beijing was entering into an agreement with Rajiv Gandhi on improving bilateral relations, it was secretly entering an agreement with Islamabad for assistance in the missile field. Another example is China's decision in 2001 to assist Pakistan in the construction of the Gwadar port on the Balochistan coast, which will reduce Pakistan's present dependence on Karachi port, which is within easy reach of the Indian navy, and give the Pakistani navy a greater operational flexibility. The threat from Pakistan, meanwhile, has always remained and will continue to remain of a very high order due to the following reasons:

- Pakistan's inability to reconcile itself to the loss of Jammu and Kashmir and its obsessive urge to gain control of this territory by hook or by crook.
- Its equally obsessive urge to avenge its defeat at the hands of India in 1971 and its loss of the then East Pakistan.
- The predominant role of the revenge-seeking Pakistani army in its national security management, with practically no role for an elected political leadership in this matter.
- Its refusal to work for a reduction of tension and for the improvement of relations in other fields until a negotiated solution could be found to the Kashmir question.
- The complexes and the feelings of insecurity from which the Pakistan army suffers vis-a-vis its Indian counterpart.
- The role of the pan-Islamic extremist elements in moulding perceptions towards India, whether in the civil society or in the national security apparatus.

Its 1971 defeat at the hands of India brought home to Pakistan the ground reality that it could never hope to achieve its territorial objective through a conventional war on India. It therefore embarked on a policy of waging a proxy war through the use of terrorism as a weapon against the Indian state.

Pakistan had been using terrorism against the Indian state since 1956 when the Naga insurgency broke out. Whereas its use of terrorism against India before 1971 was a defensive measure to keep the Indian security forces preoccupied with internal security duties so that they could not pose a threat to it, its use after 1971 was an aggressive measure having the dual objective of continuing to keep the Indian security forces bleeding and preoccupied with internal security duties and achieving its strategic objective of annexing Jammu and Kashmir without the direct use of its army in a conventional war. Until Pakistan achieved a military nuclear capability in the late 1980s, which was subsequently openly demonstrated in the Chagai nuclear tests of 1998, it kept its proxy war restricted to the training and arming of Indian separatist groups, whether in Punjab or Kashmir, which had taken to arms against the government of India due to various grievances.

The acquisition of the military nuclear capability made the Pakistani military leadership conclude that the possibility of an Indian-imposed conventional war in retaliation for its proxy war had been reduced considerably, if not largely eliminated, and hence it could further escalate its proxy war by training, arming and infiltrating into India its own nationals under the guise of jihadi volunteers from different pan-Islamic organizations to intensify the jihad against India. Until 1995, the role of these mercenaries was largely confined to Jammu and Kashmir, but since then Pakistan's Inter-Services Intelligence has been using them in other parts of India too.

Pakistan looks on its nuclear arsenal and its missile delivery capability not as a weapon of deterrence to deter India from using its nuclear capability against it, but as a weapon of intimidation to prevent India from retaliating against it through its armed forces for its proxy war and as a weapon of psychological pressure by creating fears of a possible nuclear holocaust and thereby moving the rest of the world, particularly the US, to exercise pressure on India on the Jammu and Kashmir issue.

Its consistent refusal to subscribe to the no first use of nuclear weapons declaration and its repeated reiteration of its readiness to make first use of its nuclear weapons to prevent the Indian army from over-running its large cities and crushing its army are part of its intimidatory tactics.

The nuclear threat from Pakistan is compounded by the presence of pan-Islamic jihadi elements which justify the use of the weapons of mass destruction to protect Islam, if necessary. The possibility of the nuclearization of terrorism originating from the terrorist hub of Pakistan is a matter of great concern not only to India, but also to the international community as a whole, confronted with the threat of pan-Islamic jihadi terrorism.

Since President General Pervez Musharraf seized power on October 12, 1999, Pakistan has embarked on a policy of over-projecting its nuclear and missile capability in order to reassure its own population of the adequacy of its capability and to intimidate India and prevent a retaliatory conventional strike against its proxy war.

# Bibliography


Alam, Aftab : *US Policy Towards South Asia: Special Reference to Indo-Pak Relations*, Raj, Delhi, 1998.

Alastair Lamb, Kashmir: *A Disputed Legacy 1846–1990*, Hertingfordbury, Herts: Roxford Books, 1991.

Allen Carlson, *Unifying China, Integrating with the World: Securing Chinese Sovereignty in the Reform Era*, Stanford: Stanford University Press, 2005.

Amitabh Sikdar: *India and China : Strategic Energy Management and Security*, Manas, Delhi, 2009.

Anderson, J.: *Transnational Democracy: Political Spaces and Border Crossings*, Routledge: London and New York, 2002.

Anil, K.C.: *Military and Democracy in South Asia : Challenges, Politics and Power*, Sumit Enterprises, Delhi, 2009.

Benjamin, Joseph : *China-Pak Relations : Prospect and Retrospect*, Reference Press, Delhi, 2004.

Bhat, T.P. : *India and China : Trade Complementarities and Competitiveness*, Bookwell, Delhi, 2008.

Bort, E.: *Boundaries and Identities: The Eastern Frontier of the Asia*, Edinburgh: International Social Sciences Institute, University of Edinburgh, 1996.

Chitkara, M.G. : *China-Pak Relations Challenges Before New Millennium*, APH, Delhi, 2001.

Coakley, J.: *The Territorial Management of Ethnic Conflict*, London: Frank Cass, 2003.

Deepak, B R : *India and China : 1904-2004 : A Century of Peace and Conflict*, Manak, Delhi, 2005.

Dixit, J.N. : *India and Regional Developments : Through the Prism of Indo-Pak Relations*, Gyan, Delhi, 2004.

Donnan, H. and Wilson, T. M.: *Borders: Frontiers of Identity, Nation and State*, Oxford: Berg, 1999.

Gao, Mobo: *The Battle for China's Past: Mao and the Cultural Revolution,* London, Pluto Press, 2008.

Ghosh, Ajoy : *Indo-Pak Conflict : Threat to South Asian Security*, Reference Press, Delhi, 2003.

Gupta, Alka R. : *Indo-Pak Security Discourse : South Asian Context*, Radha Pub, Delhi, 2010.

Gupta, S.: *Disrupted Borders: An Intervention in Definitions of Boundaries*, London: River Oram Press, 1993.

Huntington, S.P.: *The China Defence Modernisation Military and the State*, N.Y., Vintage Books, 1964.

Imtiaz, A.: *State and Foreign Policy: India's Role in South Asia*, New Delhi, Vikas, 1993.

Jagannath P. Panda: *China's Path to Power : Party, Military and the Politics of State Transition*, Pentagon, Delhi, 2010.

Jha, Prem Shankar : *India and China : The Battle Between Soft and Hard Power*, Penguin Books India, Delhi, 2010.

Kunju, N. : *Indo-Pak : Nuclear Cold War*, Reliance, Delhi, 2002.

Nayyar, K K : *National Security : Military Aspects*, Rupa, Delhi, 2003.

Phuskele, Preeti : *India and China : Emerging Superpowers*, ICFAI University, Delhi, 2009.

Prabir De: *India and China in an Era of Globalisation : Essays on Economic Cooperation*, Bookwell, Delhi, 2005.

Rosen, P.: *Societies and Military Power: India and its Armies*, Ithaca, Cornell University Press, 1996.

Thampi, Madhavi : *India and China in the Colonial World*, Social Science Press, Delhi, 2010.

Theodore, William : T*he Buddhist Tradition in India, China and Japan,* New York: Vintage Books, 1972.

# Index

## S



## T



❑❑❑